THE ICON
PROGRAMMING
LANGUAGE

Ralph E. Griswold · Madge T. Griswold

The Icon Programming Language

Prentice-Hall Software Series
Brian W. Kernighan, advisor

The Icon Programming Language

Ralph E. Griswold and Madge T. Griswold

Department of Computer Science
The University of Arizona
Tucson, Arizona   85721

PRENTICE-HALL, INC., Englewood Cliffs, New Jersey   07632

Library of Congress Cataloging in Publication Data

Griswold, Ralph E. (date)
 The Icon programming language.

 (Prentice-Hall software series)
 Includes bibliographical references and index.
 1. Icon (Computer program language) I. Griswold,
Madge T. (date). II. Title. III. Series.
QA76.73.119G74   1983   001.64'24   82-24078
ISBN 0-13-449777-5

Printed in the United States of America

10 9 8 7 6 5 4 3 2 1

ISBN 0-13-449777-5

PRENTICE-HALL INTERNATIONAL, INC., *London*
PRENTICE-HALL OF AUSTRALIA PTY. LIMITED, *Sydney*
EDITORA PRENTICE-HALL DO BRASIL, LTDA., *Rio de Janeiro*
PRENTICE-HALL OF CANADA, INC., *Toronto*
PRENTICE-HALL OF INDIA PRIVATE LIMITED, *New Delhi*
PRENTICE-HALL OF JAPAN, INC., *Tokyo*
PRENTICE-HALL OF SOUTHEAST ASIA PTE. LTD., *Singapore*
WHITEHALL BOOKS LIMITED, *Wellington, New Zealand*

CONTENTS

PREFACE   **xiii**

ACKNOWLEDGMENTS   **xviii**

**Part I
BASICS**

1

GETTING STARTED   **1**

1.1 Program Structure *1*
1.2 Success and Failure *4*
1.3 Control Structures *6*
1.4 Procedures *6*
1.5 Expression Syntax *8*
1.6 Notation and Terminology *10*

2
CONTROL STRUCTURES 12

2.1 Loops *12*
2.2 Selecting Expressions *15*

3
NUMBERS 19

3.1 Numeric Literals *19*
3.2 Numerical Computation *20*
3.3 Numerical Comparison *21*
3.4 Augmented Assignment *22*
3.5 Random Numbers *23*

4
CHARACTER SETS AND STRINGS 24

4.1 Character Sets *25*
    4.1.1 Cset Literals *25*
    4.1.2 Built-in Csets *25*
    4.1.3 Operations on Csets *26*
    4.1.4 Conversion between Csets and Strings *26*
4.2 Strings *27*
    4.2.1 String Literals *27*
    4.2.2 String Size *28*
    4.2.3 Concatenation *28*
    4.2.4 Substrings *29*
    4.2.5 Lexical Comparison *33*
    4.2.6 String-Valued Functions *34*
4.3 String Analysis *38*
    4.3.1 Locating Substrings *39*
    4.3.2 Lexical Analysis *40*
    4.3.3 Range Restriction *44*

5
STRUCTURES 48

5.1 Lists *48*
    5.1.1 List Creation *48*
    5.1.2 List Referencing *50*
    5.1.3 List Concatenation *52*
    5.1.4 List Sections *53*
    5.1.5 Queue and Stack Access to Lists *53*

5.1.6   Sorting Lists   *54*
5.1.7   Properties of Lists   *55*
5.2   Tables   *56*
     5.2.1   Table Creation and Referencing   *56*
     5.2.2   Sorting Tables   *57*
5.3   Records   *58*

6

DATA TYPES   61

6.1   Type Determination   *61*
6.2   Type Conversion   *62*
     6.2.1   Implicit Type Conversion   *63*
     6.2.2   Explicit Type Conversion   *64*
6.3   The Null Value   *65*
6.4   Sorting Mixed Types   *66*

7

PROCEDURES   68

7.1   Procedure Declarations   *68*
7.2   The Scope of Identifiers   *69*
7.3   Procedure Invocation   *72*
7.4   Returning from a Procedure   *73*
7.5   Procedures as Values   *74*
7.6   Recursive Calls   *74*

8

EXPRESSION EVALUATION   80

8.1   Results and Outcomes   *80*
8.2   The Evaluation of Arguments   *82*
8.3   Dereferencing   *84*
8.4   Mutual Evaluation   *85*

9

INPUT AND OUTPUT   88

9.1   Files   *88*
9.2   Input   *90*
9.3   Output   *91*

10
MISCELLANEOUS OPERATIONS   94

10.1 Comparing Values *94*
10.2 Copying Values *96*
10.3 Exchanging Values *96*
10.4 String Images *97*
10.5 Tracing *99*
10.6 Other Information about Procedures *100*
10.7 Environmental Information *101*

Part II
ADVANCED FEATURES

11
GENERATORS   103

11.1 The Concept of Generators *103*
11.2 Result Sequences *104*
11.3 Contexts for Generation *104*
    11.3.1 Iteration over Result Sequences *104*
    11.3.2 Goal-Directed Evaluation *106*
11.4 Argument Evaluation *107*
11.5 Generator Expressions *109*
    11.5.1 Alternation *109*
    11.5.2 Integer Sequences *110*
    11.5.3 Limiting Generation *111*
    11.5.4 Repeated Alternation *112*
    11.5.5 Element Generation *112*
11.6 Generators in String Analysis *115*
11.7 Procedures as Generators *116*
11.8 Backtracking and Reversible Effects *119*
    11.8.1 Control Backtracking *119*
    11.8.2 Data Backtracking *120*

12
STRING SCANNING   122

12.1 The Concept of String Scanning *122*
12.2 The Scanning Operation *124*
12.3 Matching Functions *126*
12.4 Scanning Keywords *127*
12.5 String Analysis Functions *128*
12.6 Nested Scanning *129*

12.7   Returning Values from Scanning   *129*

13
CO-EXPRESSIONS 132

13.1   Co-Expression Operations   *132*
    13.1.1   Creating Co-Expressions   *132*
    13.1.2   Activating Co-Expressions   *133*
    13.1.3   The Size of Co-Expressions   *134*
    13.1.4   Refreshing Co-Expressions   *134*
13.2   Using Co-Expressions   *135*
13.3   Modeling Generative Control Structures   *137*
13.4   Coroutine Programming   *138*
    13.4.1   Additional Co-Expression Facilities   *138*
    13.4.2   Using Co-Expressions as Coroutines   *138*

Part III
PROGRAMMING TECHNIQUES

14
PROGRAMMING WITH GENERATORS 141

14.1   The Applicability of Generators   *141*
14.2   Condensing Expressions   *142*
14.3   Infinite Result Sequences   *144*
14.4   Limitations on the Use of Generators   *146*
14.5   Nested Iteration   *147*
14.6   Backtracking   *148*

15
HIGH-LEVEL STRING PROCESSING 155

15.1   The Generality of String Scanning   *155*
    15.1.1   Integrating Scanning with Other Operations   *155*
    15.1.2   The Order of Matched Substrings   *156*
15.2   Pattern Matching   *158*
    15.2.1   Matching Expressions   *158*
    15.2.2   Matching Procedures   *160*
15.3   Grammars and Languages   *161*
    15.3.1   Recognizers   *163*
    15.3.2   Parsers   *166*

16
LIST PROCESSING   170

16.1   Trees   *170*
16.2   Dags   *174*
16.3   Graphs with Cycles   *177*

17
MAPPINGS AND LABELINGS   181

17.1   Mapping Techniques   *181*
    17.1.1   Transpositions   *181*
    17.1.2   Positional Transformations   *185*
17.2   Labelings   *186*
    17.2.1   Manipulating Decks of Cards   *186*
    17.2.2   Manipulating Graphs   *189*

Part IV
SAMPLE PROGRAMS

18
LARGE INTEGERS   192

18.1   Representing Large Integers   *192*
18.2   Addition of Large Integers   *193*
    18.2.1   A String Representation   *193*
    18.2.2   A List Representation   *195*
    18.2.3   A Linked-List Representation   *197*
18.3   Multiplying Large Integers   *198*

19
SYMBOLIC ALGEBRA   201

19.1   Infix-to-Prefix Conversion   *201*
19.2   Symbolic Evaluation   *206*
19.3   Symbolic Differentiation   *207*

20
RANDOM STRINGS   211

20.1   Representing Grammars   *211*
    20.1.1   Grammar Input   *211*
    20.1.2   Internal Representation of Grammars   *212*
20.2   Processing Grammars   *213*

20.3   The Generation Process   *215*
20.4   Generation Specifications   *216*
20.5   The Complete Program   *217*

APPENDIXES

A
ICON SYNTAX   221

B
MACHINE DEPENDENCIES AND LIMITS   238

C
RUNNING AN ICON PROGRAM   240

D
ERRORS   246

E
SUMMARY OF BUILT-IN OPERATIONS   251

F
SOLUTIONS TO SELECTED EXERCISES   281

REFERENCES   303

INDEX   305

PREFACE

Icon is a high-level, general-purpose programming language that contains many features for processing nonnumeric data, particularly for textual material consisting of strings of characters. Icon was designed to aid in analyzing natural languages, reformatting data, transforming computer programs, generating computer programs, manipulating formulas, formatting documents, and so forth. It is suited to situations where a quick solution is needed, one that can be obtained with a minimum of time and programming effort. Icon is extremely useful for "one-shot" programs and for speculative efforts such as computer-generated poetry, in which a proposed problem solution is more heuristic than algorithmic. It also excels for very complicated problems.

In its focus on solutions for nonnumerical problems, Icon continues the tradition of SNOBOL4 [1]. However, Icon has modern control structures, and its facilities for string analysis and synthesis are more extensive than those of SNOBOL4. While string analysis and synthesis, together with goal-directed evaluation, are just a part of the pattern-matching mechanism in SNOBOL4, these features are an integral part of Icon, making possible a wide variety of programming techniques.

There are several general characteristics of Icon that contribute to its "personality". It is an expression-based language with a syntax similar to Algol 68 [2] and Pascal [3]. Icon has many of the traditional control structures that are found in other programming languages, but it lacks labels and go-tos. Superficially, Icon programs resemble those in many other modern programming languages.

In Icon, strings of characters are values in their own right, as opposed to being treated as arrays of characters. Strings may be arbitrarily long, although there are both practical considerations and physical limitations. Icon has neither storage declarations nor explicit allocation and deallocation operations; management of storage for strings and other values is handled automatically.

There are no type declarations in Icon; it is an "untyped" language in which a variable may have values of different types during program execution. Type conversion is automatic. For example, a numeric value read into a program as a string is converted automatically to a number if it is used in a numerical operation. Error checking is rigorous; a value that cannot be converted to a required type in a meaningful way causes termination of program execution with a diagnostic message.

Like SNOBOL4, but unlike most other programming languages, operations in Icon may succeed or fail. Algol-like programming languages have conditional operations (such as the comparison of the magnitudes of integers) that produce Boolean values *true* or *false* depending on whether or not a condition is satisfied. A control structure such as

$$\text{if } i < j \text{ then } expr_1 \text{ else } expr_2$$

is "driven" by the Boolean value produced by the expression $i < j$. Therefore, if the value of i is less than the value of j, $i < j$ produces *true* and $expr_1$ and is evaluated. If i is not less than j, $i < j$ produces *false* and $expr_2$ and is evaluated. Icon has a control structure that is identical in appearance to this one. In Icon, however, the control structure is driven by the success or failure of $i < j$. The distinction is not just a matter of terminology but goes to the heart of the language.

Consider the Icon function find(s1, s2), which produces the position at which s1 occurs as a substring of s2. Depending on the values of s1 and s2, there may or may not be such a position. If there is such a position, it is produced as the value of find, while if there is not such a position, find fails. This allows find to be used both in the control clause of a control structure such as an **if-then-else** expression and in ordinary computational contexts where its value is useful. This use of success and failure contrasts with languages like PL/I [4], in which the function INDEX produces zero if s1 is not a substring of s2. A test for a zero value can be made, of course, but this is cumbersome.

Another example of the usefulness of producing a meaningful value when a conditional operation succeeds occurs in comparison operations. A comparison operation produces the value of its right argument if it succeeds. Therefore,

$$i < j$$

produces the value of j if the comparison succeeds. Consequently,

$$i < j < k$$

which groups as

$$(i < j) < k$$

succeeds if the value of j is between the values of i and k. In many programming languages, such a construction is either erroneous or meaningless.

One of the more unusual features of Icon is its concept of *generators*, expressions that may produce more than one value. The function find, described previously, illustrates the possibilities. Consider, for example,

find("th", "this thesis is the best one")

Here th occurs at three positions in the second argument: 1, 6, and 16. In most programming languages, such a situation is resolved by selecting one position for the value of the function (the first position is most often the rule). This interpretation discards potentially useful information, however. Icon generalizes the concept of expression evaluation to allow an expression to produce more than one result. These results are produced in sequence as determined by context. One context is the iteration control structure

every *expr₁* **do** *expr₂*

which evaluates *expr₂* for every result produced by *expr₁*. An example is

every i := find(s1, s2) do write(i)

which writes all the positions at which s1 occurs as a substring of s2.

It is worth noting here that a number of other programming languages have constructions called generators. CLU [5] is an example. In most languages, however, generators are confined to particular operations on certain kinds of values. In Icon, generators are completely general and may occur in any computation. Generators in themselves lend conciseness and expressive power.

Perhaps the most significant aspect of Icon is *goal-directed* evaluation. This term suggests that the evaluation of expressions is purposeful, as it is in pattern matching in SNOBOL4. Here the purpose is to achieve success for expression evaluation, that is, some result. In most programming languages, such a concept is meaningless; all expressions produce a result (but not necessarily a computationally useful one). The usefulness of goal-directed evaluation in Icon comes from the capability of generators to produce more than a single result. Consider, for example,

if find(s1, s2) = **10 then** *expr₁* **else** *expr₂*

The intuitive meaning of this expression is: "If s1 occurs as a substring of s2 at a position that is equal to 10, then evaluate *expr₁*; otherwise evaluate *expr₂*". This is, in fact, exactly what this expression does in Icon. Furthermore, this works even if **s1** also occurs at positions less than 10 or greater than 10. Without generators, it is necessary to look through successive substrings.

Neither generators nor goal-directed evaluation depends on any particular feature for processing strings; **find** is useful pedagogically, but there are many possibilities in numerical computation. Furthermore, Icon allows programmers to write their own generators, and there is no limit to the range of their applicability.

Since Icon is oriented toward the processing of textual data, it has a large repertoire of functions for operating on strings, of which **find** is only one example. Icon also has a high-level *string scanning* facility. String scanning, like pattern matching in SNOBOL4, establishes a *subject* that is the focus for string-processing operations. Scanning operations apply to this subject. As operations on the subject take place, the *position* in the subject may be changed. A scanning expression has the form

> **s** ? *expr*

where **s** is the subject and *expr* contains scanning operations on this subject.

Matching functions change the position in the subject and produce the substring of the subject that they "match". For example, **tab(i)** moves the position to **i** and produces the substring between the previous and new positions. A simple example of string scanning is

> **text ? write(tab(find("the")))**

which writes the initial substring of **text** up to the first occurrence of **the**. The function **find** is the same as the one given earlier. In string scanning, the second argument of **find** is the subject and need not be given explicitly. Note that any operation, such as **write**, can appear in string scanning.

With procedures and generators, string scanning can be used to formulate pattern matching similar to that of SNOBOL4. Unlike pattern matching in SNOBOL4, string scanning is integrated into the rest of Icon. String analysis, string synthesis, and other kinds of computation can be used in combination.

This book is divided into four parts. Part I covers the basic features of Icon, including its basic string-processing facilities. None of the material in this part relies on generators; it describes only the subset of Icon that is similar in nature to several other programming languages. Part II introduces more advanced features, including generators, goal-directed evaluation, string scanning, and co-expressions. Part III is devoted to programming techniques: how to program with generators, string processing techniques, list processing, and so forth. In Part IV several substantial Icon programs are presented to illustrate how the features of Icon can be used in combination and how specific problems are handled. There are exercises at the end of each chapter.

Appendix A summarizes the syntax of Icon. Machine dependencies and implementation limits are described in Appendix B. Appendix C describes how to run Icon programs and Appendix D summarizes error messages. Appendix E is a quick reference guide to the functions, operations, and control structures of Icon. Solutions to selected exercises are given in Appendix F.

The reader of this book should have a general understanding of the concepts of computer programming languages and a familiarity with the current terminology in the field. Programming experience with other programming languages, such as Pascal or Algol, is desirable. SNOBOL4 programmers will find familiar concepts, sometimes cast differently, in Icon.

Icon, like many other programming languages, evolved through a series of versions and has been implemented on a variety of computers. This book describes Version 5 of Icon, which is written in C [6] and is designed to run under the UNIX[†] operating system [7]. Version 2, which differs in several respects from Version 5, is available for a number of computers. The differences between Versions 2 and 5 are described in Reference 8.

[†]UNIX is a trademark of Bell Laboratories.

ACKNOWLEDGMENTS

The original version of Icon was designed by Ralph Griswold, Dave Hanson, and Tim Korb. It was implemented by Dave Hanson, Tim Korb, and Walt Hansen. Subsequent design changes that culminated in Version 5 were made by Cary Coutant, Ralph Griswold, and Steve Wampler. Cary Coutant and Steve Wampler implemented Version 5. Bill Mitchell contributed to subsequent implementation efforts. In addition to the persons mentioned, who were primarily responsible for the design and implementation of Icon, many others, too numerous to acknowledge individually, contributed ideas and made suggestions that shaped the final result.

Several of the program examples used in this book were derived from programs written by students in computer science courses at The University of Arizona. In addition, individual contributions were made by Allan Anderson, Debbie Coutant, Ward Cunningham, and Steve Wampler. The authors gratefully acknowledge the assistance of the persons who read draft copies of this book. Debbie Coutant, Rebecca Griswold, Dave Hanson, Brian Kernighan, and Bill Mitchell provided helpful suggestions on the presentation of the material and pointed out a number of errors. Special thanks go to Cary Coutant and Steve Wampler, who provided particularly helpful, detailed, and insightful criticisms.

The support of the National Science Foundation under Grants MCS75-01397, MCS79-03890, and MCS81-01916 was instrumental in the original conception of Icon and has been invaluable in its subsequent development.

Ralph E. Griswold and Madge T. Griswold

The Icon Programming Language

1

GETTING STARTED

This chapter introduces a few basic concepts of Icon, enough to get started. Subsequent chapters discuss these concepts in greater detail.

1.1 PROGRAM STRUCTURE

An Icon program consists of declarations and expressions. The declarations define information that must be known before program execution begins, such as procedures and the properties of identifiers. The expressions constitute the executable part of the program.

A good way to learn a programming language is to write programs. There is a fine tradition for beginning a new programming language by writing a program that produces a greeting. In Icon this takes the form

```
procedure main()
    write("Hello world")
end
```

This program writes Hello world to the output file.

The reserved words procedure and end bracket the procedure declaration. The procedure name is main; every program must have a procedure with the name main. Execution of every program begins at main. Most programs contain several procedures, although this program contains only one.

The expressions within the procedure declaration are evaluated when the procedure is called. The call of the function write simply writes its argument, a string that is given literally in enclosing quotation marks. When a procedure reaches the end, it returns. When the main procedure returns, program execution stops.

To illustrate the use of procedures, the preceding program can be divided into two procedures as follows:

```
procedure main()
    hello()
end

procedure hello()
    write("Hello world")
end
```

Note that **main** and **hello** are procedures, while **write** is a function that is built into the Icon language. Procedures and functions are used in the same way. The only distinction between the two is that functions are built into Icon, while procedures are declared in programs. The procedure **hello** writes the greeting and returns to **main**. The procedure **main** then returns, terminating program execution.

Expressions in the body of a procedure are evaluated in the order in which they appear. Therefore, the program

```
procedure main()
    write("Hello world")
    write("    this is a new beginning")
end
```

writes two lines:

```
Hello world
    this is a new beginning
```

Procedures may have parameters, which are given in a list enclosed in the parentheses that follow the procedure name in the declaration. For example, the program

```
procedure main()
    greet("Hello", "world")
end

procedure greet(what, who)
    write(what)
    write(who)
end
```

writes

Hello
world

Like most programming languages, Icon has both values and variables that have values. This is illustrated by

```
procedure main()
    line := "Hello world"
    write(line)
end
```

The operation

```
line := "Hello world"
```

assigns the value **Hello world** to the identifier **line**. The value of **line** is then passed to the function **write**.

Identifiers must begin with a letter, which may be followed by other letters, digits, and underscores. Upper- and lowercase letters are distinct. Examples of identifiers are **comp**, **Label**, **test10**, and **entry_value**. There are other kinds of variables besides identifiers; these are described in Chapters 4 and 5.

Note that there is no declaration for the identifier **line**. Scope declarations, which are described in Chapter 7, are optional for local identifiers. In the absence of a scope declaration, an identifier is assumed to be local to the procedure in which it occurs, as is the case with **line**.

Local identifiers are created when a procedure is called and are destroyed when the procedure returns. No other procedure call can access these identifiers.

Most identifiers are local. The default to local is an example of a design philosophy of Icon: Common usages usually default automatically without the need for the programmer to write them out.

Icon has no type or storage declarations. Any variable can have any type of value. Storage that is needed for values is handled automatically without the need for the programmer to be concerned.

The character # in a program signals the beginning of a comment. The # and the remaining characters on the line are ignored when the program is translated. An example of the use of comments is

```
#   This procedure illustrates the use of parameters. The
#   first parameter provides the message, while the second
#   parameter specifies the recipient.
#
procedure greet(what, who)
    write(what)                        # message
    write(who)                         # recipient
end
```

Note that the end of a line terminates a comment. Each line of a multiline comment must have a #.

If a # occurs in a quoted literal, it stands for itself and does not signal the beginning of a comment. Therefore,

```
write("#======#")
```

writes

```
#======#
```

1.2 SUCCESS AND FAILURE

The function **read** reads a line from the input file. For example,

```
write(read())
```

reads a line and writes it out. Note that the value produced by **read()** is the argument of **write**.

The function **read** is one of a number of expressions in Icon that may either *succeed* or *fail*. If an expression succeeds, it produces a value, such as a line from the input file. If an expression fails, it produces no value. In the case of **read**, failure occurs when the end of the input file is reached.

Expressions that may succeed or fail are called *conditional expressions*. Comparison operations, for example, are conditional expressions. The expression

```
count > 0
```

succeeds if the value of **count** is greater than 0 but fails if the value of **count** is not greater than 0.

As a general rule, failure occurs if a relation does not hold or if an operation cannot be performed but is not actually erroneous. For example, failure occurs when an attempt is made to read but when the end of the input file has been reached.

Two other conditional expressions are find(s1, s2) and match(s1, s2). These functions succeed if s1 is a *substring* of s2 but fail otherwise. A substring is a string that occurs in another string. The function find(s1, s2) succeeds if s1 occurs anywhere in s2, while match(s1, s2) succeeds only if s1 is an *initial* substring that occurs at the beginning of s2. For example,

find("on", "slow motion")

succeeds, since on is a substring of slow motion, but

find("on", "radio noise")

fails, since on is not a substring of radio noise because of the intervening space between the o and the n. Similarly,

match("on", "slow motion")

fails, since on does not occur at the beginning of slow motion. On the other hand,

match("slo", "slow motion")

succeeds, since slo is an initial substring of slow motion.

If an expression that fails is an argument in another expression, the other expression fails also, since there is no value for the argument. For example, in

write(read())

if read() fails, there is nothing to write. The function write is not called and the whole expression fails.

The context in which failure occurs is important. Consider

line := read()
write(line)

If read() succeeds, the value it produces is assigned to line. If read() fails, however, no new value is assigned to line, because read() is an argument of the assignment operation. Conceptually, there is no value to assign to line if read() fails, so no assignment is performed. In this case the value of line is left unchanged. The assignment is *conditional* on the success of read(). Since

line := read()

and

write(line)

are separate expressions, the failure of read() does not affect write(line); it just writes the previous value of line.

1.3 CONTROL STRUCTURES

Control structures use the success or failure of one expression to govern the evaluation of others. For example,

```
while line := read() do
    write(line)
```

repeatedly evaluates **read()**. Each time **read()** succeeds, the value that it produces is assigned to **line** and **write(line)** is evaluated to write the value that is read. When **read()** fails, however, the assignment operation fails and the loop terminates. In other words, the success or failure of the expression following **while** controls evaluation of the expression following **do**.

Note that assignment is an expression. It can be used anywhere that any expression is allowed.

Words, such as **while** and **do**, that distinguish control structures are reserved and cannot be used as identifiers. A complete list of reserved words is given in Appendix A.

The **if-then-else** control structure allows the selection of one of two expressions to evaluate, depending on the success or failure of a conditional expression. For example,

```
if count > 0 then write("positive") else write("nonpositive")
```

writes **positive** if the value of count is greater than 0, but writes **nonpositive** if the value of count is not greater than 0.

1.4 PROCEDURES

Procedures are the major logical units of a program. Each procedure in a program typically performs a logical task. In short programs there may be only a single main procedure. Other procedures may be useful in a variety of programs. Some examples follow.

The following procedure prints only the lines that contain the string **s**.

```
procedure locate(s)
    while line := read() do
        if find(s, line) then write(line)
end
```

For example, **locate("fancy")** writes all the lines of the input file that contain an occurrence of the string **fancy**.

This procedure is more useful if it also writes the numbers of the lines that contain **s**. To do this, it is necessary to count each line as it is read.

```
procedure locate(s)
    lineno := 0
    while line := read() do {
        lineno := lineno + 1
        if find(s, line) then write(lineno, ": ", line)
    }
end
```

The braces in this procedure enclose a *compound expression*, which in this case consists of two expressions. One expression increments the line number and the other writes the line if it contains the desired substring. Compound expressions must be used wherever one expression is expected but several are needed.

Note that **write** is called with three arguments in this procedure. The function **write** can be called with many arguments; the values of the arguments are written one after another, all on the same line. In this case there is a line number, followed by a colon and space, followed by the line itself.

To illustrate the use of this procedure, consider an input file that consists of the following song from Shakespeare's play *The Merchant of Venice*:

Tell me, where is fancy bred,
Or in the heart or in the head?
How begot, how nourished?
    Reply, reply.
It is engender'd in the eyes,
With gazing fed; and fancy dies
In the cradle where it lies:
  Let us all ring fancy's knell;
I'll begin it, − Ding, dong, bell.

The lines written by **locate("fancy")** are:

1: Tell me, where is fancy bred,
6: With gazing fed; and fancy dies
8:    Let us all ring fancy's knell;

This example illustrates one of the more important features of Icon: the automatic conversion of values from one type to another. The first argument of **write** in this example is an integer. Since **write** expects to write strings, this integer is converted to a string without requiring the programmer to specify the conversion. This is another example of a default, which makes programs shorter and saves the programmer from having to specify routine actions where they clearly are the natural thing to do.

Like other expressions, procedure calls may produce values. The reserved word **return** is used to indicate a value to be returned from a procedure call. For example,

```
procedure countm(s)
   count := 0
   while line := read() do
      if match(s, line) then count := count + 1
   return count
end
```

produces a count of the number of input lines that begin with **s**.

A procedure call also may fail. This is indicated by the reserved word **fail**, which causes the procedure call to return but fail instead of producing a value. For example,

```
procedure countm(s)
   count := 0
   while line := read() do
      if match(s, line) then count := count + 1
   if count > 0 then return count else fail
end
```

produces a count of the number of lines that begin with **s**, provided that the count is greater than 0. The procedure fails, however, if no line begins with the string **s**.

1.5 EXPRESSION SYNTAX

Icon has several types of expressions, as illustrated in the preceding sections. A literal such as **"Hello world"** is an expression that designates a value literally. Identifiers, such as **line**, are also expressions.

Function calls, such as

> **write(line)**

and procedure calls, such as

> **greet("Hello", "world")**

are expressions in which parentheses separate the operation to be performed from its arguments.

The syntax for operations is more concise, using symbols to stand for the computations to be performed. For example, $-i$ produces the negative of **i**, while $i + j$ produces the sum of **i** and **j**. Operations and functions essentially are equivalent; the difference is in their syntax. The term argument is used for both to describe the expressions on which they operate.

Infix operations, such as $i + j$ and $i * j$ have precedences that determine which operations apply to which arguments when they are used in combination. For example, i + j * k

groups as

    i + (j * k)

since multiplication has higher precedence than addition, as is conventional in numerical computation.

Associativity determines how expressions group when there are several occurrences of the same operation in combination. For example, subtraction associates from left to right so that

    i − j − k

groups as

    (i − j) − k

On the other hand, assignment associates from right to left so that

    x := y := 0

groups as

    x := (y := 0)

The precedences and associativities of various operations are mentioned as the operations are introduced in subsequent chapters. Appendix A summarizes the precedences and associativities of all operations.

Parentheses can be used to group expressions differently from the way they would group according to precedence and associativity, as in

    (i + j) * k

Since there are many operations in Icon with various precedences and associativities, it is safest to use parentheses to assure that operations group in the desired way, especially for operations that are not used frequently.

Where the expressions in a compound expression appear on the same line, they must be separated by semicolons. For example,

```
while line := read() do {
    count := count + 1
    if find(s, line) then write(line)
    }
```

can also be written as

```
while line := read() do
    {count := count + 1; if find(s, line) then write(line)}
```

Programs usually are easier to read if the expressions in a compound expression are written on separate lines, however.

Unlike many programming languages, Icon has no statements. It just has expressions. Even control structures, such as

$$\text{if } expr_1 \text{ then } expr_2 \text{ else } expr_3$$

are expressions. The value returned by such a control structure is the value of $expr_2$ or $expr_3$, whichever is selected. Even though control structures are expressions, they usually are not used in such a way that the values they produce are important. That is, they usually stand alone as if they were statements, as illustrated by the examples in this chapter.

Keywords, consisting of the character **&** followed by one of a number of specific words, are used to designate significant values. For example, the value of **&time** is the number of milliseconds that a program has been in execution.

There are many other kinds of expressions in Icon. These are introduced in subsequent chapters. The details of expression syntax are summarized in Appendix A.

Any argument of a function, procedure, operation, or control structure may be any expression, however complicated that expression is. There are no distinctions among the kinds of expressions; any kind of expression can be used in any context where an expression is legal.

Of course the result produced by an expression must be appropriate for the context in which it is used. Therefore,

```
1 := 2
```

is considered to be syntactically correct, but it is erroneous when evaluated, since the left argument of an assignment expression must be a variable. Such an error causes program execution to terminate with a diagnostic message.

1.6 NOTATION AND TERMINOLOGY

In describing what operations and functions do, the fact that their arguments may be syntactically complicated is not significant. It is the values produced by these expressions that are important.

Icon has several types of data: strings, integers, real numbers, and so forth. Many functions and operations require specific types of data for their arguments. Single letters, sometimes followed by numbers, are used in this book to indicate the arguments of operations and functions. The letters are chosen to indicate the types that operations and functions expect. These letters usually are taken from the first character of the type name. For example, i indicates an argument that is expected to be an integer, while s indicates an argument that is expected to be a string. For example, −i indicates the operation of computing the negative of the integer i, while i1 + i2 indicates the operation of adding the integers i1 and i2. This notation is extended following usual mathematical conventions, so that j and k also indicate integers, while n and m are used for numbers that may be integers or real numbers. Other types are indicated in a similar fashion. Finally, x and y are used for arguments that are of unknown or irrelevant types. Chapter 6 discusses types in more detail.

This notation does not mean that arguments of operations and functions must be written as identifiers. As mentioned previously, any argument of any operation or function can be an expression, no matter how complicated that expression is. The use of letters to stand for expressions is just a device that is used in this book for conciseness and to emphasize the required data types of arguments. In situations where the type produced by an expression is not important, the notation *expr*, *expr$_1$*, *expr$_2$*, ... is used. Therefore,

> while *expr$_1$* do *expr$_2$*

emphasizes that the control structure is concerned with the evaluation of its arguments, not with their values or their types.

In describing functions, phrases such as "the function match(s1, s2) ... " are used to indicate the name of a function and the number and types of its arguments. Strictly speaking, match(s1, s2) is not a function but rather a *call* of the function match. The shorter phraseology is used when there can be no confusion about its meaning. Similarly, other readily understood abbreviations are used. For example, "an integer between 1 and i" sometimes is used in place of "an integer between 1 and the value of i".

As shown by examples in this chapter, different typefaces are used to distinguish program material and terminology. The sans-serif typeface denotes literal program text, such as procedure and read(). The bold typeface denotes program constructions, such as **while-do** expressions, while italics are used for expressions in general, such as *expr*.

EXERCISES

1.1.[*]   Modify the second version of locate(s) given in §1.4 so that it returns a count of the number of lines that are written but fails if no lines are written.

1.2.   Why is it necessary for subtraction to associate from left to right? Why is it more useful for assignment to associate from right to left than from left to right?

---

[*]Exercises marked by stars have solutions in Appendix F.

2

CONTROL STRUCTURES

In the absence of control structures, expressions are evaluated in the order in which they appear in a procedure. Control structures can be used to evaluate expressions repeatedly or to select one of several expressions to evaluate. The expression that controls the loop or selection is called the *control expression*.

2.1 LOOPS

There are two control structures that evaluate an expression repeatedly, depending on the success or failure of a control expression:

> while *expr₁* do *expr₂*

described earlier, and

> until *expr₁* do *expr₂*

which repeatedly evaluates $expr_2$ until $expr_1$ succeeds. In both cases $expr_1$ is evaluated before $expr_2$. The **do** clauses are optional in **while** and **until** expressions. For example,

> while write(read())

copies the input file to the output file.

A related control structure is

> not *expr*

which fails if *expr* succeeds, but which succeeds if *expr* fails. Therefore, until $expr_1$ do $expr_2$

and

while not $expr_1$ do $expr_2$

are equivalent. The form that is used should be the one that is most natural to the situation in which it occurs.

The precedence of not is higher than that of any infix operation. For example,

not find(s1, s2) = 10

groups as

(not find(s1, s2)) = 10

It is advisable to use parentheses for grouping in expressions containing not to avoid such unexpected results.

The **while** and **until** control structures produce loops that normally are terminated only by the failure or success of their control expressions. Sometimes it is necessary to exit from a loop, independent of the evaluation of its control expression.

The **break** expression causes immediate termination of the loop in which it occurs. The following program illustrates the use of the **break** expression:

```
procedure main()
    while line := read() do
        if match("stop", line) then break
        else write(line)
end
```

This program copies the input file to the output file but stops if an input line beginning with the substring stop is encountered.

Sometimes it is useful to skip to the beginning of the control expression of a loop. This can be accomplished by the **next** expression. For example,

```
procedure main()
    while line := read() do
        if match("comment", line) then next
        else write(line)
end
```

copies the input file to the output file, omitting lines that begin with the substring comment.

The **break** and **next** expressions may appear anywhere in a loop but apply only to the innermost loop in which they occur. For example, if loops are nested, a **break** expression exits only from the loop in which it appears, not from any outer loops. The use of a **break** expression to exit from an inner loop is illustrated by the following program, which copies the input file to the output file, but which omits lines between lines that begin with skip and end, inclusive.

```
procedure main()
    while line := read() do
        if match("skip", line) then   # check for lines to skip
            while line := read() do    # skip loop
                if match("end", line) then break
                else next
        else write(line)               # write line in main loop
end
```

There is one other looping control structure:

    repeat *expr*

This control structure evaluates *expr* repeatedly, regardless of whether it succeeds or fails. A **repeat** loop can be terminated by a **break** expression. Repeat loops are useful when the controlling expression cannot be placed conveniently at the beginning of the loop.

Consider an input file that is organized into several sections. The first line in each section is a header, and the end of a section is identified by a line beginning with end. The following program counts the number of lines in each section and writes the header for the section followed by the count.

```
procedure main()
    repeat {                              # exit repeat if eof
        if not (headline := read()) then break
        count := 1
        while line := read() do {    # exit while if "end"
            count := count + 1
            if match("end", line) then break
            }
        write(headline, " : ", count)
        }
end
```

In this procedure it is convenient to use a repeat loop, since the first line of each section is treated specially.

Another way to exit from a loop (or any expression) is by stop(s), which writes s and then terminates program execution. The expression stop(s) is particularly useful for terminating program execution if an erroneous situation is detected at a place where it is awkward to exit by any other means.

For example, if each header in the preceding example is supposed to begin with the substring procedure, a test for this can be added as follows:

```
procedure main()
    repeat {
        if not (headline := read()) then break
        if not match("procedure", headline)
        then stop("erroneous header")
        :
        :
```

2.2 SELECTING EXPRESSIONS

The most common form of selection occurs when one or another expression is evaluated, depending on the success or failure of a control expression. As described Chapter 1, this is performed by

$$\text{if } expr_1 \text{ then } expr_2 \text{ else } expr_3$$

which evaluates $expr_2$ if $expr_1$ succeeds but evaluates $expr_3$ if $expr_1$ fails.

If there are several possibilities, **if-then-else** expressions can be chained together, as in

```
if match("begin", line) then depth := depth + 1
else if match("end", line) then depth := depth - 1
else other := other + 1
```

The **else** portion of this control structure is optional:

$$\text{if } expr_1 \text{ then } expr_2$$

evaluates $expr_2$ only if $expr_1$ succeeds. The **not** expression is useful in this abbreviated **if-then** form:

$$\text{if not } expr_1 \text{ then } expr_2$$

evaluates $expr_2$ only if $expr_1$ fails.

If there is a "dangling" else in nested **if-then-else** expressions, the **else** clause is grouped with the nearest preceding if. Consider, for example, the following section of a program for analyzing mailing lists:

```
if find("Mr.", line) then
if find("Mrs.", line)
then mm := mm + 1
else mr := mr + 1
```

These lines group as

```
if find("Mr.", line) then {
   if find("Mrs." ,line) then mm := mm + 1
   else mr := mr + 1
   }
```

Braces or parentheses can be used to force expressions to group in any desired way.

The value produced by

if *expr₁* then *expr₂* else *expr₃*

is the value produced by the selected expression. Since **if-then-else** is an expression, its value can be used in another, enclosing expression. An example is

k := (if i > j then i else j)

which assigns the larger of i or j to k. It generally is considered better style to rephrase such computations as

if i > j then k := i else k := j

but it is possible and sometimes useful to use a control structure just like any other expression that produces a value.

The precedence of then and else is lower than the precedence of any infix operation, so the previous example groups as

if i > j then k := i else (k := j)

as is usually desired.

While **if-then-else** selects an expression to evaluate, depending on the success or failure of the control expression, it is often useful to select an expression to evaluate, depending on the *value* of a control expression. The **case** control structure provides selection that is based on a value and has the form

```
case expr of {
   case-clause
        .
        .
        .
   }
```

The expression after case is a control expression whose value controls the selection. There can be several **case** clauses. Each has the form

expr₁ : *expr₂*

The value of the control expression is compared with the value of *expr₁* in each **case** clause in the order in which the **case** clauses appear. If the values are the same, the corresponding *expr₂* is evaluated, and its value becomes the value of the entire **case** expression. If the values of the control expression and *expr₁* are different, or if *expr₁* fails, the next **case** clause is tried.

There is also an optional **default** clause that has the form

default : *expr*₂

If no comparison of the value of the control expression with *expr₁* is successful, *expr₂* in the **default** clause is evaluated, and its value becomes the value of the **case** expression. The **default** clause may appear anywhere in the list of **case** clauses, but it is evaluated last. Since the **default** clause is evaluated last, it is good programming style to place it last in the list of **case** clauses.

Once an expression is selected, its value becomes the value of the **case** expression. Subsequent **case** clauses are not processed, even if the selected expression fails. A **case** expression itself fails if (1) its control expression fails, (2) if the selected expression fails, or (3) if no expression is selected.

Any kind of value can be used in the control expression. For example,

```
case s of {
    "begin" :  depth := depth + 1
    "end"   :  depth := depth − 1
    }
```

increments depth if the value of s is the string begin but decrements depth if the value of s is the string end. Since there is no **default** clause, this **case** expression fails if the value of s is neither begin nor end. In this case, the value of depth is not changed.

The values in the **case** clauses do not have to be constants; they can be produced by expressions. For example,

```
case i of {
    j + 1   :  write("high")
    j − 1   :  write("low")
    j       :  write("even")
    default :  write("out of range")
    }
```

writes one of four strings, depending on the relative values of i and j.

EXERCISES

2.1.* Write a program that writes the last line of the input file.

2.2.* Write a program that copies the input file to the output file, omitting the even-numbered lines.

2.3.[*]   Write a procedure first(i) that copies the first i lines of the input file to the output file, failing if there are less than i lines of input.

2.4.   Write a procedure omit(s) that copies the input file to the output file, omitting lines that contain the substring s.

2.5.   Write a procedure skipto(s) that reads and discards input lines until a line beginning with the substring s is found, returning this line but failing if no such line is found.

2.6.   Write a procedure both(s1, s2) that counts the number of input lines in which both s1 and s2 occur as substrings.

2.7.[*]   Write a procedure exor(s1, s2) that counts the number of input lines that contain either of the substrings s1 or s2 but not both.

2.8.   Write a program that determines if the input file has properly nested occurrences of braces but fails otherwise. For example,

```
while line := read() do {
        if find(s, line) then {
            write(line)
            scount := scount + 1
        }
    }
```

is properly nested, but

```
while line := read() do {
    if find(s, line) then
        write(line)
        scount := scount + 1
        }
    }
```

is not properly nested. For simplicity, assume that there is at most one occurrence of a brace on any one line.

3

NUMBERS

Numerical computation in Icon is similar to that in most programming languages. The usual operations on integers and real numbers (floating-point numbers) are supported. Integers are converted to real numbers automatically in mixed-mode operations that involve both integers and real numbers.

3.1 NUMERIC LITERALS

Integers are represented literally in the usual way. For example, **36** represents the integer 36 and **1024** represents the integer 1,024. Real numbers can be represented literally using either decimal or exponent notation. For example, **27e2** and **2700.0** are equivalent and represent the real number 2,700.0.

Bases other than 10 can be used for integer literals. Such *radix literals* have the form irj, where i is a base-10 integer that specifies the base for j. For example, **2r11** represents the integer 3, while **8r10** represents 8. The base can be any value from 2 through 36; the letters **a**, **b**, ..., **z** are used to specify "digits" in j that are larger than 9. For example, **16ra** represents 10, while **36rcat** represents 15,941.

See Appendix A for additional details of the syntax of numeric literals.

3.2 NUMERICAL COMPUTATION

There are two prefix operations for numerical computation. The operation +n produces the numeric value of n, while −n produces the negative of n.

The infix operations for numerical computation are as follows:

expression	operation	relative precedence	associativity
n + m	addition	1	left to right
n − m	subtraction	1	left to right
n * m	multiplication	2	left to right
n / m	division	2	left to right
n % m	remaindering	2	left to right
n ∧ m	exponentiation	3	right to left

All of these infix operations have precedence higher than that of assignment. Consequently,

    n := n + 1

groups as

    n := (n + 1)

As a general rule, prefix operations have higher precedence than infix operations. For example,

    −n + 3

groups as

    (−n) + 3

The operation

    n % m

produces the remainder of n divided by m with the sign of n. For example,

    −10 % 3

produces −1, but

    10 % −3

produces 1.

In integer division the remainder is discarded; that is, the value is truncated. For example,

    −7 / 2

produces −3.

Division by zero and raising a negative real number to a real power are erroneous. Such an error causes program execution to terminate with a diagnostic message.

The function **abs**(n) produces the absolute value of n. For example,

abs(−7 / 2)

produces 3.

Any numerical computation that involves a real number produces a real number. For example,

n := 10 + 3.14159

assigns 13.14159 to n.

3.3 NUMERICAL COMPARISON

The numerical comparison operations are

n < m	less than
n <= m	less than or equal to
n = m	equal to
n >= m	greater than or equal to
n > m	greater than
n ~= m	not equal to

A comparison operation produces the value of its right argument if the specified relation holds, but fails if the relation does not hold. For example,

n < m

succeeds and produces the value of m if the value of n is less than the value of m, but fails otherwise.

The comparison operations associate from left to right, which allows compound comparisons to be written in a natural way. For example,

1 <= n <= 10

groups as

(1 <= n) <= 10

and succeeds if the value of n is between 1 and 10, inclusive.

The comparison operations all have the same precedence, which is lower than that of any numerical computation operation, but higher than that of assignment. Therefore,

$$n > m + 1$$

groups as

$$n > (m + 1)$$

while

$$n := m > 10$$

groups as

$$n := (m > 10)$$

Note that this expression assigns the value 10 to n if the comparison succeeds.

3.4 AUGMENTED ASSIGNMENT

One of the most common operations in programming is incrementing the numerical value of a variable, as in

$$n := n + 1$$

In order to make such operations more concise and to avoid two references to the same variable, Icon has *augmented assignment* operations that combine assignment with the computation to be performed. For example,

$$n +:= 1$$

adds one to the value of n.

There are augmented assignment operations corresponding to all infix operations (except the assignment operations themselves); the := is simply appended to the operator symbol. For example,

$$n *:= 10$$

is equivalent to

$$n := n * 10$$

Similarly,

$$n >:= m$$

assigns the value of m to n if the value of n is greater than the value of m. This may seem a bit strange at first sight, since most programming languages do not treat comparisons as computations, but this feature of Icon sometimes can be used to advantage.

3.5 RANDOM NUMBERS

The operation ?i produces a number from a pseudo-random sequence. If the value of i is a positive integer i, the value produced by ?i is an integer j in the range $1 \leq j \leq i$. If the value of i is 0, the value produced by ?i is a real number r in the range $0.0 \leq r < 1.0$.

For example, the expression

> if ?2 = 1 then "H" else "T"

produces the string H or T with approximately equal probability.

The pseudo-random sequence is produced by a linear congruence relation starting with an initial seed value of 0. This sequence is the same from one program execution to another, allowing programs to be tested in a reproducible environment. The seed can be changed by assigning an integer value to &random. For example,

> &random := 0

resets the seed to its initial value.

EXERCISES

3.1.[*]   Assuming that the input file consists of lines each of which contains a single number, write programs that

(a) compute the sum of the numbers,

(b) compute the average of the numbers, and

(c) determine the largest and smallest numbers.

3.2.   Write a procedure that computes the greatest common divisor of two positive integers.

3.3.[*]   Write a procedure that computes factorials.

3.4.   Write a procedure that computes binomial coefficients.

4

CHARACTER SETS
AND STRINGS

Different computer systems have character sets of different sizes: 128 and 256 are common. Most characters have graphic representations, such as the characters **A** and **$**. Some characters, such as the linefeed, have interpretations for input and output. Since the hardware representation of a character is just a bit pattern or *code*, different assignments of graphics to codes produce different orderings or *collating sequences* of the graphics according to the numerical values of their codes. Of course, it is customary to assign letters to codes so that the numerical order of the codes corresponds to the alphabetical order of the letters. Different systems disagree, however, on the relative order of digits and letters, as well as upper- and lowercase letters, to say nothing of the punctuation marks. Consequently, sorting, which usually relies on the numerical values of codes, may produce different results on different computer systems.

The character set Icon uses is fixed in size and ordering and is independent of the computer system on which Icon runs. This character set has 256 characters, the first 128 of which are interpreted as ASCII. See Appendix A for a listing of the ASCII collating sequence and graphics. The last 128 characters have no graphics but may be used for labeling objects (see Chapter 17).

Icon has no character data type, but it has two data types that are composed of characters. *Csets* are sets of characters, while *strings* are sequences of characters. These two organizations of characters are useful for representing various kinds of data and operating on data in different ways.

4.1 CHARACTER SETS

Since there are only 256 different characters, the number of possible csets, while large, is small compared to the number of possible strings. Nonetheless csets are useful for representing relationships among characters. For example, sharing a common property, such as being a lowercase letter, is naturally represented by set membership.

4.1.1 Cset Literals

Csets are represented literally by surrounding the characters by single quotation marks. For example,

> vowel := 'aeiou'

assigns a cset containing five characters to vowel. Since there is no concept of order in a cset, the order in which the characters appear in a cset literal is irrelevant and duplicate characters have no effect. Therefore,

> vowel := 'uoieaou'

assigns the same cset to vowel as the previous expression.

All the characters within quotation marks are taken literally, whether or not they have associated graphics. For example, ' ' is the literal representation of the cset consisting of a single space. To allow any character to be represented literally, escape sequences are used. In quoted literals the character \ (backslash) "escapes" the character that follows it, giving it a special interpretation. Two useful escape sequences are \', which stands for the single quotation mark, and \n, which stands for a newline (linefeed) character. Therefore, '\'' is the literal representation for the cset consisting of a single quotation mark, while '\n' is the literal representation for the cset consisting of a newline character. Another escape sequence is \b, which stands for a backspace character. A complete list of escape sequences is given in Appendix A.

4.1.2 Built-in Csets

Some useful csets are built into Icon as the values of keywords. The value of &cset is the set of all 256 characters. The value of &ascii consists of the 128 ASCII characters of &cset, while &lcase consists of the lowercase letters and &ucase consists of the uppercase letters.

4.1.3 Operations on Csets

There are five operations on csets:

expression	*operation*
*c	size
~c	complement
c1 ** c2	intersection
c1 ++ c2	union
c1 −− c2	difference

Intersection has the same precedence as multiplication, while union and difference have the same precedence as addition and subtraction. The three infix operations on csets associate from left to right.

The size of a cset is the number of characters that it contains. For example, *'aeiou' and *'uoieaou' both produce the integer 5.

The complement of a cset is taken with respect to &cset. For example, ~&lcase produces a cset of all characters that are not lowercase letters.

The union of two csets consists of all characters that are in either cset. For example,

&lcase ++ &ucase

produces a cset that consists of all letters.

The intersection of two csets consists of all characters that are in both csets. For example,

'Spanish' ** 'armada'

produces a cset that consists of the single character a.

The difference of two csets consists of all characters in the first that are not in the second. For example,

'egotist' −− 'twist'

produces the cset 'ego'.

4.1.4 Conversion between Csets and Strings

As described in Chapter 1, Icon automatically converts values from one type to another according to context. This conversion applies to csets and strings. For example, the following procedure produces a cset of all the characters that occur in the input file.

```
procedure inset()
   chars := ''
   while line := read() do
      chars := chars ++ line
   return chars
end
```

The cset **chars** originally starts out empty, given literally by enclosing no characters in quotes. Then the characters in each line of the input file are added to **chars**. In the union operation, the value of **line** is a string that is automatically converted to a cset.

As described in Chapter 3, there are augmented assignment operations for all infix operations except the assignment operations themselves. Using augmented assignment and omitting the unnecessary auxiliary identifier **line**, the preceding procedure can be written more compactly as

```
procedure inset()
   chars := ''
   while chars ++:= read()
   return chars
end
```

4.2 STRINGS

Strings are used more frequently than csets because the sequential organization of strings allows the representation of complex relationships among characters. Written text, such as this book, is just a sequence of characters. Most of the data processed by computers consists of sequences of characters, especially when it is read in, written out, and stored in files.

4.2.1 String Literals

As described earlier, strings are represented literally with surrounding double quotation marks. For example,

```
vowel := "aeiou"
```

assigns the string **aeiou** to **vowel**. Unlike csets, the order of characters in a string is significant, as are duplicate characters. For example,

```
vowel := "uoieaou"
```

assigns a different value to **vowel** than the previous expression; it is longer, and the characters **u** and **o** occur twice.

The escape sequences used in cset literals can also be used in string literals. In addition, \" stands for a double quotation mark. Therefore,

write("What I want to say is\n\"Hello world\"")

produces

What I want to say is
"Hello world"

4.2.2 String Size

The size of a string is the number of characters in it. The operation ∗s produces the size of s. For example,

∗"Hello world"

produces the integer 11.

There is no practical limit to the size of a string, although very large strings are awkward and expensive to manipulate. The smallest string is the *empty string*, which contains no characters and has size zero. The empty string is represented literally by "".

4.2.3 Concatenation

One of the more commonly used operations on strings is *concatenation*,

s1 || s2

which produces a string consisting of the characters in s1 followed by those in s2. For example,

"Hello " || "world"

produces the string Hello world.

Concatenation associates from left to right and its precedence is higher than that of the numerical comparison operations, but lower than that of addition. Concatenation usually does not occur in combination with numerical computation, however.

The empty string is the identity with respect to concatenation; concatenating the empty string with another string just produces the other string. The empty string therefore is a natural initial value for building up a string value by successive concatenations. For example, suppose that the input file consists of a number of lines, each of which contains a single word. Then the following procedure produces a list of these words with each followed by a comma.

```
procedure wordlist()
   wlist := ""                          # initialize wlist
   while word := read() do
      wlist := wlist || word || ","
   return wlist
end
```

The augmented assignment operation for concatenation is particularly useful for appending strings onto an evolving value. For example,

```
wlist ||:= word || ","
```

is equivalent to

```
wlist := wlist || word || ","
```

4.2.4 Substrings

Since a string is a sequence of characters, any subsequence or substring is also a string. A substring is simply a portion of another string. For example, **Cl** is a substring of **Cleo**, as are **leo** and **e**. **Co**, however, is not a substring of **Cleo**, since **C** and **o** do not occur consecutively in **Cleo**. Any string is a substring of itself. The empty string is a substring of every string.

In Icon, substrings are specified by position. Positions are numbered from left to right starting at 1, and are between characters (so that a substring is between positions). The positions for **Cleo** are

```
C   l   e   o
↑   ↑   ↑   ↑   ↑
1   2   3   4   5
```

Therefore, **Cl** is the substring between positions 1 and 3, **leo** is the substring between positions 2 and 5, and **e** is between positions 3 and 4.

Range specifications.   A substring is produced by a subscripting expression, in which a *range specification* enclosed in brackets gives the positions that bound the desired substring. One form of range specification is $i:j$, where i and j are the bounding positions. For example,

```
"Cleo"[1:3]
```

produces **Cl**. Range specifications usually are applied to identifiers, as in

```
text[1:4]
```

which produces the first three characters of **text**, those between positions 1 and 4. If the value of **text** is less than three characters long, the subscripting expression fails. This is another example of the design philosophy of Icon: If an operation cannot be performed, it does not produce a result. In this case the failure occurs because the specified substring does not exist.

Expressions can be used to provide the bounds in range specifications. For example,

        text[2:*s]

produces the substring of **text** between 2 and the size of **s**. Similarly, any expression whose value is a string can be subscripted, as in

    s := read()[2:10]

which assigns a substring of a line of input to **s**. Note that this expression may fail for two reasons: if **read** fails because there is no more input, or if **read** produces a line that is not long enough. Expressions containing such *ambiguous failure* should be avoided, since they can be the source of subtle programming errors.

The following program illustrates the use of substrings to copy the input file to the output file, limiting the length of the output lines to 60 characters.

```
procedure main()
    while line := read() do {
        line := line[1:61]              # truncate
        write(line)
        }
    end
```

If a line is longer than 60 characters, it is truncated before it is written. Note that

    write(line[1:61])

does not work properly in place of the two lines in the previous procedure, since the subscripting expression fails if a line is less than 60 characters long. There is no output for such lines.

The two positions in a range specification can be given in either order. The leftmost position need not be given first; only the bounding positions are significant. Therefore, **line[1:4]** and **line[4:1]** are equivalent.

Range specifications may also be given by a position and an offset from that position. The range specification **i+:j** specifies a substring starting at **i** of size **j**. The offset can be negative: **i−:j** specifies a substring starting at **i** but consisting of the **j** characters to the left of **i**, rather than to the right. For example,

    write(line[1+:60])

writes the first 60 characters of **line**, as does

write(line[61−:60])

It usually is more natural to work from left to right, using a positive range specification. However, the character positions can be specified either from left to right, as previously, or from right to left. In right-to-left specifications, positions start at 0 beyond the rightmost (last) character, and then become increasingly negative toward the beginning of the string. The right-to-left positions for **Cleo** are

```
  C  l  e  o
  ↑  ↑  ↑  ↑  ↑
 −4 −3 −2 −1  0
```

Right-to-left position specifications are called *nonpositive specifications*. Note that there are two ways of specifying each position in a string: positive and nonpositive. Nonpositive specifications are particularly useful when the length of a string is not known. For example,

write(line[−3:0])

writes the last three characters of **line**, while

write(line[2:0])

writes all the characters of **line** except the first. Note that positive and nonpositive specifications can be mixed.

Nonpositive specifications are merely a convenience; actual positions are always positive.

If a substring consists of only a single character, it can be specified by the position before it. Therefore,

write(line[2])

writes the second character of **line** and is equivalent to

write(line[2+:1])

Similarly,

last := line[−1]

assigns the last character of **line** to **last**.

Assignment can be made to a subscripted variable to change the substring corresponding to the range specification. Consequently, if the value of **word** is **two**,

word[2] := "o"

changes the value of **word** to **too**. Similarly,

word[−1] := ""

deletes the last character of **word** so that its value becomes **to**.

Note that assignment to change a substring may change the length of a string. Assignment to change a substring only is a shorthand notation for concatenation. For example,

word[2] := "o"

is shorthand for

word := word[1] || "o" || word[3:0]

If two identifiers have the same string value, changing a substring in one does not change the value of the other. Therefore, in

line := read()
image := line
line[2+:3] := ""

the value of **image** is not changed by the assignment to **line[2+:3]**. A new value is assigned to **line**, but not to **image**.

Assignment can be made to a subscripting expression to change the value of a string only if the range specification is applied to a variable. For example,

"Cleo"[1] := "K"

is as meaningless as

1 := 2

Both are erroneous.

Random subscripts.   The operation **?s** produces a randomly selected subscript of **s** and is equivalent to

s[?∗s]

if **s** is not empty. If **s** is empty, **?s** fails. For example,

?"HT"

produces the string **H** or **T** with approximately equal probability.

If **s** is a string-valued variable, assignment can be made to **?s** to replace a randomly selected character of **s**. For example,

?s := ""

deletes a randomly selected character of **s**.

4.2.5 Lexical Comparison

Strings can be compared for their relative magnitude in a manner similar to the comparison of numbers, but the comparison is based on lexical (alphabetical) order rather than numerical value. Lexical order is based on the collating sequence of characters. The character c1 is lexically less than c2 if c1 appears before c2 in the collating sequence. Characters are represented internally in Icon as 8-bit binary numbers, so 01000001 is less than 01100001, for example. Since the binary number 01000001 (octal 101) corresponds to the letter A, while 01100001 (octal 141) corresponds to the letter a, A is less than a in the ASCII collating sequence. That is, A is lexically less than a.

For longer strings, lexical order is determined by the lexical order of their characters, from left to right. Therefore, AB is less than aA and aB is less than ab. If one string is an initial substring of another, the shorter string is lexically less than the longer. For example, Aba is lexically less than Abaa. The empty string is lexically less than any other string. Two strings are lexically equal if and only if they are the same size and are identical, character by character. There are six lexical comparison operations:

s1 << s2	lexically less than
s1 <<= s2	lexically less than or equal
s1 >> s2	lexically greater than
s1 >>= s2	lexically greater than or equal
s1 == s2	lexically equal
s1 ~== s2	lexically not equal

All the lexical comparison operations associate from left to right and have the same precedence as the numerical comparison operations. A lexical comparison operation produces the value its right argument, provided that the comparison succeeds. Therefore, the expression

    s1 << s2 << s3

succeeds and produces s3, provided s2 is strictly between s1 and s3 in lexical order.

The use of lexical comparison is illustrated by the following program, which determines the lexically largest and smallest lines in the input file.

```
procedure main()
    min := max := read()              # initial min and max
    while line := read() do
  ,   if line >> max then max := line
        else if line << min then min := line
    write("lexically largest line is: ", max)
    write("lexically smallest line is: ", min)
end
```

This program can be rephrased in a way that is more idiomatic to Icon by using augmented assignment operations:

```
procedure main()
    min := max := read()              # initial min and max
    while line := read() do
        if max <<:= line then next
        else min >>:= line
    write("lexically largest line is: ", max)
    write("lexically smallest line is: ", min)
end
```

4.2.6 String-Valued Functions

When producing formatted output, it is often useful to have "fields" of a specific width that line up in columns. There are three functions that position a string in a field of a specified width, aligning the string in the field at the right, left, or in the center.

right(s1, i, s2).   The function right(s1, i, s2) produces a string of size i in which s1 is positioned at the right and s2 is used to pad out the remaining characters to the left. For example,

```
right("Detroit", 10, "+")
```

produces

```
+++Detroit
```

Note that enough copies of s2 are concatenated on the left to make up the specified size. If s2 is omitted, spaces are used for padding.

If the size of s1 is greater than i, it is truncated at the left so that the value is of size i. Therefore,

```
right("Detroit", 6)
```

produces

etroit

The value of s2 usually is a one-character string, but it may be of any length. The resulting string is always of size i, however; any extra characters that might result from appending copies of s2 are discarded. For example,

right("Detroit", 10, "+*")

produces

+*+Detroit

Note that the padding string is truncated at the right.

A common use of right is to position data in columns. The following program, which prints out a table of the first four powers of the integers from 1 to 10, illustrates such an application:

```
procedure main()
   i := 0
   while i < 10 do {
      i +:= 1
      write(right(i, 5), right(i ∧ 2, 8), right(i ∧ 3, 8),
         right(i ∧ 4, 8))
      }
end
```

The output written by this program is

1	1	1	1
2	4	8	16
3	9	27	81
4	16	64	256
5	25	125	625
6	36	216	1296
7	49	343	2401
8	64	512	4096
9	81	729	6561
10	100	1000	10000

left(s1, i, s2).   The function left(s1, i, s2) is similar to right(s1, i, s2) except that the direction is reversed: s1 is placed at the left, padding is done on the right, and truncation (if necessary) is done at the right. Therefore,

left("Detroit", 10, "+")

produces

Detroit+++

and

left("Detroit", 6)

produces

Detroi

The padding string is truncated at the left if necessary.

center(s1, i, s2).   The function center(s1, i, s2) centers s1 in a string of size i, padding on the left and right, if necessary, with s2. If s1 cannot be centered exactly, it is placed to the left of center. Truncation is then done at the left and right if necessary. Therefore,

center("Detroit", 10, "+")

produces

+Detroit++

while

center("Detroit", 6)

produces

etroit

repl(s, i).   When several copies of the same string are to be concatenated, it is more convenient (and more efficient) to use repl(s, i), a function that produces the concatenation of i copies of s. For example,

repl("+*+", 3)

produces

+*++*++*+

The expression repl(s, 0) produces the empty string.

reverse(s).   The function reverse(s) produces a string consisting of the characters of s in reversed order. For example,

reverse("string")

produces gnirts.

trim(s, c).   The function trim(s, c) produces a string consisting of the initial substring of s with the omission of any trailing characters contained in c. That is, it trims off any characters in c. If c is omitted, spaces are trimmed. For example,

>   trim("Betelgeuse   ")

produces **Betelgeuse** (without the trailing spaces), while

>   trim("Betelgeuse", &lcase)

produces just **B**.

map(s1, s2, s3).   The function map(s1, s2, s3) produces a string resulting from a character mapping of s1 in which each character of s1 that appears in s2 is replaced by the corresponding character in s3. Characters of s1 that do not appear in s2 are not changed.   For example,

>   map("mad hatter", "a", "+")

produces

>   m+d h+tter

and

>   map("mad hatter", "aeiou", "12345")

produces

>   m1d h1tt2r

Several characters in s2 may have the same corresponding character in s3. Therefore,

>   map("mad hatter", "aeiou", "+++++")

produces

>   m+d h+tt+r

In case a character appears more than once in s2, the rightmost correspondence with s3 applies. Duplicate characters in s2 provide a way to mask out unwanted characters. For example, marking the positions of vowels in a string can be accomplished by mapping every vowel into a vertical bar and mapping all other characters into a space. An easy way to do this is to set up a correspondence between every character and a space and then append the correspondences for the vowels:

```
s2 := &cset || "AEIOUaeiou"
s3 := repl(" ", *&cset) || "||||||||||"
```

In this correspondence, s2 is a string consisting of all characters followed by the vowels, 266 characters in all, since the vowels are duplicated. The value of s3 is 256 spaces followed by 10 vertical bars. The last 10 characters in s2 and s3 override the previous correspondences between the vowels and spaces. The following program illustrates an application of such a mapping:

```
procedure main()
    s2 := &cset || "AEIOUaeiou"
    s3 := repl(" ", *&cset) || "||||||||||"
    while line := read() do {
        write(line)
        write(map(line, s2, s3))
        }
end
```

Consider the following input file consisting of a stanza from "The Rime of the Ancient Mariner" by Coleridge:

```
The Sun came up upon the left,
Out of the sea came he!
And he shone bright, and on the right
Went down into the sea.
```

For this input file, the output for the previous program is

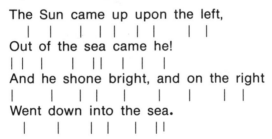

4.3 STRING ANALYSIS

String analysis involves locating the positions of specified substrings or characters in strings. These positions, in turn, can be used to extract substrings using range specifications.

4.3.1 Locating Substrings

find(s1, s2).   The function find(s1, s2) produces the position in s2 at which s1 occurs as a substring. It fails if s1 is not a substring of s2. If s1 occurs as a substring of s2 at more than one place, the first (leftmost) position is produced. For example,

find("the", "The theory is fallacious")

produces 5, while

find("Theory", "The theory is fallacious")

fails.

An example of the use of find is given by the following procedure, which writes a vertical bar beneath the leftmost location of s in each line of input.

```
procedure lmark(s)
   while line := read() do {
      write(line)
      write(repl(" ", find(s, line) − 1), "|")
      }
   return
end
```

Note that if s does not occur in line, find(s, line) fails and no vertical bar is written. An example of output written by lmark("not"), when applied to a portion of a song from Shakespeare's play *As You Like It*, is

```
Freeze, freeze, thou bitter sky,
That dost not bite so nigh
         |
As benefits forgot:
Though thou the waters warp,
Thy sting is not so sharp,
             |
As friend remember'd not.
                    |
```

match(s1, s2).   If s1 occurs as an initial substring of s2, the function match(s1, s2) produces the position in s2 at the end of s1. It fails if s1 is not an initial substring of s2. For example,

match("The", "The theory is fallacious")

produces 4, while

match("theory", "The theory is fallacious")

fails, since **theory** is not an initial substring of the second argument.

The function **match(s1, s2)** is usually used to check whether a string has a specific initial substring, as illustrated by the procedures in §1.4. The value it produces usually is uninteresting, since it is just one greater than the size of **s1**.

4.3.2 Lexical Analysis

The analysis of strings that is concerned with the characters that they contain is called lexical analysis. There are four lexical analysis functions.

any(c, s).   If the first character of **s** is in the cset **c**, **any(c, s)** produces the position after that character. It fails otherwise. For example,

any('aeiouAEIOU', "Our conjecture has support")

produces 2, while

any('aeiou', "Our conjecture has support")

fails.

The use of **any(c, s)** is illustrated by the following program, which writes out only those input lines that begin with a character in **c**:

```
procedure icwrite(c)
   while line := read() do
      if any(c, line) then write(line)
   return
end
```

For the stanza from "The Rime of the Ancient Mariner" used in §4.2.6, the lines written by **icwrite('AEIOU')** are

Out of the sea came he!
And he shone bright, and on the right

Note that **any** resembles **match**, except that the **any** depends on the initial character, not an initial substring, and that any one of several of initial characters may be specified. Like **match**, the value produced by **any** is usually uninteresting; it is the success or failure that is significant.

upto(c, s).   If **s** contains a character in **c**, **upto(c, s)** produces the position of (before) that character. It fails otherwise. If a character in **c** occurs more than once in **s**, the first position is produced. For example,

upto('aeiou', "Our conjecture has support")

produces 2.

The function upto(c, s) is much like find(s1, s2). The difference is that the value produced by upto depends on any one of a number of characters, rather than on a specific substring.

The use of upto is illustrated by the following program, which writes the initial string up to a punctuation mark or a space (a "word" in textual material):

```
procedure main()
    wchar := &lcase ++ &ucase
    pchar := '.,:;?! '
    while line := read() do
                                        # get to first letter
        if line := line[upto(wchar, line):0]
        then write(line[1:upto(pchar, line)])
end
```

The first expression in the **do** clause has the effect of deleting any initial characters other than letters, such as indenting spaces, that may occur at the beginning of line. If the line starts with a letter, upto produces 1 and the value of line is not changed by the assignment. If line does not contain a letter, however, no value is written and the next line is read.

The result of applying this procedure to the song given in §4.3.1 is

```
Freeze
That
As
Though
Thy
As
```

many(c, s). If s begins with a string of characters in c, many(c, s) produces the position after this initial substring. It fails otherwise. For example,

many('aeiouAEIOU', "Our conjecture has support")

produces 3. The function many(c, s) is similar to match(s1, s2), except that the initial substring may consist of any of the characters in c rather than a specific string. It is similar to any(c, s), except that the initial substring may be arbitrarily long (it must be at least one character long, however).

In some respects, many is the converse of upto. For example, the program given previously for producing initial words can be reformulated as follows:

```
procedure main()
   wchar := &lcase ++ &ucase
   while line := read() do
      if line := line[upto(wchar, line):0]
      then write(line[1:many(wchar, line)])
end
```

This program produces the same results as the one given earlier if the input file is the same. The two programs do not produce the same results for all input files, however. The first procedure defines a word by exclusion (anything up to a specific set of characters), while the second procedure defines a word by inclusion (upper- and lowercase letters). Definition by exclusion presents several problems. Many characters besides the punctuation marks given that are not ordinarily considered to be contained in words. Quotation marks and parentheses are examples. While additions can be made to the set of characters that terminates a word, it is not easy to decide when to stop. Furthermore, if a line contains only a single word that is not followed by one of the characters in **pchar**, the first procedure does not work properly, since **upto** only succeeds if a terminating character is found.

While **many** does not require a terminating character, words may contain characters other than letters. For example, apostrophes and dashes can be added to **wchar**:

   wchar := &lcase ++ &ucase ++ '\'−'

None of these approaches defines a word precisely, of course.

bal(c1, c2, c3, s).   The function bal(c1, c2, c3, s) is useful in applications that involve the analysis of formulas, expressions, and other strings that have balanced bracketing characters. Mathematical expressions are representative of such balanced strings.

The function bal(c1, c2, c3, s) is like upto(c, s), except that c2 and c3 specify sets of bracketing characters that must be balanced in the usual algebraic sense up to a character in c1 in the string s. For example,

   bal('−', '(', ')', "−35")

produces 1 but

   bal('+', '(', ')', "((2*x)+3)+(5*y)")

produces 10. Note that the position of the first + is not preceded by a string that is balanced with respect to parentheses:

   ((2*x)+3)+(5*y)
     ↑   ↑

The bracketing characters need not be parentheses. The expression

bal(',', '[', ']', "[+, [2, 3]], [*, [5, 10]]")

produces 10.

In determining whether or not a string is balanced, a count is kept start-ing at zero as characters in s are examined. If a character in c1 is encountered and the count is zero, bal(c1, c2, c3, s) produces that position. Otherwise, if a character in c2 is encountered, the count is incremented, while the count is decremented if a character in c3 is encountered. Other characters leave the count unchanged.

If the counter ever becomes negative, or if the count is positive after ex-amining the last character of s, bal fails.

All characters in c2 and c3 have equal status; bal cannot be used to determine proper nesting of different bracketing characters. For example, the value produced by

bal('+', '([', ')]', "([a+b))+c]")

is 8.

If c2 and c3 both contain the same character, its presence in c2 counts; it has no effect as a character in c3.

If c1 is omitted, &cset is assumed. If c2 and c3 are omitted, left and right parentheses are used for the bracketing characters. That is,

bal(, , , s)

is equivalent to

bal(&cset, '(', ')', s)

The use of bal is illustrated by the following program, which writes a vertical bar under the leftmost operator following an initial balanced substring in lines of the input file:

```
procedure main()
    while line := read() do {
        write(line)
        write(repl(" ", bal('+−*/', , , line) − 1), "|")
    }
end
```

An example of the output produced by this program is

```
      y
      x−x∗z
      |
      ((z+y))+y/z−(x)
           |
      z+y−(z∗(x/(z)+x∗y))−z∗z/x+(x+y+x)
      |
      (y)∗(x)
      |
      ((z))+(z)
            |
      z−x
      |
      (z)/x+y
         |
      (z−(y)+y∗(y/x))
      z+(((y))/(y))−z
      |
      x+(y)
      |
      z/(y)+y∗y
         |
```

Note that no vertical bar is written for expressions that do not have an initial balanced substring that is followed by one of the operator symbols.

4.3.3 Range Restriction

All the string and lexical analysis functions may have two additional arguments that restrict the range in which the analysis is done. For example, upto(c, s, i, j) restricts the value to positions between i and j in s. Therefore,

upto('aeiou', "The theory is fallacious", 5, 11)

produces 7. Note that this is a position in s; the value produced by

upto('aeiou', "The theory is fallacious"[5:11])

is 3.

An omitted value of j is equivalent to 0 and restricts the value to positions between i and the end of the string.

Like range specifications, the range restriction arguments can be given either as positive or nonpositive position specifications and can be given in either order. For example, find(s1, s2, 0, −10)

restricts the range in s2 to the last 10 characters.

Range restriction allows the string and lexical analysis functions to be used to advance through strings. An example is the following program, which writes all the words in the input file.

```
procedure main()
    wchar := &lcase ++ &ucase ++ '\'−'
    while line := read() do {
        i := 1
        while j := upto(wchar, line, i) do {
            i := many(wchar, line, j)
            write(line[i:j])
            }
        }
end
```

In this program i and j advance through the value of line as successive letters are found and passed over. Note that the success of

j := upto(wchar, line, i)

assures the success of

i := many(wchar, line, j)

The result for the quotation from Shakespeare given earlier is

Freeze
freeze
thou
bitter
sky
    .
    .
    .
friend
remember'd
not

EXERCISES

4.1.[*]   Write a program that determines the number of different characters that occur in the input file.

4.2.   Write a procedure space(s) that produces a string consisting of the characters in s interspersed with spaces. For example,

space("Hello world")

should produce

H e l l o   w o r l d

4.3.[*]   Write a procedure rotate(s, i) that produces the value of s rotated to the left i characters. For example,

rotate("abcde", 3)

should produce

deabc

4.4.   Write a procedure that converts strings to the form of Icon string literals. Insert escape sequences for " and \.

4.5.   Write a program that produces a weight conversion table consisting of the equivalent values of pounds, ounces, kilograms, and grams for weights from 1 to 10 pounds in increments of one-tenth of a pound.

4.6.   Write a procedure that enciphers the input file by using a simple substitution cipher. Write a corresponding procedure that deciphers the results.

4.7.[*]   Write a procedure delete(s, c) that produces a string in which all characters in c that occur in s are deleted. For example,

delete("becomes", 'aeiou')

should produce bcms.

4.8.   A palindrome is a string, such as madam, that reads the same forward and backward. In palindromic sentences, spaces and punctuation marks are ignored and upper- and lowercase letters are considered to be equivalent, as in

A man, a plan, a canal − Panama!

Write a procedure palin(s) that succeeds if s is a palindromic sentence, but fails otherwise.

4.9.   Write a program that counts the number of lines, words, and characters in the input file.

4.10.[*]   Write a program that writes the lines of the input file with dashes under each word.

4.11.   Write a procedure that is similar to **wordlist** as given in §4.2.3, but without the assumption that there is only a single word in each line of the input file. Do not put duplicate words in the list.

4.12.   Write a program that writes vertical bars under every operator that follows an initial balanced substring in lines of the input file. For example, the input line

```
        X—X*Z
```

should produce the output lines

```
        X—X*Z
         |  |
```

5

STRUCTURES

Structures are aggregates of variables. Icon has two kinds of built-in structures: lists and tables. Records, which are similar to lists, also can be declared. Different kinds of structures have different access methods and organizations. Structures are created during program execution.

5.1 LISTS

Lists in Icon have two roles. In one role, they are one-dimensional arrays that can be subscripted by position. In the other role, they can be manipulated by stack and queue access functions and grow and shrink automatically. The two ways of manipulating lists can be used in combination.

5.1.1 List Creation

One way to create a list is to place brackets around a list of expressions:

$$[expr_1, expr_2, \ldots, expr_n]$$

This expression produces a list of n values produced by $expr_1$, $expr_2$, ..., $expr_n$. For example,

```
oracles := ["Delphi", "Heracles", "Claros"]
```

assigns a list of three strings to oracles. Similarly,

powers := [i, i ∧ 2, i ∧ 3, i ∧ 4]

assigns a list of four integers to **powers**.

The values in a list do not have to be of the same type. For example,

city := ["Tucson", 400000, "Arizona", "Pima"]

assigns a list of four values to **city**, three of which are strings and one of which is an integer.

The values in a list may be of any type. For example,

expression := ["+", ["a"], ["*", ["c"], ["d"]]]

assigns a list of three values to **expression**. The first value is a string, while the second and third values are other lists, and so on. Such a list can be thought of as representing a tree in which the first value in the list is associated with the position in the tree and subsequent values represent subtrees. The tree for **expression** can be visualized as

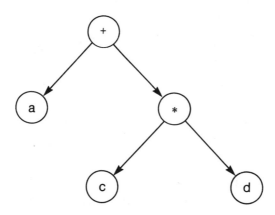

The function

list(i, x)

creates a list of i values, each of which has the value of **x**. For example,

vector := list(100, 0.0)

assigns to **vector** a list of 100 values, each of which is 0.0.

An *empty list*, which contains no value, can be created by [] or list(0). The size of a list is produced by the same operation that is used for strings. For example, ∗**vector** produces 100, while ∗[] produces 0.

5.1.2 List Referencing

The values in a list are referenced, or *subscripted*, by position much as the characters in a string are. For example,

```
write(oracles[2])
```

writes **Heracles**. Similarly,

```
i := 0
while i < *a do {
    i +:= 1
    write(a[i])
}
```

writes all the values in the list **a**. Since the position can be computed in the sub-scripting expression, this loop can be written more compactly as

```
i := 0
while i < *a do write(a[i +:= 1])
```

A value in a list can be changed by assignment to its position, which may be specified positively or nonpositively. For example,

```
oracles[−1] := "Branchidae"
```

changes the last value of **oracles**, so that the list becomes

```
["Delphi", "Heracles", "Branchidae"]
```

Similarly,

```
city[2] +:= 1000
```

changes the second value in **city** to 401,000.

As for string subscripting, list subscripting fails if the position specified does not correspond to a value in the list, that is, if the subscript is out of range. This failure can be used in place of an explicit check on the size of a list. There-fore, the values of a list can be written by

```
i := 0
while write(a[i +:= 1])
```

The following program, which tabulates word lengths, illustrates a typi-cal use of lists.

```
procedure main()
    wchar := &lcase ++ &ucase ++ '\'–'
    wordlength := list(10, 0)          # initial zero counts
    while line := read() do {
        i := 1
        while j := upto(wchar, line, i) do {
            i := many(wchar, line, j)
            wordlength[*line[i:j]] +:= 1
            }
        }
    write("word length    count:\n")
    i := 0
    while i < *wordlength do {
        i +:= 1
        write(left(i || ":", 12), right(wordlength[i], 3))
        }
end
```

The values in **wordlength** accumulate counts of word lengths from 1 to 10. After the input file has been processed, the results are written out. The output for the song from *As You Like It* given in §4.3.1 is as follows:

```
word length    count:

1:             1
2:             5
3:             6
4:             7
5:             2
6:             7
7:             0
8:             2
9:             0
10:            0
```

Note that any word that is longer than 10 characters is not tabulated; the expression

    wordlength[*line[i:j]] +:= 1

fails, since the subscript is out of range for word sizes greater than 10.

Lists are one dimensional, but a list of lists can be used to simulate a multidimensional array. The following procedure constructs an i-by-j array in which each value is x:

```
procedure array(i, j, x)
   a := list(i, 0)
   k := 0
   while a[k +:= 1] := list(j, x)
   return a
end
```

For example,

   board := array(8, 8, 0)

assigns to **board** an 8-by-8 array in which each value is 0. A list reference can be subscripted so that

   board[2][4]

references the value in "row" 4 of "column" 2 of **board**.

   The operation ?a produces a randomly selected reference to the list **a**. If **a** is empty, ?a fails. If **a** is a variable, assignment can be made to ?a to change the subscripted value. For example,

   ?a := 0

assigns 0 to a randomly selected position in **a**.

5.1.3 List Concatenation

   Lists can be concatenated, but the list concatenation operation has three vertical bars to distinguish it from string concatenation. An example is

   city := city ||| [1883]

which assigns the list

   ["Tucson",400000, "Arizona", "Pima",1883]

to **city**. An empty list is an identity with respect to list concatenation.

   As for other infix operations, there is an augmented assignment operation for list concatenation operation, as in

   city |||:= [1883]

   Note that both arguments in list concatenation must be lists;

   city |||:= 1883

is erroneous.

5.1.4 List Sections

A list section is a list composed of a sequence of values from another list. List sections are like substrings, except that they are distinct from the list from which they are obtained, instead of being a part of it. List sections are produced by range specifications applied to lists, much as substrings are produced by range specifications applied to strings. For the value of city given in the preceding section, the value of

city[3:5]

is the list

["Arizona", "Pima"]

There is one other important distinction between subscripting lists and strings: If a is a list, a[i] refers to the ith *value* in the list, while a[i:j] is a *list* consisting of the values between positions i and j in a. In particular, a[i:j] is a list that is distinct from a, and assignment cannot be made to it to change a.

5.1.5 Queue and Stack Access to Lists

Queue and stack access functions provide ways to add values to lists and to remove them from lists.

The function put(a, x) adds the value x to the right end of the list a, increasing the size of a by 1. One use of put is to build a list whose size cannot be determined when it is created. For example, the following procedure returns a list of all words in the input file.

```
procedure words()
   wchar := &lcase ++ &ucase ++ '\'–'
   wordlist := []
   while line := read() do {
      i := 1
      while j := upto(wchar, line, i) do {
         i := many(wchar, line, j)
         put(wordlist, line[i:j])     # add to list
         }
      }
   return wordlist
end
```

Since put adds values at the right end, the words in the list are in the order that they appear in the input file. That is, the first value in the list is the first word, the second value is the second word, and so on.

Values are removed from a list by the converse operation, get(a). Each time get(a) is evaluated, it removes a value from the left end of a and produces this value. If a is empty, get(a) fails.

For example, the following program uses the procedure words to produce a list of words and then writes out only those words that begin with an uppercase letter:

```
procedure main()
    wlist := words()
    while word := get(wlist) do
        if any(&ucase, word) then write(word)
end
```

When the execution of this program is complete, the list wlist is empty, since each call of get removes a value from it.

The functions put and get constitute a queue access method for lists; put(a, x) adds x to the right end of a, and get(a) removes a value from the left end of a.

There are two functions that provide a corresponding stack access method for lists. The function push(a, x) adds x to the left end of a and pop(a) removes a value from the left end of a. For example, if the expression

```
put(wordlist, line[i:j])
```

in the procedure words given previously is replaced by

```
push(wordlist, line[i:j])
```

the list that is produced has the words in the opposite order from the order in the input file: the first word in the list is the last in the input file, and so on.

Note that get(a) and pop(a) both remove a value from the left end of a. The two names for the same function are provided to accommodate the usual terminology for queue and stack access methods. The function pull(a) removes a value from the right end of a, so push and pull also provide a queue access method. The four functions together provide an access method for double-ended queues, or *deques*.

The functions put(a, x) and push(a, x) produce a.

5.1.6 Sorting Lists

The function sort(a) produces a list that is a copy of a but with the values sorted. In sorting, strings are sorted in nondecreasing lexical order (see §4.2.5), while integers are sorted in nondecreasing numerical order (see §3.3). For example, if the value of oracles is a list produced by

```
oracles := ["Delphi", "Heracles", "Claros"]
```

then the value of

sort(oracles)

is

["Claros", "Delphi", "Heracles"]

Similarly, if the last line in the preceding procedure **words** is

return sort(wordlist)

the list produced is sorted in lexical order.

In lists that contain both strings and integers, the integers are placed before the strings in the sorted copy. For values of other types, see §6.4.

5.1.7 Properties of Lists

Lists are created during program execution. A list value is a reference (pointer) to a structure. Furthermore, assignment does not make copies of structures. There are several consequences of these properties of lists that may not be immediately obvious. Consider

```
index := list(50, 0)
temp := index
temp[1] := 1
```

Since the assignment of the value of **index** to **temp** does not copy the value of **index**, **index** and **temp** both have the *same* list as value. Therefore, the assignment of 1 to **temp**[1] changes the contents of the list that **temp** and **index** share as their value. The effect is as if

index[1] := 1

had been evaluated.

Consider also

```
cycle := ["x"]
put(cycle, cycle)
```

These expressions construct a loop in which **cycle** is its own value. This can be visualized as follows:

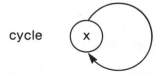

Since assignment does not copy structures, the result of an expression such as

$$a1 := a2 := list(i, 0)$$

is to assign the *same* list to both **a1** and **a2**. Subsequently, assignment to a position in **a2** changes the value of that position in **a1**, and conversely. Similarly, the effect of

$$a := list(3, list(5, 0))$$

is to assign the *same* list of five values to each of the three values in **a**. Compare this to the procedure for constructing two-dimensional arrays that is given in §5.1.2.

5.2 TABLES

A table is a set of pairs of values: an *entry value* and a corresponding *assigned value*. Tables resemble lists, except that the entry values, or "subscripts", need not be integers but can be values of any type. Tables are much like the symbol tables found in typical compilers, but lookup and insertion are taken care of automatically.

5.2.1 Table Creation and Referencing

A table is created by the function

$$table(x)$$

where **x** is the initial assigned value for new entries in the table. Table references are similar to array references in appearance. For example, if **words** is a table created by

$$words := table(0)$$

then

$$words["The"] := 1$$

assigns the value 1 to the entry The in **words**. Subsequently,

$$write(words["The"])$$

writes **1**.

An assigned value can be changed, as in

$$words["The"] := words["The"] + 1$$

Augmented assignment is particularly useful for tables. The expression

$$words["The"] +:= 1$$

performs the same operation as the preceding expression, but The is looked up only once, not twice.

When a table is first created, it is empty and has a size of zero. Every time a value is assigned to a new entry, the size of the table increases by 1. The operation *t produces the size of t.

An entry is added to a table only when an assignment is made to an entry value. Therefore, if **way** has not been assigned a value in **words**, the expression

> words["way"]

produces the initial assigned value of 0, but **way** is not added to the table and the size of the table does not change. On the other hand,

> words["way"] +:= 1

adds **way** to **words** and increases the size of **words** by 1.

The operation ?t produces a randomly selected reference to the table t. If t is empty, ?t fails. If t is a variable, assignment can be made to ?t to change the assigned value. For example,

> ?t +:= 1

increments the assigned value of a randomly selected entry in t.

Since tables often are used to count values, a typical initial assigned value is 0. For example, the following procedure produces a table of counts of the number of times each different word occurs in the input file.

```
procedure tabwords()
   wchar := &lcase ++ &ucase ++ '\'—'
   words := table(0)
   while line := read() do {
      i := 1
      while j := upto(wchar, line, i) do {
         i := many(wchar, line, j)
         words[line[i:j]] +:= 1     # increment count
         }
      }
   return words
end
```

5.2.2 Sorting Tables

The function sort(t, i) produces a sorted list from the table t. The size of the sorted list is the same as the size of the table. Each value in the list is itself a list of two values: an entry value and the corresponding assigned value. If i is 1, these lists are in the sorted order of the entry values. If i is 2, the lists are in the sorted order of the assigned values. If i is omitted, 1 is assumed.

Since the entry values in tables usually depend on the data in the input file, the actual entry values typically are not known. This is the case in the table produced by the procedure **tabwords**, since there is no way to predict what words may occur in the input file. If the entry values in a table are not known, the only way to determine them is to sort the table. For example, the following program prints a count of word occurrences in the input file, using the procedure **tabwords**:

```
procedure main()
    wlist := sort(tabwords())        # get sorted list
    i := 0
    while pair := wlist[i +:= 1] do
        write(left(pair[1], 12), right(pair[2], 3))
end
```

The output for the song from *As You Like It* is

```
As             2
Freeze         1
That           1
Though         1
Thy            1
        .
        .
        .
not            3
remember'd     1
sharp          1
sky            1
        .
        .
        .
```

5.3 RECORDS

Records are similar to lists, except that records are fixed in size and the values in them are referenced by field names instead of by integer positions. Records, like procedures, are declared and are global to the entire program. A record declaration cannot appear within a procedure declaration. The declaration of a record with n fields has the form

   record *name*(*field$_1$*, *field$_2$*, ..., *field$_n$*)

where *name* is the name of the record and *field$_1$*, *field$_2$*, ..., *field$_n$* are the field names associated with the record. The syntax of record names and field names is the same as the syntax for identifiers (see §1.1). An example of a record declaration is record complex(rpart, ipart)

Such a record declaration could be used to represent complex numbers with real and imaginary parts. On the other hand, the record declaration

    record employee(name, age, ssn, salary)

could be used to represent an employee whose name, age, social security number, and salary are attributes of interest.

An instance of a record is created by a *record constructor* function corresponding to the record name and with values as specified in the record declaration. For example,

    origin := complex(0.0, 0.0)

assigns a **complex** record with zero real and imaginary parts to origin, while

    clerk := employee("John Doe", 36, "123−45−6789", 14000.00)

assigns an **employee** record to clerk.

The field names are used to reference the fields as qualifiers to expressions whose values are records. For example, the value of

    origin . rpart

is 0.0. Field references, like list and table references, are variables, and values can be assigned to the corresponding fields. Therefore,

    origin . ipart := 6.0

changes the imaginary part of origin to 6.0.

The field reference operation associates from left to right. Consequently,

    x.y.z

groups as

    (x.y).z

where y and z are field names. The field reference operation has higher precedence than any other operation, including the prefix operations. This is an exception to the general rule that prefix operations have higher precedence than infix operations. As a result,

    −x.y

groups as

    −(x.y)

Fields also can be referenced by position like lists. For example, origin[2] +:= 2.5

adds 2.5 to the ipart field of origin.

If x is a record, the operation ?x produces a randomly selected reference to a field of x. The size of a record is produced as for other kinds of structures. For example, *origin produces 2.

EXERCISES

5.1.   Modify the program in §5.1.2 that tabulates word lengths so that there is no output for counts of zero.

5.2.[*]   Write a program that copies the input file to the output file with the order of the lines reversed, so that the first line written is the last line read, and so on.

5.3.   Modify the procedure words in §5.1.5 so that duplicate words are not added to the list.

5.4.   Modify the program in §5.2.2 that counts word occurrences so that the output is written in order of increasing count.

5.5.[*]   Write a program that tabulates word lengths without restriction on the length that a word may have.

5.6.[*]   Write a procedure that converts the string representation of a complex number, such as 3.2+5.1i, to a **complex** record.

5.7.[*]   Write a procedure that converts a **complex** record to the string representation of a complex number.

5.8.[*]   Write procedures that add, subtract, multiply, and divide complex numbers.

6

DATA TYPES

There are ten built-in data types in Icon:

co-expression	null
cset	procedure
file	real
integer	string
list	table

Record declarations add new types.

6.1 TYPE DETERMINATION

Sometimes it is useful, especially in program debugging, to be able to determine the type of a value. The function type(x) produces a string that is the name of the type of x. For example,

    write(type("Hello world"))

writes string.

Similarly,

    if type(i) == "integer" then write("type checks")

writes type checks if the value of i is an integer.

Functions, which are simply built-in procedures, are of type **procedure**. For example, the value of type(write)

is procedure.

As described in §5.3, a record declaration adds a type to the built-in repertoire of Icon. For example, the declaration

        record complex(rpart, ipart)

adds the type **complex**. If a **complex** record is assigned to origin, as in

        origin := complex(0.0, 0.0)

then the value of

        type(origin)

is complex.

6.2 TYPE CONVERSION

In many cases, values of one type can be converted to values of another type. The possible type conversions are given in the following table. The usual letters that serve as abbreviations for type names in expressions are indicated in the left column. With three exceptions, these letters correspond to the initial letter of the type name. The letter **e** is used for co-expressions, while **c** is used for csets. Since the letter **l** is difficult to distinguish typographically, the letter **a** (for "array") is used for lists. The letter **u** is used for null, since **n** is used elsewhere for numeric types.

type in		*type out*									
		e	c	f	i	a	u	p	r	s	t
co-expression	e	✔									
cset	c		✔		?				?	✔	
file	f			✔							
integer	i		✔		✔				✔	✔	
list	a					✔					
null	u						✔				
procedure	p							✔			
real	r		✔		?				✔	✔	
string	s		✔		?				?	✔	
table	t										✔

The symbol ✔ indicates a conversion that is always possible, while **?** indicates a conversion that may or may not be possible, depending on the value of the data to be converted. The checks on the diagonal do not represent actual conversions, since nothing needs to be done to convert a value to its own type.

A string can be converted to a numeric type only if it "looks like a number". For example, **1500** can be converted to the integer 1,500, but **a1500** cannot be converted to an integer. Signs and radix literals are allowed in conversion from string to numeric types. For example, **−2.5** can be converted to −2.5 and **16ra** can be converted to 10. Spaces are ignored in strings that are converted to numeric types. The empty string is not convertible to zero.

Since numbers are limited in size, the strings that can be converted to numbers are correspondingly limited. See Appendix B for information about limitations on the sizes of numbers.

When csets are converted to strings, the characters are put in lexical order. For example, conversion of **&lcase** to a string produces

abcdefghijklmnopqrstuvwxyz

When a cset is converted to a numeric type, it is first converted to a string, and then string-to-numeric conversion is performed.

A real number can be converted to an integer provided the real number is not too large. Any fractional part is discarded in the conversion.

Type conversions take two forms: *implicit* and *explicit*.

6.2.1 Implicit Type Conversion

Implicit conversion occurs in contexts where the type of a value that is expected by an operation is different from the type that is given. For example, in

write(*line)

the integer produced by *line is converted to a string in order to be written. Similarly, in

i := upto("aeiou", line)

the string **aeiou** is automatically converted to a cset.

In some situations, implicit conversion can be used to convert a value to a desired type directly. For example,

n := +s

is a way of converting a string that looks like a number to an actual number.

Implicit type conversion sometimes may occur unexpectedly. For example, a comparison operation produces the value of its right argument, converted to the type expected by the comparison. Therefore,

i := j > "20"

assigns the integer 20, not the string 20 to i, provided the comparison succeeds.

Unnecessary type conversion can be a significant source of program inefficiency. Since there is no direct evidence of implicit type conversion, this problem can go unnoticed. For example, in an expression such as

upto("aeiou", line)

the first argument is converted from a string to a cset every time the expression is evaluated. If this expression occurs in a loop that is evaluated frequently, program execution speed may suffer considerably. Where a cset is expected, it is important to use a cset literal or some other cset-valued expression that does not require conversion.

An implicit type conversion that cannot be performed is an error and causes program execution to terminate with a diagnostic message. For example,

n +:= "a"

is erroneous.

Implicit type conversion is not performed for comparing values in **case** clauses or for determining the entry values in tables. For example,

t[1]

and

t["1"]

reference different entries in t.

6.2.2 Explicit Type Conversion

Explicit conversion is performed by functions whose names correspond to the desired types. For example,

s := string(x)

converts x to a string and assigns that string value to s. The other explicit type-conversion functions are cset(x), integer(x), and real(x). The function numeric(x) converts strings to their corresponding numeric values if possible. This function is useful for converting a value that may represent either an integer or a real number. For example,

numeric("10.0")

produces 10.0, but

integer("10.0")

produces 10.

Explicit conversions sometimes can be used as a way of performing computations that otherwise would be difficult. For example,

s := string(cset(s))

eliminates duplicate characters of s and puts the remaining characters in lexical order.

If an explicit type conversion cannot be performed, the type conversion function fails. For example,

numeric("a")

fails. Explicit type conversion therefore can be used to test the convertibility of a value without risking a program error.

6.3 THE NULL VALUE

The null value is a single, unique value of type **null**. The keyword &null produces the null value, and all identifiers have the null value initially.

The use of the null value in most computations is erroneous. This prevents the accidental use of an uninitialized identifier in a computation. For example, if no value has been assigned to x, evaluation of the expression

j := x + 10

causes program termination with a diagnostic message.

The null value also is provided automatically for expressions that are omitted. For example, in

vector := list(100)

the omitted second argument is equivalent to the null value. The result is a list with 100 null values. Since the null value cannot be used in most computations, care should be taken to specify appropriate initial values for structures. Similarly,

words := table()

creates a table in which the default assigned value is null. Consequently,

words["The"] +:= 1

is erroneous, since this expression attempts to add 1 to the null value.

Assignment is indifferent to the null value. Therefore,

x := &null

assigns the null value to x.

There are two operations that succeed or fail, depending on whether or not an expression has the null value. The operation

/x

succeeds and produces the null value if x produces the null value, but it fails if x produces any other value.

The operation

\x

succeeds and produces the value of x if that value is any value except the null value, but fails if x produces the null value. This operation is useful for determining whether or not a variable has been assigned a value.

These operations produce variables to which assignment can be made, provided they succeed. For example,

/x := 0

assigns 0 to x if x has the null value, while

\x := 0

assigns 0 to x if x does not have the null value.

As in all operations, the arguments of these operations can be expressions. For example, if a table is created with the null initial assigned value, as in

t := table()

then

\t[word]

succeeds if the entry word in t has been assigned a nonnull value; otherwise, this expression fails.

6.4 SORTING MIXED TYPES

If a list or table that contains various types of values is sorted, the values are first sorted by type. The order of types in sorting is as follows:

null
integer
real
string
cset
file
co-expression
procedure
list
table
record types

For example,

sort([[ ], write, 1, 2.0])

produces

[1, 2.0, write, [ ]]

As described in §5.1.6, strings are sorted in nondecreasing lexical order, while integers and real numbers are sorted in nondecreasing numerical order. The order for values of other types is unpredictable. There is no sorting among records of different types; all records are treated as one type in sorting.

EXERCISES

6.1.   Assuming that each line of the input file is supposed to consist of a single number, write a program that checks the input file to be sure it contains only numeric values.

6.2.*   Write a procedure **hexcvt(s)** that converts strings representing hexadecimal numbers to their numerical equivalents. For example, hexcvt("a7") should produce 167.

6.3.   Write a program that writes the lines of the input file that contain duplicate characters.

7

PROCEDURES

Procedures and functions are very similar in Icon. The main difference is that procedures are declared in programs, while functions are built into the language. Procedures and functions are used the same way. Both procedures and functions are values in Icon, and they can be assigned to variables and passed as arguments to procedures like any other values. Icon has no block structure, and procedure declarations cannot be nested.

7.1 PROCEDURE DECLARATIONS

Procedures serve to declare the scope of identifiers and enclose the executable portions of a program. A procedure declaration has the form

procedure *name* (*parameter-list*)
    local-declarations
    initial-clause
    procedure-body
end

The procedure name is an identifier. The procedure itself is a value. It is assigned to the identifier that is the name of the procedure prior to the beginning of program execution.

The parameter list, which is optional, consists of identifiers separated by commas:

identifier, identifier, ...

These identifiers are local to the procedure and are not accessible elsewhere in the program. Different procedure declarations can have parameters with the same names, but parameters with the same names in different procedures have no connection with each other.

Other identifiers may be declared local to a procedure in optional local declarations, which have the form

local *identifier-list*   .

The reserved word **dynamic** is synonymous with **local**. There may be more than one local declaration in a procedure.

The **initial** clause, which is also optional, has the form

initial *expr*

where *expr* is an expression that is evaluated the first time that the procedure is called. Use of the **initial** clause is discussed in the §7.2.

The body of the procedure consists of a sequence of expressions that is evaluated when the procedure is called.

Representative procedure declarations appear in preceding chapters but without declarations for local identifiers. A typical procedure with local declarations is

```
procedure exor(s1, s2)
    local count, line
    count := 0
    while line := read() do
        if find(s1, line) then {
            if not find(s2, line) then count +:= 1
            }
        else if find(s2, line) then count +:= 1
    return count
end
```

7.2 THE SCOPE OF IDENTIFIERS

The identifiers in the parameter list and the identifiers in the local declarations of a procedure are local to calls of that procedure and are accessible only to expressions in the body of that procedure. Identifiers can be made global and accessible to all procedures in a program by global declarations, which have the form

global *identifier-list*

Global declarations are on a par with procedure declarations and they may not appear inside procedure declarations. If an identifier that is declared global also appears in a parameter list or local declaration, that name refers to the local identifier in the procedure, not to the global identifier. A declaration of a global identifier need not appear before the appearance of the identifier in a procedure.

Global identifiers are used to share values among procedures. Suppose, for example, procedures **p1** and **p2** both need to increment the same counter. Then the following format could be used.

```
global counter

procedure p1()
    .
    .
    counter +:= 1
    .
    .
end

procedure p2()
    .
    .
    counter +:= 1
    .
    .
end
```

Procedures names are global, as are the names of record types. Field names are not identifiers; they apply to the entire program and are not affected by scope declarations.

Identifiers that are not declared to be global are local to the procedure in which they occur, whether or not they are declared local in that procedure. This default scope interpretation saves writing but may lead to errors. For example, a global declaration, perhaps unrelated to the procedure containing an undeclared local identifier, can cause that identifier to be interpreted as global. It is good practice to declare all local identifiers explicitly.

Local identifiers normally come into existence when a procedure is called and are destroyed when the procedure returns; they are only accessible during the duration of the procedure call. Identifiers can be made *static* by using the declaration

static *identifier-list*

A static identifier is created the first time the procedure is called and is not destroyed when the procedure returns. It retains its value for subsequent calls of that procedure. Therefore, a static identifier can provide "memory" for the procedure.

Static identifiers are useful when a procedure that is called many times uses a value that must be computed but is always the same. Consider the program in §4.3.2 that writes the first word of each line of the input file. This program can be adapted to other uses more easily if it is divided into two procedures: one that produces the words and another that writes them. In this way, the words can be used in different ways without changing the procedure that produces them. An example is

```
procedure main()
    while write(fword())
end

procedure fword()
    local wchar, line
    wchar := &lcase ++ &ucase ++ '\'-'
    while line := read() do
        if line := line[upto(wchar, line):0]
        then return line[1:many(wchar, line)]
end
```

Note that the value assigned to **wchar** is computed every time **fword** is called. This unnecessary computation can be avoided by making **wchar** a static identifier and computing its value only once the first time that **fword** is called:

```
procedure fword()
    static wchar
    local line
    initial wchar := &lcase ++ &ucase ++ '\'-'
    while line := read() do
        if line := line[upto(wchar, line):0]
        then return line[1:many(wchar, line)]
end
```

A more sophisticated use of static identifiers is to maintain the state of a computation from one call of a procedure to the next. For example, the programs in Chapters 4 and 5 that process all the words in the input file would be simpler and clearer if they used a common procedure that produced the next word from the input file every time it was called. Such a procedure requires memory, since when it returns a word there still may be other words on the last line that was read. One formulation of such a procedure is

```
procedure nword()
    static wchar, line, i, j
    initial {
        wchar := &lcase ++ &ucase ++ '\'−'
        if line := read() then i := 1 else fail
    }
    repeat {
        while j := upto(wchar, line, i) do {
            i := many(wchar, line, j)
            return line[i:j]
        }
        if line := read() then i := 1 else fail
    }
end
```

In the **initial** clause a line is read and i is assigned the value 1. If the input file is empty, however, the procedure fails. If the input file is not empty, the **while** loop is evaluated repeatedly. If a word is found, it is returned. Note that a return terminates any loops in which it appears. If no word is found, a line is read and, because of the outer **repeat** loop, the **while** loop is evaluated again. This procedure fails when the end of the input file is reached, indicating that there are no more words. Note that a line is read the first time the procedure is called. On subsequent calls, evaluation begins with the first expression in the procedure body, which starts by evaluating the **while** loop with the preceding values of line, i, and j.

One programming error that is difficult to locate is the failure to declare a static identifier, even though it is assigned a value in an **initial** clause. In this case, the procedure works properly the first time it is called, but this value is discarded when the procedure returns. When the procedure is called again, the identifier then has the null value.

7.3 PROCEDURE INVOCATION

Procedures are invoked by procedure calls, which have the form

>   *expr* (*argument-list*)

where an argument list is a sequence of expressions separated by commas:

> $expr_1$, $expr_2$, $expr_3$, ...

Usually, *expr* is an identifier given in a procedure declaration, but see §7.5. Normally, there are as many arguments as there are parameters. For example, exor("Mr.", "Mrs.")

is a call of the procedure **exor** given in §7.1. The values of the expressions in the argument list are assigned to the identifiers in the parameter list (**s1** and **s2** in this case). Evaluation then starts at the beginning of the body of the procedure in **exor**.

Arguments are transmitted by value; there is no call-by-reference or other method of argument transmission. Note, however, that a structure value, such as a list, is a reference (pointer) to the actual structure.

If the evaluation of any argument fails, the procedure is not invoked and the calling expression fails. Evaluation then continues with the next expression following the call. See §8.2 for the details of argument evaluation.

7.4 RETURNING FROM A PROCEDURE

Evaluation of the expression

return *expr*

causes a return from the procedure call in which it occurs. The value of *expr* becomes the value of the procedure call, and evaluation resumes at the place where the call was made.

The precedence of **return** is lower than that of any infix operation, so

return i + j

groups as

return (i + j)

The procedures given earlier illustrate the return of specifically computed values. The *expr* following **return** is optional. If *expr* is omitted, the null value is returned. This is useful in procedures that do not have a value to return and corresponds to the initial null value of identifiers. If *expr* is present but fails, the procedure call fails. If the value of an expression is to be returned, the expression must begin on the same line as the **return**. In

return
    expr

the null value is returned and *expr* is never evaluated.

The **fail** expression causes a procedure to return and fail explicitly, as illustrated in previous examples.

An implicit **fail** expression is provided at the end of the procedure body. Consequently, a procedure that returns by flowing off the end of the procedure body fails. It is important to provide an explicit **return** expression at the end of such a procedure body unless failure is intended.

7.5 PROCEDURES AS VALUES

As mentioned in §7.1, a procedure declaration constructs a procedure and assigns it to the identifier that is the name of the procedure. Functions, which are built-in procedures, also are values and are preassigned to global identifiers. For example, **write** is a global identifier.

Since procedures are values, they may be assigned to variables, passed as arguments to functions, and so forth. Therefore,

> print := write

assigns the procedure for **write** to **print**, and **print(s)** subsequently performs the same operations as **write(s)**.

Ordinarily, functions are not used in this way, but it is possible. In fact, if a procedure is declared with the name **write**, the declared procedure value replaces the built-in procedure, which is then inaccessible to the program. It is good practice to avoid choosing names for declared procedures that are the same as the names for built-in procedures.

Although the procedure that is applied in a procedure call usually is produced by an identifier, it can be the value of any expression. Therefore,

> plist := [upto, any, many]

constructs a list of procedures and

> plist[2](c, s)

is equivalent to

> any(c, s)

The procedure that is applied in a call is just the "zeroth" argument; it is evaluated before the other arguments.

7.6 RECURSIVE CALLS

It is common in mathematics to define functions recursively in terms of themselves. The Fibonacci numbers provide a classic example:

$$f(i) = 1 \qquad\qquad i = 1, 2$$
$$f(i) = f(i-1)+f(i-2) \qquad i > 2$$
$$f(i) \qquad\qquad\qquad \text{undefined otherwise}$$

The sequence of Fibonacci numbers for $i = 1, 2, 3, \ldots$ is $1, 1, 2, 3, 5, 8, 13, \ldots$.

Since a procedure can contain calls to itself, this mathematical definition can be transcribed quite mechanically into a procedure that computes the Fibonacci numbers:

```
procedure fib(i)
    if i = 1 then return 1
    if i = 2 then return 1
    return fib(i − 1) + fib(i − 2)
end
```

Recursive calls rely on the fact that the identifier for the procedure name is global. For example, within the procedure body for **fib, fib** is a global identifier whose value is the procedure itself.

While a recursive definition may be elegant and concise, the use of recursion for computation may be very inefficient, especially when it depends on the computation of previous values. For example, to compute **fib(5)**, it is necessary to compute **fib(4)** and **fib(3)**. The computation of **fib(4)** also requires the computation of **fib(3)**, and so on. Sometimes, redundant computations can be avoided by finding an iterative solution (see the exercises at the end of this chapter). In some cases iterative solutions may be difficult to formulate. The classic example is Ackermann's function:

$$
\begin{array}{ll}
a(i,j) = j+1 & i = 0, \ j \geq 0 \\
a(i,j) = a(i-1, 1) & i > 0, \ j = 0 \\
a(i,j) = a(i-1, a(i,j-1)) & i > 0, \ j > 0 \\
a(i,j) & \text{undefined otherwise}
\end{array}
$$

One method for avoiding redundant computation in recursive procedures is to *tabulate* the procedure so that the values of previous computations are remembered [9]. These values can then be looked up instead of being recomputed. A static identifier can be used to provide the memory. Consider the following reformulation of **fib(i)**:

```
procedure fib(i)
    static fibmem
    local j
    initial {
        fibmem := table()
        fibmem[1] := fibmem[2] := 1
        }
    if j := \fibmem[i] then return j
    else return fibmem[i] := fib(i − 1) + fib(i − 2)
end
```

A table is assigned to the static identifier **fibmem** when the procedure is called the first time, and the values for 1 and 2 are placed in this table. If the desired value is in the table, \fibmem[i] produces it and it is returned. If a value is not in the table, \fibmem[i] fails, since the null value is the specified initial assigned value for entries that are not in the table. If the value is not in the table, it is computed and stored in the table before returning. Note that the computation still is recursive, but no value is computed recursively more than once.

While the classic definitions of recursive functions come from mathematics, there are many applications of recursion to computations that are not mathematical in nature. Many of these occur in situations where a structure can be defined recursively and in which computations on such a structure therefore can be formulated recursively.

Arithmetic expressions can be defined recursively, for example. Consider the following definition of a simple type of expression:

1. An *expression* is a *term* or a *term* followed by a + followed by an *expression*.

2. A *term* is an *element* or an *element* followed by a * followed by a *term*.

3. An *element* is one of the characters x, y, z or an *expression* enclosed in parentheses.

Therefore, *expression*, *term*, and *element* are defined recursively in terms of each other. Ultimately, these *nonterminal symbols* lead to strings composed of the *terminal symbols*

$$+ \quad * \quad x \quad y \quad x \quad (\quad)$$

For example, x is an *element* and also, by (2), a *term*. Similarly, x*y is a *term* and also, by (1), an *expression*. Both y+x*z and z+(x*z) are *expressions*, and so on.

The strings of terminal symbols that can be derived from the definition of a nonterminal symbol are called the *language* that the nonterminal symbol generates.

The generation of representative examples of the language for a nonterminal symbol is an interesting problem. Such examples may provide insight into the structure of the language that the nonterminal symbol generates. If the language corresponds to an interesting programming language, a stock of such examples may be useful in testing compilers or other processors for the language.

One way to generate representative examples of such a language is to write procedures for the nonterminal symbols in which the possibilities given in the definition are selected at random. The random choice produces results that are representative of the different possibilities, instead of getting stuck in a rut (such as always producing x for an element).

The recursive definitions for expressions given here can be translated mechanically into procedures that produce examples. For these definitions, such procedures are as follows:

```
procedure expression()
   return case ?2 of {
      1  :  term()
      2  :  term() || "+" || expression()
      }
end

procedure term()
   return case ?2 of {
      1  :  element()
      2  :  element() || "*" || term()
      }
end

procedure element()
   return case ?4 of {
      1  :  "x"
      2  :  "y"
      3  :  "z"
      4  :  "(" || expression() || ")"
      }
end
```

Consequently, there are two possible choices for an expression, and the value of ?2 is used to select one of these in a **case** expression. Note that the value produced by the **case** expression is returned by the procedure.

Examples of results produced by expression() are

```
y
x*x*z
((z+y))+y*z+(x)
z+y+(z*(x*(z)+x*y))*z*z+x+(x+y+x)
(y)*(x)
z
((z))+(z)
z+x
(z)*x+y
(z+(y)+y*(y*x))
z+(((y))*(y))+z
y*z
x+(y)
z+(y)+y*y
```

One problem in recursive generation of this kind is that the recursion can get out of hand, either producing impossibly long results or else continuing to call first one procedure and then another until the storage available for computation is exhausted (every call of a procedure requires some storage to keep track of information that must be restored when the procedure returns). The previous procedures have this problem.

One way to reduce the possibility of runaway recursion is to bias the selection so that it is more likely that the procedure will return than call other procedures. The procedure **element** has such a bias built into it, since three out of four of the choices return immediately. Bias can be added to a procedure like **expression** by favoring the first choice, which only contains one call, as opposed to the second, which contains two calls. For example, this procedure could be rewritten as

```
procedure expression()
    return case ?3 of {
        1 :  term()
        2 :  term()
        3 :  term() || "+" || expression()
        }
end
```

EXERCISES

7.1. The procedure fib(i) in §7.6 does not check that the Fibonacci sequence is defined for the given value of i. Modify the procedure so that it fails if i is less than 1. What might be done if the value of i is not an integer?

7.2. Write an iterative procedure fib(i) that computes the ith Fibonacci number without using tabulation.

7.3.* Write a procedure acker(i, j) that computes Ackermann's function. *Warning:* The value of Ackermann's function and the time required to compute it increase *very* rapidly as the values of the arguments increase.

7.4. The "chaotic sequence" [10] is defined as follows:

$$q(i) = 1 \qquad\qquad\qquad\qquad\qquad i = 1,\ 2$$
$$q(i) = q(i - q(i-1)) + q(i - q(i-2)) \quad i > 2$$
$$q(i) \qquad\qquad\qquad\qquad\qquad\text{undefined otherwise}$$

Write a procedure that computes $q(i)$. Compute $q(i)$ for $i = 1, 2, \ldots,$ 17.

7.5. Provide tabulation for the computation of the chaotic sequence in Exercise 7.4 and compute $q(i)$ for $i = 1, 2, \ldots, 500$.

7.6.* Provide tabulation for acker(i, j) in Exercise 7.3 and compute acker(3, 3).

7.7. Write a procedure comb(s, i) that produces all combinations of characters from s taken i at a time. For example, comb("abcd", 3) should produce

```
abc
abd
acd
bcd
```

7.8. Add the infix operators − and / to the definition of expressions given in §7.6.

8

EXPRESSION EVALUATION

8.1 RESULTS AND OUTCOMES

Some expressions in Icon produce values, while others produce variables to which values can be assigned. A numerical operation produces a value, while a list reference such as a[i], produces a variable. Assignment operations also produce their left arguments as variables. In Icon, the term *result* denotes either a value or a variable. Therefore, the phrase "the result produced by an expression" is used, whether the expression produces a value or a variable. On the other hand, an expression that fails does not produce a result. The terms *succeeds* and *produces a result* are synonymous, as are *fails* and *does not produce a result*.

The keyword &fail produces no result and can be used to indicate failure explicitly.

To make it easier to describe the evaluation of expressions, the term *outcome* is used to denote the consequence of evaluating an expression, whether it be success (with some result) or failure. For example, the outcome of evaluating a compound expression

$$\{expr_1;\ expr_2;\ \ldots;\ expr_n\}$$

is the outcome of evaluating $expr_n$. Therefore, if $expr_n$ fails, the compound expression fails, while if $expr_n$ produces a result, the compound expression produces that result.

Control structures in Icon are expressions, and they can be used wherever any expression is allowed. For example, a control structure can be used as an argument to a function, although such usage generally is awkward. Since Icon control structures are expressions, their outcomes are nonetheless important in some situations.

The outcome of the control structure

> if $expr_1$ then $expr_2$ else $expr_3$

is the outcome of $expr_2$ or $expr_3$, whichever is selected. Therefore, if $expr_2$ is selected and it fails, the entire control structure fails. If the **else** clause is omitted and the control expression fails, the entire control structure fails. Therefore,

> if $expr_1$ then $expr_2$

is equivalent to

> if $expr_1$ then $expr_2$ else &fail

If the selected expression produces a variable, the entire control structure produces this variable. For example,

> (if i > j then a[i] else a[j]) := 0

assigns 0 to a[i] if i is greater than j, but assigns 0 to a[j] otherwise. Unless the value to be assigned is produced by a complicated expression, it generally is clearer to duplicate the assignment in the two arms of the **if-then-else** expression, as in

> if i > j then a[i] := 0 else a[j] := 0

Like **if-then-else**, the outcome of a **case** expression is the outcome of the expression in the selected case clause.

Looping control structures such as

> while $expr_1$ do $expr_2$

and

> until $expr_1$ do $expr_2$

ordinarily are used for the computations that are performed by $expr_2$. When a loop terminates, the control structure itself produces no result; that is, it fails. Therefore, such a control structure should not be used in a context where its failure to produce a result might affect the outcome of another expression. Normally, this not a problem, since it is unusual to use a looping control structure as an argument to another expression. See §12.2, however.

The **break** expression described in §2.1 has an optional argument:

> break $expr$

If $expr$ is omitted, the null value is provided. When a **break** expression is used to exit from a loop, the outcome of *expr* becomes the outcome of the loop. For example,

```
cap := while line := read() do
   if any(&ucase, line) then break line
```

assigns to cap the first line of the input file that begins with an uppercase letter.

The **break** expression, like the **return** expression, has low precedence, so

```
break i + j
```

gròups as

```
break (i + j)
```

The argument of a **break** expression can be any expression, even another **break** expression. This makes it possible to exit from nested loops. Consider a variation on the procedure words in §5.1.5 in which a limit on the size of the list that is produced is specified as a parameter:

```
procedure words(k)
   local wchar, wordlist, line, i, j
   wchar := &lcase ++ &ucase ++ '\'−'
   wordlist := []
   while line := read() do {
      i := 1
      while j := upto(wchar, line, i) do {
         i := many(wchar, line, j)
         put(wordlist, line[i:j])
         if *wordlist = k then break break
         }
      }
   return wordlist
end
```

If the size of wordlist reaches k, both loops are exited and the **return** expression is evaluated next.

8.2 THE EVALUATION OF ARGUMENTS

The arguments in function calls, procedure calls, and operations are evaluated in the same way. The term function is used in this section to include all three cases.

The arguments of a function are evaluated from left to right. If evaluation of an argument fails, the remaining arguments are not evaluated and the function is not invoked. Instead, the function call fails. Consequently, if there is no result for an argument of a function, the function call produces no result. For example, in

upto(&lcase, read())

the first argument is evaluated first and produces a cset. The second argument,

read()

is evaluated next. If it succeeds, the function upto is called with the values of the two arguments. If evaluation of read() fails, however, upto is not called, and the entire expression fails. Therefore, the failure of an argument is "inherited" by the call in which it appears.

If such a function call is used in an assignment operation, such as

loc[i] := upto(&lcase, read())

the arguments of the assignment operation are evaluated first. The first argument, loc[i], may produce a variable or it may fail, depending on the values of loc and i. If the evaluation of this argument fails,

upto(&lcase, read())

is not evaluated. In particular, read is not called and no line is read. The assignment operation is not performed, and the entire expression fails.

An omitted argument in a function call defaults to the null value. In the case of trailing arguments, the commas can be omitted as well. For example,

trim(text)

is equivalent to

trim(text,)

and also to

trim(text, &null)

The interpretation of the null value depends on the particular function. For example, a null-valued second argument in trim is interpreted as ' ', a cset containing the space character. Such default interpretations allow frequently used argument values to be omitted. See Appendix E for a complete list of interpretations for omitted arguments.

If more arguments are given in a function call than the function expects, the additional arguments are evaluated, but their values are discarded. If an additional argument fails, however, the function is not invoked and the function call fails.

8.3 DEREFERENCING

Where a variable is produced by an expression, but a value is needed, the value of the variable is obtained automatically. This process is called *dereferencing.* Dereferencing, like type conversion, occurs implicitly. For example, in

> write(line)

the variable line is dereferenced to produce its value, which is then written.

In most cases the result in a **return** expression is dereferenced and a value is returned. Exceptions occur for global identifiers, structure references, and subscripted global string-valued identifiers. In these cases, a variable is returned, and a value can be assigned to the function call that returns this variable. Consider the following procedure, which returns the largest value in the list a:

```
procedure maxel(a)
    local i, j, max
    j := i := 1
    max := a[1]
    while i < *a do {
        i +:= 1
        if max <:= a[i] then j := i
        }
    return a[j]
end
```

Since the result that is returned is a list reference and hence a variable, a value can be assigned to it. For example,

> maxel(a) := 0

replaces the maximum value in a by 0.

The possibility of such an assignment can be prevented by use of the explicit dereferencing operation .x, which produces the value of x. For example, if the **return** expression in the previous procedure is changed to

> return .a[j]

an attempt to assign a value to the result produced by the procedure is erroneous.

The dereferencing operation can be applied to any expression, not just one that produces a variable. Consequently, it is not necessary to know whether or not an expression produces a variable in order to apply the dereferencing operation to it. Dereferencing is indifferent to the null value.

In a function call, implicit dereferencing is done by the function itself after all arguments have been evaluated and passed to it. Consider write(line, line := read())

In this expression a new value is assigned to line when the second argument,

line := read()

is evaluated. When write is called, its two arguments are dereferenced. At this time, they both have the same value, and two copies of the newly read line are written, not the former value of line followed by the newly read value.

While expressions with side effects such as the preceding generally should be avoided, explicit dereferencing can be used to prevent unexpected results from side effects, as in

write(.line, line := read())

8.4 MUTUAL EVALUATION

Sometimes the mutual success of a number of expressions is important, even though there is no computation to perform on their results. *Conjunction*, denoted by

$expr_1$ & $expr_2$

is an operation that simply produces the result of evaluating $expr_2$. In this sense, conjunction performs no computation. Since it is an operation, its arguments are evaluated, and both must succeed for the conjunction to succeed. For example,

(i < j) & (m < n)

succeeds only if i is less than j and m is less than n. Similarly,

upto(' ', line1) & upto(' ', line2)

succeeds only if both line1 and line2 contain a space.

The precedence of conjunction is lower than that of any other infix operation. Consequently,

i < j & m < n

groups as

(i < j) & (m < n)

On the other hand,

i := upto(' ', line1) & upto(' ', line2)

groups as

(i := upto(' ', line1)) & upto(' ', line2)

This expression assigns the position of the first space in line1, not line2, to i. Furthermore, the assignment is performed even if line2 does not contain a space. Care should be taken to use parentheses where they are appropriate in complex expressions involving conjunction.

If the mutual success of several expressions is needed, conjunction can be compounded, as in

$$expr_1 \ \& \ expr_2 \ \& \ \ldots \ \& \ expr_n$$

This notation is cumbersome, especially if the expressions are themselves complex. An alternative is *mutual evaluation*, denoted by

$$(expr_1, expr_2, \ldots, expr_n)$$

which evaluates $expr_1$, $expr_2$, ..., $expr_n$ just like the evaluation of the arguments in a function call. If all the expressions produce results, the result of mutual evaluation is the result of $expr_n$. Otherwise, the mutual evaluation expression fails. The effect is exactly the same as in a compound conjunction. For example,

i := (upto(' ', line1), upto(' ', line2))

assigns to i the position of the first space in line2, provided both line1 and line2 contain a space.

Sometimes a number of expressions need to be mutually evaluated, but a result other than the last one is desired. The expression

$$expr(expr_1, expr_2, \ldots, expr_n)$$

produces the result of $expr_i$, where the value of *expr* is the integer i, provided that all the expressions produce a result. If any of the expressions fails, however, the mutual evaluation expression fails. For example, the value of

i := 1(upto(' ', line1), upto(' ', line2))

assigns to i the position of the first space in line1, provided both line1 and line2 contain a space.

The value of *expr* can be negative, in which case the result is selected from right to left in the manner of nonpositive position specifications.

If the value of *expr* is out of range, the mutual evaluation expression fails. For example,

$$3(expr_1, expr_2)$$

always fails, regardless of whether or not $expr_1$ and $expr_2$ produce results.

Although mutual evaluation has the same syntax as a function call, there is no ambiguity. If the value of *expr* is an integer i, the result is the result of *expr$_i$*. If the value of *expr* is a function, however, the function is called with the arguments, and the outcome of the expression is the outcome of the function call.

EXERCISES

8.1.   Write a procedure index(a, i, j) that produces the variable in row i and column j of a, where a is an array produced by the procedure array(i, j, x) in §5.1.2.

8.2.   Write a procedure place(a, i, j) that produces the variable in row i and column j of an array a, provided the the value of the variable is the null value, but fails otherwise.

8.3.*   Rewrite Exercise 2.6 using mutual evaluation.

9

INPUT AND OUTPUT

Input and output in Icon are sequential and line oriented. There are neither random access facilities nor format conversions. Input and output are necessarily somewhat machine and system dependent; where there are such dependencies, this chapter refers to the UNIX operating system.

9.1 FILES

All reading and writing in earlier examples are from *standard input* to *standard output*. In an interactive system, such as UNIX, standard input often comes from the user's terminal and standard output often is written to this terminal. These standard files are implicit in reading and writing operations; they are the default files that are used in case no specific files are given.

Values that are of type file are used to reference actual files of data that are external to the program. There are three predefined values of type file:

&input   standard input
&output   standard output
&errout   standard error output

Standard input and output normally are used for input and output. They can be connected to specific files when Icon is run. This allows a program to use any input and output files without having to incorporate the names of the files in the text of the program. By convention, standard error output is used for error messages so that such messages are not mixed up with normal output.

While many programs can be written to use just standard input and output, sometimes it is necessary to use other files. For example, some programs must read from several files or write to several files.

How files are named is a property of the operating system under which Icon runs, not a property of Icon itself. For example, when Icon runs under UNIX, UNIX file naming conventions apply.

The name of a file is specified when it is opened for reading or writing; at this point a value of type file is created in the program and connected with the actual file that is to be read or written. The function

> open(s1, s2)

opens the file with name s1 according to options given in s2 and produces a value of type file that can be used to reference the named file.

The options given in s2 specify how the file is to be used. These options are inherently somewhat dependent on the operating system, although some options are common to all operating systems. The common options are

r	open for reading
w	open for writing
a	open for writing in append mode

See Appendix B for other options. If the option is omitted, r is assumed. For example,

> intext := open("shaw.txt")

opens the file **shaw.txt** for reading and assigns the resulting value to **intext**. The omission of the second argument with the subsequent default to r is common practice in Icon programming.

A file that is opened for reading must already exist; if it does not, the **open** function fails. A file that is opened for writing may or may not already exist. If it does not exist, a new file with the name s1 is created. If this is not possible (there may be various reasons, depending on the environment), the **open** function fails. If the file does exist, the previous contents of the file are destroyed unless the **a** option is used, in which case new output is written at the end of old data. Some files may be protected to prevent them from being modified; **open** fails if an attempt is made to open such a file for writing.

Since **open** may fail for a variety of reasons, it is good practice to check for possible failure, even if it is not expected. An example is

> if intext := open("shaw.txt") then *expr*
> else stop("cannot open input file")

This also can be formulated as

```
if not (intext := open("shaw.txt"))
then stop("cannot open input file")
else expr
```

The function **close(f)** closes the file **f**. This has the effect of physically completing output for **f**, such as flushing output buffers, and making the file inaccessible for further input or output. A file that has been closed can be opened again for input or output.

If several files are used, it is good practice to close files when they are no longer needed, since most operating systems allow only a few files to be open at the same time. See Appendix B. All open files are closed automatically when program execution terminates.

9.2 INPUT

The function **read(f)** reads the next line from the file referenced by **f**. If **f** is omitted, standard input is assumed, as is illustrated in earlier examples. For example, the following program copies **shaw.txt** to standard output.

```
procedure main()
    if not (intext := open("shaw.txt"))
    then stop("cannot open input file")
    while write(read(intext))
end
```

A file of textual data, such as a source program, is a sequence of lines (in some kinds of files, such as binary data files, the concept of a line is meaningless). A line is a logical unit, usually related to the way that the text is created. As far as Icon is concerned, a line is just a string; it *is* the value produced by reading. Lines are separated from each other in different ways by different operating systems. In UNIX, lines are separated by newline characters (line feeds). Therefore, **read(f)** produces the string up to the next newline character; the newline character itself is discarded.

When there is no more data in a file, **read** fails. This end-of-file condition can be used to terminate a loop in which the read occurs, as illustrated in earlier examples.

Sometimes it is useful to be able ignore the line structure of a file or to read a binary file that does not have line structure. This can be done by

```
reads(f, i)
```

where **f** is the file that is read and **i** specifies how many characters are to be read. If **f** is omitted, standard input is assumed. If **i** is omitted, 1 is assumed.

The function **reads**(f, i) reads a string of i characters; newlines are included. If there are not i characters remaining, only the remaining characters are read. In this case the value produced is shorter than i. The function **reads** fails if there are no characters remaining in the file.

9.3 OUTPUT

The function

>   write(x1, x2, ..., xn)

writes strings. What **write** does depends on the types of its arguments. The simplest case is

>   write(s)

which simply writes a line consisting of the string s to standard output. The function **write** automatically appends a newline character, so s becomes a new line at the end of the file.

If there are several string arguments, as in

>   write(s1, s2, ..., sn)

then s1, s2, ..., sn are written in sequence and a newline character is appended. Therefore, the line consists of the concatenation of s1, s2, ..., sn, although the concatenation is done on the file, not in the Icon program. When several strings are to be written in succession on the same line, it is much more efficient to use **write** with several arguments than to actually concatenate the strings in the program.

The most general case is

>   write(x1, x2, ..., xn)

where x1, x2, ..., xn may have various types. If the *i*th argument, xi, is not a string, it is converted to a string if possible as described in §6.2 and then written. If xi is a file, subsequent output is directed to that file. The following program, for example, copies **shaw.txt** to standard output and also copies it to **shaw.cpy**:

```
procedure main()
    if not (intext := open("shaw.txt"))
    then stop("cannot open input file")
    if not (outtext := open("shaw.cpy","w"))
    then stop("cannot open output file")
    while line := read(intext) do {
        write(line)
        write(outtext, line)
        }
end
```

The output file can be changed in midstream. Therefore,

```
write(&errout, s1, &output, s2)
```

writes **s1** to standard error output and **s2** to standard output. A separate line is written to each file; a newline is appended whenever the file is changed.

If the ith argument, **xi**, is not a file and is not convertible to a string, program execution terminates with a diagnostic message. There is one exception; the null value is treated like an empty string. Therefore,

```
write()
```

writes an empty line (newline character) to standard output.

The function

```
writes(x1, x2, ..., xn)
```

is like **write**, except that newline characters are not appended to the output. One line on a file can be built up using **writes** several times. Similarly, prompting messages to users of interactive programs can be produced with **writes** to allow the user at a computer terminal to enter input on the same visual line as the prompt. For example, the following program prompts the user for the names of the input and output files for a file copy.

```
procedure main()
    writes("specify input file: ")
    repeat {
        if intext := open(read()) then break
        writes("cannot open input file, respecify: ")
        }
```

```
    writes("specify output file: ")
    repeat {
        if outtext := open(read(),"w") then break
        writes("cannot open output file, respecify: ")
        }
    while write(outtext, read(intext))
end
```

In addition to writing, the functions **write** and **writes** produce the last string written. For example,

```
    last := write("The final value is ", count)
```

assigns the value of **count** to **last**. The value produced is always a string because all values that are written are converted to strings.

The function

```
    stop(x1, x2, ..., xn)
```

writes output in the manner of **write** and then terminates program execution as described in §2.1. Output is written to standard error output unless another file is specified.

EXERCISES

9.1.   Write a procedure **laminate(f1, f2, f3)** that performs a line-by-line concatenation of corresponding lines from **f1** and **f2** and writes the result to **f3**. If the files are of different lengths, provide empty lines for the shorter file.

9.2.[*]   Write a program that copies a binary file from standard input to standard output.

10

MISCELLANEOUS OPERATIONS

10.1 COMPARING VALUES

Five of the ten built-in data types in Icon, **cset**, **integer**, **null**, **real**, and **string**, have the property of having "unique" values. This means that equivalent values of these types are indistinguishable, regardless of how they are computed. For example, there is just one distinguishable integer 0. This value is the same, regardless of how it is computed.

Whether or not two numbers are the same is determined by a numerical comparison operation. Therefore,

$$(1 - 1) = (2 - 2)$$

succeeds, because the two arguments have the same value (by definition).

The property of uniqueness is natural for numbers and is essential for numerical computation. The uniqueness of csets and strings is not a necessary consequence of their inherent properties, but it plays an important role in Icon. For example,

$$("ab" \mathbin{||} "cd") == ("a" \mathbin{||} "bcd")$$

succeeds because both arguments have the same value, even though they are computed in different ways.

Numerical and string comparisons are restricted to specific data types, although type conversions are performed automatically as described in §6.2.1. For example, csets are converted to strings in string comparison operations.

There is also a general value comparison operation

    x === y

which compares arbitrary values x and y, as well as the converse operation

    x ~=== y

Unlike string comparison, value comparison fails if x and y do not have the same type: No implicit type conversion is performed. For the types that have unique values, value comparison succeeds if the values are the same, regardless of how they are computed. For other types, value comparison succeeds only if the values are *identical*.

Lists may be equivalent but not identical. For example,

    [] === []

fails because the two empty lists are not identical, even though they are equivalent in size and contents. Assignment does not copy structures. Consequently, in

    a := []
    a === a

the comparison succeeds, because the two arguments have identical values.

Value comparison is used implicitly in **case** expressions and table references. For example, if the value of x is the integer 1,

    case x of {
        "1": *expr*
        .
        .

the first **case** clause is not selected, since the types of the values compared are different. Similarly,

    t["abcdefghijklmnopqrstuvwxyz"]

and

    t[&lcase]

reference different values in the table t, but

    t["abcdefghijklmnopqrstuvwxyz"]

and

    t[string(&lcase)]

reference the same value, since string values are unique.

10.2 COPYING VALUES

Any value can be copied by copy(x). For lists, tables, and records, a physical copy of x is made and is distinct from x. For example, in

    a := []
    a === copy(a)

the comparison fails.

Only the list itself is copied; values contained in the copy are the same as in the original list (copying is "one level"). For example, in

    a1 := []
    a2 := [a1]
    a3 := copy(a2)
    a3[1] === a2[1]

the comparison succeeds, since both a2[1] and a3[1] are the same list, a1.

For values other than lists, tables, and records, copy(x) simply produces the value of x; no actual copy is made. Therefore,

    write === copy(write)

succeeds.

10.3 EXCHANGING VALUES

The operation

    x :=: y

exchanges the values of x and y. For example, after evaluating

    s1 := "begin"
    s2 := "end"
    s1 :=: s2

the value of s1 is end and the value of s2 is begin.

The exchange operation associates from right to left and returns its left argument as a variable. Consequently,

    x :=: y :=: z

groups as

    x :=: (y :=: z)

Like assignment, the exchange operation is indifferent to the null value.

Exchange can be used on any kind of variable. For example,

    a[1] :=: a[−1]

exchanges the first and last values of the list **a**. Similarly, suppose

    deck := &lcase || &ucase

represents a deck of cards in which each character stands for a different card. Then the following procedure can be used to shuffle the deck [11].

```
procedure shuffle(s)
  local i
  i := *s
  while i >= 2 do {
    s[?i] :=: s[i]
    i −:= 1
    }
  return s
end
```

In this procedure the loop starts with the last character of **s** and exchanges it with a randomly selected character from **s**. As the value of i is decremented, the process is repeated for successively smaller portions of **s**.

It is also possible to exchange substrings of different sizes, as in

    word1[1+:2] :=: word2[2+:3]

The subscripted variables may be the same and the ranges may even overlap, although such operations are likely to be confusing.

10.4 STRING IMAGES

When debugging a program it is often useful to know what a value is. Its type can be determined by **type(x)** as described in §6.1, but that is not helpful if the actual value is of interest. Its value can be written, provided it is of a type that can be converted to a string, although there is no way to differentiate different types whose written values are the same, such as the integer 1 and the string "1".

The function **image(x)** provides a representation of **x** that both distinguishes its type and provides information about its value. The function **image(x)** always produces a string; the format of this string depends on the type of **x**.

If **x** is a string or cset, enclosing quotes are provided. For example, image("Hello world")

produces

"Hello world"

while

image('Hello world')

produces

' Hdelorw'

Note that the characters in the image of a cset are in lexical order. Escape sequences are provided as needed in the images of quoted literals as described in §4.1.1 and §4.2.1.

The data type and current size are given for lists and tables. For example,

image([1, 4, 9, 16])

produces

list(4)

Although functions and procedures are of the same type, they are distinguished in string images. For example,

image(main)

produces

procedure main

while

image(trim)

produces

function trim

In the case of a record declaration such as

record complex(rpart, ipart)

the record constructor is distinguished from built-in functions, so

image(complex)

produces

record constructor complex

On the other hand, **complex** values have the same kind of string image that other structures have:

image(complex(0.0, 0.0))

produces

record complex(2)

Some built-in values have string images consisting of the keyword that produces the value. For example,

image()

produces

&null

10.5 TRACING

Procedure tracing is the main debugging tool in Icon. Tracing is controlled by &trace. If &trace is zero (its initial value), there is no tracing. If the value of &trace is nonzero, a diagnostic message is written to standard error output each time a procedure is called or returns. The value of &trace is decremented by 1 for each message, so the value assigned to &trace can be used to limit the amount of trace output. On the other hand,

&trace := −1

allows tracing to continue indefinitely or until another value is assigned to &trace.

The diagnostic messages produced by tracing show a substantial amount of information: the name of the file containing the program, the line that causes the tracing, procedures called, values returned, and so on. The vertical bars indicate, by way of indentation, the level of procedure call.

An example of tracing for the first method of computing the Fibonacci numbers given in §7.6 is

```
fib.icn: 9      | fib(5)
fib.icn: 5      | | fib(4)
fib.icn: 5      | | | fib(3)
fib.icn: 5      | | | | fib(2)
fib.icn: 4      | | | | fib returned 1
fib.icn: 5      | | | | fib(1)
fib.icn: 3      | | | | fib returned 1
fib.icn: 5      | | | fib returned 2
fib.icn: 5      | | | fib(2)
fib.icn: 4      | | | fib returned 1
fib.icn: 5      | | fib returned 3
fib.icn: 5      | | fib(3)
fib.icn: 5      | | | fib(2)
fib.icn: 4      | | | fib returned 1
fib.icn: 5      | | | fib(1)
fib.icn: 3      | | | fib returned 1
fib.icn: 5      | | fib returned 2
fib.icn: 5      | fib returned 5
```

The name of the file containing the program is fib.icn. The initial call, fib(5), is on line 9, which is in the main procedure used for testing. Note the redundant computations.

10.6 OTHER INFORMATION ABOUT PROCEDURES

Other information can be obtained about procedure activity without resorting to tracing. The value of &level is the current level of procedure call. &level is initially 1 when the procedure main is called to initiate program execution. &level is automatically incremented by 1 each time a procedure is called and decremented by 1 each time a procedure returns.

The function display(i, f) writes a list of identifiers and their values in i levels of procedure calls, starting at the current level. The output is written to the file f. An omitted value of i defaults to &level, while an omitted value of f defaults to &errout. All local and global identifiers referenced in the procedure are included. The function call display(1) includes only identifiers in the currently active procedure. The function call display(&level) includes all procedures leading to the currently active procedure, while display(0) includes only global identifiers.

An example of the output of display() is given by the following program:

```
procedure main()
    local intext
    if not (intext := open("shaw.txt"))
    then stop("cannot open input file")
    write(linecount(intext))
end

procedure linecount(file)
    local count, line
    count := 0
    while line := read(file) do
        if find("stop", line) then break
        else count +:= 1
    display()
    return count
end
```

which produces the display output

```
linecount local identifiers:
    file = file(shaw.txt)
    count = 378
    line = "stop"
main local identifiers:
    intext = file(shaw.txt)
global identifiers:
    main = procedure main
    linecount = procedure linecount
    open = function open
    stop = function stop
    write = function write
    read = function read
    find = function find
    display = function display
```

Note that values are displayed in the manner of **image(x)**.

10.7 ENVIRONMENTAL INFORMATION

Keywords provide the means for obtaining information about the environment in which an Icon program runs. The value of **&date** is the current date in the form yyyy/mm/dd. For example, the value of **&date** for June 27, 1982 is 1982/06/27. The value of **&dateline** is the date and time of day in a format that is easy to read. An example is

Sunday, June 27, 1982   7:21 am

The value of **&clock** is the current time in the form **hh:mm:ss**. For example, the value of **&clock** for 7:21 a.m. is **07:21:00**. The value of **&time** is the elapsed CPU time in milliseconds, measured from the beginning of program execution.

The value of **&host** is the location, operating system, and computer on which Icon is running. An example is

University of Arizona, UNIX Version 7, PDP–11/70

The value of **&version** is the name and version number of the Icon implementation. An example is

Icon Version 5.5 compiler, September 1982

EXERCISES

10.1.[*] Write a procedure that shuffles the values in a list.

10.2.[*] Write a program that counts the number of times each character occurs in the input file. Include newline characters. Produce the output in a form in which every character can be recognized.

10.3. Trace **acker(3, 3)** for the solutions to Exercises 7.3 and 7.6.

10.4.[*] Write a procedure that produces a trace of the depth of recursion in the computation of Ackermann's function. Do not use tabulation.

10.5. Trace the procedures given in §7.6 that produce expressions and observe the recursive calls among the procedures for the nonterminal symbols.

10.6.[*] Write a procedure **pause(i)** that loops for i milliseconds before returning.

11

GENERATORS

11.1 THE CONCEPT OF GENERATORS

In the Part I of this book, only two possible outcomes of expression evaluation are considered: success and failure, one result or no result. Many expressions in Icon are capable of generating more than one result. Such expressions are called *generators*.

Consider the function find("th", s2). The positions at which th occurs as a substring of s2 are shown below for three values of s2.

when she wins she is pleased

when he discusses this point, he is quite eloquent
                 ↑

the central theme of his thesis involves three points
↑   ↑   ↑   ↑

In the first case, th does not occur as a substring of s2. In the second case, th occurs as a substring of s2 at position 19. In the third case, it occurs at four positions: 1, 13, 26, and 42. In the first case, find("th", s2) fails. In the second case, it produces 19. In the third case, it produces 1 but is capable of producing three more results.

A number of other functions are capable of producing more than one result. For example, upto(c, s) is capable of producing all the positions at which a character in c occurs in s.

If an expression is capable of producing more than one result, the results are produced in sequence according to the context in which the expression appears. In this context, the term outcome is extended to describe the sequence of results that an expression produces. The ways in which results are produced are discussed in detail in subsequent sections.

11.2 RESULT SEQUENCES

The *result sequence* for an expression consists of the results the expression is capable of producing. The results an expression actually produces depend on the context in which the expression is evaluated, which is described in §11.3. For the examples given in the preceding section, the result sequences are {}, {19}, and {1, 13, 26, 42}. The empty sequence, {}, is synonymous with failure.

The result sequence for a literal, such as 1, consists of the value of the literal, {1} in this case. The result sequence for a variable, such as x, also consists of just the variable, {x} in this case.

From the viewpoint of result sequences, the operation of control structures depends on the length of the result sequence for the control expression. For example,

if $expr_1$ then $expr_2$ else $expr_3$

selects $expr_2$ if the length of the result sequence for $expr_1$ is greater than 0 but selects $expr_3$ otherwise.

If a generator is an argument of another expression, the result sequence for that expression depends on the result sequence for the generator. Therefore, the result sequence for

5 + find("th", s2)

is {6, 18, 31, 47} for the third value of s2 in §11.1. If the argument of an expression is a generator, the expression becomes a generator; generation is "inherited" from arguments, just as failure is.

11.3 CONTEXTS FOR GENERATION

There are two contexts in which a generator may produce more than one result: *iteration* over its result sequence and *goal-directed evaluation*.

11.3.1 Iteration over Result Sequences

The control structure

every $expr_1$ do $expr_2$

evaluates *expr₂* once for each result in the result sequence for *expr₁*. For example,

> every i := upto('aeiou', line) do write(i)

writes the positions of all the lowercase vowels in line. Note that the assignment operation inherits the results from

> upto('aeiou', line)

The **do** clause in **every-do** is optional, and auxiliary identifiers such as the one used in the preceding often can be avoided. For example,

> every write(upto('aeiou', line))

produces the same output as the preceding expression.

The usefulness of being able to iterate over a sequence of results is illustrated by the following procedure, which prints vertical bars under the first character of every occurrence of the substring **s** in the input file.

```
procedure mark(s)
   local line, marker, i
   while line := read() do {
      marker := ""              # initialize marker
      every i := find(s, line) do
         marker := left(marker, i - 1) || "|"
      write(line, "\n", marker)   # write line and marker
      }
   return
end
```

The output produced by mark("he") for the song by Shakespeare given in §1.4 is:

```
Tell me, where is fancy bred,
          |
Or in the heart or in the head?
       |  |         |  |
How begot, how nourished?
                  |
    Reply, reply.
```

It is engender'd in the eyes,
|
With gazing fed; and fancy dies

In the cradle where it lies:
| |
Let us all ring fancy's knell;

I'll begin it, − Ding, dong, bell.

The **break** and **next** expressions can be used in the **every-do** control structure in the same way they are used in other loops. For example, in

    every i := upto('aeiou', line) do
        if i <= 10 then write(i) else break

writes the positions of lowercase vowels in line, stopping when a position that
is greater than 10 is encountered.

11.3.2 Goal-Directed Evaluation

A comparison operation such as

    i > j

succeeds or fails, depending only on the values of i and j. However, in

    find(s1, s2) > 10

the comparison may succeed for some values in the result sequence for
find(s1, s2) and may fail for other values.

Evaluation of expressions in Icon is *goal-directed* in the sense that the
evaluation mechanism attempts to produce at least one result for all expressions. If a generator occurs as an argument in a conditional expression, the
generator produces results until the conditional operation succeeds or until
there are no more results. Therefore,

    (i := find(s1, s2)) > 10

succeeds for the first position greater than 10 at which s1 occurs as a substring
of s2. For the examples given in §11.1, the expression fails for the first case
but succeeds for 19 and 13, respectively, for the second and third cases.

Similarly, the expression

    if (i := find(s1, s2)) > 10 then write(i)

writes the least position greater than 10 at which s1 occurs as a substring of s2.

Since comparison operations produce the values of their right arguments, such expressions can be written more concisely by reversing the sense of the comparison and using the value it produces directly. This avoids the control structure and auxiliary identifier in the previous example:

write(10 < find(s1, s2))

Note that unlike iteration over result sequences, goal-directed evaluation causes only one result to be produced. On the other hand,

every write(10 < find(s1, s2))

writes all the positions greater than 10.

Goal-directed evaluation, which is implicit in the expression evaluation mechanism of Icon, produces the results from the result sequences for the arguments in an expression only until the expression itself produces a result. Iteration, which is explicit, produces all possible results from the arguments of an expression, regardless of whether or not the expression produces a result.

11.4 ARGUMENT EVALUATION

Expressions can have several arguments that are generators. An example is

upto(' ', line1) = upto(' ', line2)

This comparison expression succeeds if line1 and line2 have a space in the same position.

The order in which the results for upto(' ', line1) and upto(' ', line2) are produced may be important. For example, the order of evaluation determines the result sequence for the entire expression.

As mentioned earlier, arguments of expressions, except for some control structures, are evaluated from left to right. Hence upto(' ', line1) is evaluated before upto(' ', line2). Of course, if either of these expressions fails, the entire comparison expression fails. Suppose, however, that line1 and line2 have the following values from "The Rime of the Ancient Mariner":

line1 := "The air is cut away before,"
line2 := "And closes in behind."

The result sequences for upto(' ', line1) and upto(' ', line2) are {4, 8, 11, 15, 20} and {4, 11, 14}, respectively.

Intuitively, the comparison should succeed for the values 4 and 11 and have the result sequence {4, 11}. This intuitive view is correct. The sequence is produced as follows:

The first argument of the comparison is evaluated first and produces the value 4. The second argument is then evaluated and also produces the value of 4. The comparison succeeds with the value 4.

If the expression is used in a context, such as

write(upto(' ', line1) = upto(' ', line2))

the value 4 is written and evaluation of this expression stops at that point. On the other hand, evaluation continues if this expression is used in an iterative context, such as

every write(upto(' ', line1) = upto(' ', line2))

It is a general rule that the generator that produced a result last is the first to be *resumed* to produce another result. For this example,

upto(' ', line2)

is resumed and produces its second result, 11. The comparison is now performed between 4, the value previously produced by upto(' ', line1), and 11. Since this comparison fails, upto(' ', line2) is resumed again and produces its third result, 14. The comparison again fails.

When upto(' ', line2) is resumed again, it does not produce a result. The *first* argument, upto(' ', line1), is resumed at this point. It produces the result 8 and the second argument, upto(' ', line2), is *evaluated* again and produces its first result, 4.

This process continues, with the second argument being repeatedly resumed until it has no more results, in which case the first argument is resumed again and produces its third result, 11. When the second argument subsequently produces its second result, 11, the comparison succeeds. The comparison does not succeed for any subsequent combination of results from the two sequences. Therefore, the result sequence for

upto(' ', line1) = upto(' ', line2)

is {4, 11} as expected.

Iteration produces all results from all the generators in an expression in all possible ways. Hence iteration may be an expensive and computationally wasteful process. On the other hand, the left-to-right evaluation of expressions and the last-in, first-out resumption of generators produces a well-defined and exhaustive search of all possibilities during expression evaluation. This allows complicated computations to be expressed concisely and the details of the computation to be left to the expression evaluation mechanism. Without generators, computations of the kind given in the previous example often are cumbersome and difficult to formulate.

11.5 GENERATOR EXPRESSIONS

There are several control structures and operations specifically related to generators.

11.5.1 Alternation

The *alternation* control structure

$$expr_1 \mid expr_2$$

generates the sequence of results for $expr_1$ followed by the sequence of results for $expr_2$. A simple example is

        1 | 2

which has the result sequence {1, 2}. For example,

        x = (1 | 2)

succeeds if the value of x is either 1 or 2.

Alternation associates from left to right and has precedence higher than that of assignment operations, but lower than that of comparison operations. For example,

        x = 1 | 2

groups as

        (x = 1) | 2

Since alternation is a control structure that may be used in a variety of contexts, it is good practice in such situations to use parentheses to assure correct grouping.

Alternation often can be used in place of an **if-then-else** expression to achieve conciseness. For example,

        if not (intext := open("shaw.txt"))
        then stop("cannot open input file")

can be replaced by

        (intext := open("shaw.txt")) | stop("cannot open input file")

If the file is opened successfully, the second argument of the alternation control structure is not evaluated. If, however, the file is not opened successfully, the second argument is evaluated, and the program terminates with a diagnostic message. Such usages are idiomatic in Icon.

Alternation often is used to combine generators. For example, the result sequence for upto(' ', line1) | upto(' ', line2)

consists of the sequence of results for

upto(' ', line1)

followed by the sequence of results for

upto(' ', line2)

For the example in §11.4, the result sequence is {4, 8, 11, 15, 20, 4, 11, 14}. The expression

upto(' ', line1 | line2)

has the same result sequence.

11.5.2 Integer Sequences

Many computations are done for all the values of a sequence of integers at regularly spaced intervals. This fits naturally into the concept of generators. The operation

i to j by k

generates the integers from i to j, using k as the increment. For example, the result sequence for

0 to 10 by 2

is {0, 2, 4, 6, 8, 10}

The **by** clause is optional; if it is omitted, the increment is assumed to be 1. Therefore,

every write((1 to 10) ∧ 2)

writes the squares of the integers from 1 to 10.

The increment can be negative, in which case the sequence is in decreasing order, as in

every write((10 to 1 by −1) ∧ 2)

which writes the squares in decreasing order.

The words **to** and **by** are reserved and have precedence higher than that of assignment operations but lower than that of alternation. Therefore,

1 to 10 + i

groups as

1 to (10 + i)

and

```
    i := 1 to 10
```

groups as

```
    i := (1 to 10)
```

Note that an expression such as

```
    every i := j to k do p(i)
```

combines the integer sequence generator and generator iteration to produce an idiom that is equivalent to the **for** control structure of many programming languages.

As mentioned earlier, the auxiliary identifier often is not needed. For example,

```
    every write(a[1 to *a])
```

writes all the values in the list **a** and

```
    every write(fib(3 to 10))
```

writes the third through tenth values in the Fibonacci sequence described in §7.6.

11.5.3 Limiting Generation

Sometimes it is useful to be able to limit a generator to a maximum number of results. The *limitation* control structure

```
    expr \ i
```

generates at most i results from the result sequence for *expr* (the value of i is determined before *expr* is evaluated). For example,

```
    every write(upto(' ', line) \ 3)
```

writes at most the first three positions at which spaces occur in line.

The limitation control structure associates from left to right and has higher precedence than exponentiation. For example,

```
    i to j \ 10
```

groups as

```
    i to (j \ 10)
```

It is good practice to use parentheses in such expressions.

11.5.4 Repeated Alternation

Sometimes it is useful to generate a sequence of results repeatedly. The *repeated alternation* control structure,

|*expr*

repeatedly generates the result sequence for *expr*. A simple example is

|1

which generates the sequence {1, 1, ...}. Another example is

|(1 to 3)

which generates the sequence {1, 2, 3, 1, 2, 3, ...}.

Such sequences never terminate of their own accord and normally are used in situations where outside intervention prevents endless generation. For example,

every write(|(0 to 7) \ 128)

writes the octal digits 16 times.

If the result sequence for *expr* is empty, the result sequence for |*expr* is empty; it fails. Furthermore, if *expr* has a non-empty result sequence initially, but its result sequence subsequently becomes empty during the evaluation of |*expr*, the result sequence for |*expr* terminates at that point. For example, the result sequence for

|read()

consists of the lines of the input file, terminating when the end of the input file is reached.

11.5.5 Element Generation

Strings are sequences of characters, while lists and records are sequences of values of arbitrary types. Files are sequences of lines (strings), and tables can be considered to be sequences of pairs of values, although the ordering of the pairs is not defined.

There are many cases in which such *elements* are processed in order from beginning to end. While this can be done in various ways, depending on the type, the element generation operation !x does it concisely and uniformly for all the types mentioned.

For a string s, !s generates the one-character substrings of s in order from first to last, from left to right. For example,

> every write(!s)

writes the characters of s, one per line. This expression is equivalent to

> every write(s[1 to *s])

If s is a string-valued variable, the expression !s is a subscripting expression that produces a variable, just as s[i] does. For example,

> !s := ""

is equivalent to

> s[1] := ""

and deletes the first character in the value of s.

In an expression such as

> every !s := *expr*

the value of s is changed with each assignment, but the position in s is incremented repeatedly until the end of the string is reached. If the assignment changes the size of the value of s, the effect can be confusing.

The element generator can be used to generate the one-character substrings of any string, even if it is not the value of a variable. For example,

> every write(!&lcase)

writes the lowercase letters, one per line. In this expression the cset &lcase is converted to a string automatically. On the other hand, if the value of c is a cset,

> !c := "

does not delete the first character of c. Instead, it is an error, just as

> c[1] := "

is an error. The problem here is subtle. Csets cannot be subscripted, per se. When a subscript is applied to a cset, the cset is converted to a string automatically. The effect is as if the expression were

> string(c)[1] := "

The conversion of the cset to a string does not change the value of c, which is still a cset. The previous expression is equivalent to

> string(c) := string(c)[2:0]

Since string(c) does not produce a variable, a value cannot be assigned to it.

For a list a, !a generates the elements of the list in order from first to last, from left to right. The expression !a is a list reference, like a[i]. If a is a list-valued variable, a value can be assigned to !a to change that value in the list. For example,

> **every !a := 0**

sets all the elements of **a** to 0.

The elements of records are generated in order like lists.

For tables, all elements are generated but in an unpredictable order. Therefore, if **t** is a table

> **every !t := 0**

assigns 0 to all entries in **t**.

For a file **f**, **!f** generates successive lines of input from **f**. For example,

> **every write(!&input)**

copies the input file to the output file.

The familiar usage

> **while line := read() do** *expr*

also can be formulated as

> **every line := !&input do** *expr*

Generation of the lines from a file differs from that for other types, since once a line from a file is read, the position in the file is advanced. Therefore,

> **every write(!s)**
> **every write(!s)**

writes the one-character substrings of **s** twice, but

> **every write(!f)**
> **every write(!f)**

only writes the lines from file **f** once. The second expression produces no result, since the end of the file **f** is reached in the first expression. For this reason,

> **every write(!f)**

is equivalent to

> **while write(!f)**

11.6 GENERATORS IN STRING ANALYSIS

In addition to the functions find(s1, s2) and upto(c, s) described in §11.1, bal(c1, c2, c3, s) is a generator. The result sequences for these functions consist of all the positions, from left to right, at which the specified strings or characters occur.

The use of **bal** as a generator is illustrated by the following generalization of the program from §4.3.2. In the following program, every operator that follows an initial balanced substring is noted. Instead of a marker, the operator itself is written below its occurrence on the input line.

```
procedure main()
    while line := read() do {
        marker := ""
        every i := bal('+−/*',,, line) do
            marker := left(marker, i − 1) || line[i]
        write(line, "\n", marker)        # write line and marker
        }
end
```

The output from this program for the input given in §4.3.2 is:

```
y

x−x∗z
 − ∗
((z+y))+y/z−(x)
      + / −
z+y−(z∗(x/(z)+x∗y))−z∗z/x+(x+y+x)
 + −              − ∗ / +
(y)∗(x)
    ∗
z

((z))+(z)
    +
z−x
 −
(z)/x+y
  / +
(z−(y)+y∗(y/x))
```

```
z+(((y))/(y))-z
 +         -
x+(y)
 +
z/(y)+y*y
 /   + *
```

Range restrictions can be used in combination with generation. For example, the result sequence for

upto('aeiou', "The theory is fallacious", 5, 11)

is {7, 8}.

11.7 PROCEDURES AS GENERATORS

The **return** and **fail** expressions cause return from a procedure call and destruction of all local nonstatic identifiers and other information related to that call. On the other hand,

suspend [*expr*]

returns from the procedure call but leaves the call in suspension with the local identifiers intact. In this case, the procedure call can be resumed to continue evaluation from where it suspended.

The situations in which a suspended procedure is resumed are the same as those for built-in generators: iteration and goal-directed evaluation. Therefore, a procedure that suspends is a generator; each suspension produces a result in its result sequence.

An example of a procedure that is a generator follows:

```
procedure To(i, j)
    while i <= j do {
        suspend i
        i +:= 1
        }
    end
```

The result sequence for To(i, j) is the same as the result sequence for

i to j

The initial capital in To avoids conflict with the reserved word to.

When the **while** loop is complete, control flows off the end of the procedure body. This implicit return does not produce a result, so the only values produced are those from the **suspend** expression. If the value of j is less than the value of i, the **while** loop terminates without evaluating the **suspend** expression and the procedure produces no result.

The procedure **nword** in §7.2 can be rewritten as a generator so that it produces the next word from the input file every time it is resumed. This can be accomplished by suspending with each word that is found:

```
procedure genword()
    static wchar
    local line, i, j
    initial wchar := &lcase ++ &ucase ++ '\'−'
    while line := read() do {
        i := 1
        while j := upto(wchar, line, i) do {
            i := many(wchar, line, j)
            suspend line[i:j]          # produce word
        }
    }
end
```

This procedure can be used in an iterative context, such as

```
t := table(0)
every t[genword()] +:= 1
```

which tabulates the words.

Note that **line, i,** and **j** do not need to be static in this procedure. The necessary memory is provided by the procedure mechanism itself.

The **suspend** expression is like **every**; it iterates over all the results in the result sequence for its argument, suspending with each one. For example, the following procedure uses a built-in generator as the argument to **suspend** to iterate over the characters in **s** from right to left:

```
procedure rtl(s)
    suspend s[∗s to 1 by −1]
end
```

The result sequence for **rtl(s)** is the one-character strings of **s** starting with the last and finishing with the first.

The expression

suspend *expr*

does not suspend if *expr* produces no result. For example, if **s** is the empty string in the previous example, **rtl(s)** does not produce a result.

When a sequence of results is needed, procedure suspension sometimes can be used to avoid redundant computation. For example, the Fibonacci sequence described in §7.6 is produced by the following procedure.

```
procedure fibseq()
    local i, j, k
    suspend (i := 1) | (j := 1)
    repeat {
        suspend k := i + j
        i := j
        j := k
    }
end
```

Note that the first two values are produced by an alternation that has the side effect of assigning to i and j the values that are needed to compute the next result in the sequence.

The result sequence for **fibseq()** is infinite. It can be limited, however, so that only a specified number of results are produced. For example,

```
every write(fibseq() \ 20)
```

writes the first 20 Fibonacci numbers.

Procedure tracing shows the suspension and resumption of procedures, as well as calls and returns. An example of tracing for **fibseq** is

```
fibseq.icn: 12 | fibseq()
fibseq.icn: 3  | fibseq suspended 1
fibseq.icn: 12 | fibseq resumed
fibseq.icn: 3  | fibseq suspended 1
fibseq.icn: 12 | fibseq resumed
fibseq.icn: 5  | fibseq suspended 2
fibseq.icn: 12 | fibseq resumed
fibseq.icn: 5  | fibseq suspended 3
fibseq.icn: 12 | fibseq resumed
fibseq.icn: 5  | fibseq suspended 5
fibseq.icn: 12 | fibseq resumed
fibseq.icn: 5  | fibseq suspended 8
fibseq.icn: 12 | fibseq resumed
fibseq.icn: 5  | fibseq suspended 13
```

Compare this trace output to that for **fib** given in §10.5.

11.8 BACKTRACKING AND REVERSIBLE EFFECTS

11.8.1 Control Backtracking

If the evaluation of an argument of a function or operation fails, goal-directed evaluation resumes previously evaluated arguments, as described in §11.4. Similarly, if the call of a function or operation fails, goal-directed evaluation resumes the last (rightmost) argument. If this argument produces no result, the previous argument is resumed, and so on. Therefore, control may return to an earlier portion of an expression during goal-directed evaluation. This is called *control backtracking*.

If the evaluation of an expression causes side effects, such as assignments to variables, those effects normally are not reversed during control backtracking. For example, in

$$(i := j) > k$$

the value of j is assigned to i when the first argument of the comparison is evaluated. If the comparison fails, the first argument is resumed. Assignment is not a generator and it does not produce another result when it is resumed. The entire expression therefore fails. The value of j remains assigned to i even though the expression fails.

Control backtracking is restricted syntactically. One restriction occurs in compound expressions. Each expression within a compound expression is isolated with respect to control backtracking. For example, in

$$\{i := upto(' \ ', line); \ i > j\}$$

once

$$i := upto(' \ ', line)$$

is evaluated (whether it succeeds or fails), the outcome of

$$i > j$$

has no effect on it. Specifically, if

$$i > j$$

fails,

$$i := upto(' \ ', line)$$

is not resumed for another possible value. The same situation applies to the sequence of expressions in the body of a procedure; they are isolated from each other with respect to control backtracking.

In addition, the control expressions in control structures are limited to at most one result. For example, in

>   if *expr₁* then *expr₂* else *expr₃*

if *expr₁* succeeds but *expr₂* fails, *expr₁* is not resumed for another possible result, nor is *expr₃* evaluated.

11.8.2 Data Backtracking

Some programming languages support *data backtracking*, in which side effects, such as assignments, are "undone" if control backtracking goes back beyond the expression that caused the side effect. Such implicit data backtracking occurs in Icon only in string scanning (see Chapter 12). There are, however, two operations that perform explicit data backtracking: *reversible assignment* and *reversible exchange*.

Reversible assignment, denoted by

>   x <− y

is just like ordinary assignment, except that if it is resumed, the former value of x is restored. For example,

>   (i <− j) > k

assigns the value of j to i only if that value is greater than k.

Reversible exchange,

>   x <−> y

is the reversible form of the exchange operation (see §10.3); the former values of x and y are restored if the reversible exchange operation is resumed.

The reversible assignment and reversible exchange operations have the same precedence and associativity as the regular assignment and exchange operations.

EXERCISES

11.1.*   Write a program that counts the number of vowels that occur in the input file.

11.2.   Write a procedure that determines whether or not two strings have a space in the same position. Do not use generators.

11.3.   Write a procedure findi(s1, s2, i) that produces the ith position at which s1 occurs as a substring of s2 but fails if there are less than i occurrences of s1 in s2.

11.4.[*] Write an expression that has a result sequence consisting of the positive even integers {2, 4, 6, 8, ... }.

11.5.[*] Write a procedure genpos(a, x) that generates the positions in the list a at which the value of x occurs.

11.6. Write a procedure geneq(a1, a2) that generates all the values in the lists a1 and a2 that are the same.

11.7.[*] Write a procedure that generates the chaotic sequence (see Exercises 7.4 and 7.5).

11.8. Write a procedure ranseq(i) that generates a sequence of pseudo-random integers between 1 and i, inclusive.

11.9.[*] Write an expression that generates the Fibonacci sequence without using a procedure.

11.10.[*] Write a procedure allbal(c, s) that generates all the substrings of s up to a character in c that are balanced with respect to parentheses. Omit empty strings.

12

STRING SCANNING

12.1 THE CONCEPT OF STRING SCANNING

Examples in previous chapters illustrate the use of functions like upto and many to process strings. Most of these examples involve locating and processing words, although there are many other applications. In such examples, range restrictions are used to isolate the portion of a string to be analyzed, and subscripting expressions are used to produce the desired substrings. Consider again the procedure from §5.2.1 that counts words from the input file:

```
procedure tabwords()
    static wchar
    local words, line, i, j
    initial wchar := &lcase ++ &ucase ++ '\'–'
    words := table(0)
    while line := read() do {
        i := 1
        while j := upto(wchar, line, i) do {
            i := many(wchar, line, j)
            words[line[i:j]] +:= 1
            }
        }
    return words
end
```

In this procedure i and j advance through line as upto and many perform lexical analysis.

This kind of computation is cumbersome and prone to error. It is easy to make a mistake in specifying a position, to forget to set the value of i to 1 at the beginning of the **while** loop, to make a syntactic error, and so forth. The basis of such problems lies in the relatively low level of the operations, which requires the details of the computation to be specified by the programmer.

The *string scanning* facilities in Icon are designed to allow such computations to be performed at a higher level that eliminates details such as the explicit computation of indexes to keep track of positions.

The string scanning expression

   s ? *expr*

specifies, by the value of s, a subject string to which *expr* applies.

In *expr* functions like upto and many are used with only one argument. The string to which they apply is the subject of the scanning operation, and the range is implicit. For example,

   text ? upto('aeiou')

produces the position of the first vowel in text, and is equivalent to

   upto('aeiou', text)

String scanning starts at the beginning of the subject. The function **tab(i)** sets the position in the subject to i and produces the substring of the subject between the old and new positions. Therefore, **tab** provides a way of moving through the subject and producing substrings of interest. Taking this approach, the word tabulation procedure can be rephrased as follows:

```
procedure tabwords()
    static wchar
    local words, line
    initial wchar := &lcase ++ &ucase ++ '\'–'
    words := table(0)
    while line := read() do
        line ? while tab(upto(wchar)) do
            words[tab(many(wchar))] +:= 1
    return words
end
```

This procedure is the same as that given at the beginning of this chapter except for the details of the **while** loop. The value of line now is the subject of scanning and need not be specified as the argument of the lexical analysis functions. Similarly, the position in the subject is set automatically by **tab** so that the auxiliary identifiers i and j are not needed. Therefore, j := upto(wchar, line, i)

is replaced by

tab(upto(wchar))

and

i := many(wchar, line, j)
words[line[i:j]] +:= 1

are replaced by

words[tab(many(wchar))] +:= 1

Since the position in the subject is moved implicitly in string scanning, it is natural to formulate string processing in terms of movement through a string, which is the origin of the term string scanning.

12.2 THE SCANNING OPERATION

In the string scanning operation

s ? *expr*

expr usually contains operations that analyze s. These operations may produce substrings as by-products, as illustrated in the procedure for counting words. The outcome of the scanning operation is the outcome of *expr*, which may produce a substring of s. An example is

t := (s ? tab(upto(&lcase)))

which assigns to t the initial substring of s up to the first occurrence of a lower-case letter. Of course, if s does not contain a lowercase letter, the scanning operation fails and the assignment is not performed.

Augmented assignment in string scanning is often useful. For example,

s ?:= tab(upto(&lcase))

is equivalent to

s := (s ? tab(upto(&lcase)))

and assigns to s all the characters up to the first lowercase letter, which has the effect of deleting from s all trailing characters starting with the first lowercase letter.

The string scanning operation associates from left to right and has lower precedence than any infix operation except conjunction. Consequently,

```
        s ? x & y
```

groups as

```
        (s ? x) & y
```

but

```
        x := s ? y
```

groups as

```
        (x := s) ? y
```

Since an unexpected grouping in an expression containing a scanning operation may produce an error that is difficult to locate, it is good practice to use
parentheses to assure intended groupings in such situations.

String scanning is the only operation that frequently has an argument
that is a control structure. In the procedure for counting words, for example,
the right argument of the scanning operation is a **while** loop. Since looping
control structures do not produce results, the scanning operation itself fails. In
the context in which it is used in this procedure, this failure is irrelevant; it
occurs after all the desired substrings have been produced and the scanning
operation itself is not an argument of another expression. It is important to
remember, however, that such scanning operations should not be used in contexts where their failure might affect the outcome of other expressions.

A scanning expression need not produce a string. For example,

```
        write(text ? upto(&lcase))
```

writes the position of the first lowercase letter in text, and

```
        head := (text ? [tab(upto(&lcase))])
```

assigns to **head** a list that contains the string up to the first lowercase letter in
text.

Both arguments of a string scanning expression can be generators. For
example,

```
        every write((s1 | s2 | s3) ? upto(c1 | c2))
```

writes the same values as

```
        every write(upto(c1 | c2, s1 | s2 | s3))
```

Note, however, that these two expressions do not necessarily write the values in
the same order. The resumption of the arguments occurs in different orders in
the two expressions.

12.3 MATCHING FUNCTIONS

There are two *matching functions* that change the position in the subject and produce the substring between the old and new positions: tab(i) and move(i).

As indicated earlier, tab(i) sets the position to i. The function move(i), on the other hand, adds i to the position. In move(i), i can be negative, which has the effect of moving the position to the left in the subject. In tab(i), i can be a nonpositive position specification. In particular, tab(0) moves the position to the right end of the subject. The position can be moved to the left with tab(i) by specifying a position that is to the left of the current position.

Both matching functions fail if the position given is out of range of the subject.

The arguments of the matching functions can be generators. For example,

    tab(upto(&lcase) | 0)

moves the position up to a lowercase letter, if there is one, but moves it to the end if there is not.

If a matching function is resumed but has no more results to produce, it restores the position in the subject to the value it had before the matching function was evaluated. This data backtracking is like reversible assignment (see §11.6.2), except that restoration of the position in the subject is implicit.

The purpose of data backtracking in the matching functions is to make it easy to try alternative matches starting at the same position in the subject. Consider the following problem: If text contains more than two characters, produce its third character; otherwise produce all of text. A solution to this problem can be formulated as follows:

    text ? ((move(2) & move(1)) | tab(0))

The expression

    move(2) & move(1)

is the first alternative. Suppose that text is at least three characters long. The expression move(2) moves the position in the subject past the first two characters, and move(1) produces the third character, which in turn is produced by the conjunction operation. Suppose, however, there are only two characters: move(2) succeeds but move(1) fails. At this point, move(2) is resumed. It has no other result to produce but restores the position to the beginning of the subject. The second alternative, tab(0), is now evaluated and produces the entire subject. Therefore, when tab(0) is evaluated, the position is the same as it was for the first alternative. If matching functions did not perform data backtracking, it would be hard to keep track of the position in the subject, since a matching function that fails might nonetheless leave the position changed.

As described in §8.4, conjunction can be rephrased as mutual evaluation. Therefore, the previous expression can also be written as

text ? (move(2), move(1)) | tab(0)

On the other hand,

text ? 1(move(2), move(1)) | tab(0)

produces the first two characters of text if it is more than two characters long.

12.4 SCANNING KEYWORDS

The current subject and position for scanning are the values of the keywords &subject and &pos, respectively. The operation

s ? *expr*

assigns the value of s to &subject and assigns 1 to &pos. Matching functions usually are used to change the value of &pos implicitly. The value of &pos also may be changed explicitly. For example,

&pos := 1

sets the position to the beginning of the subject.

The value assigned to &pos can be nonpositive, relative to the right end of the subject. For example,

&pos := 0

sets the position to the end of the subject. The actual value assigned to &pos is the positive equivalent of 0, which depends on the size of &subject. Therefore,

&pos = 0

does *not* test whether the position is at the end of the subject; in fact, this expression always fails.

The function pos(i) does test the value of &pos; if i is not positive, it is converted to the equivalent positive position and pos(i) produces this value, provided that it is equal to &pos. It fails otherwise. Therefore, pos(0) succeeds if the position is at the end of the subject. For example,

text ? (*expr* & pos(0))

succeeds if *expr* matches all of text.

The value of &subject also may be changed by an explicit assignment. For example,

&subject := "(" || &subject || ")"

adds parentheses around the subject. Whenever the value of **&subject** is changed, **&pos** is set to 1.

While explicit references to **&pos** and **&subject** are possible, and sometimes necessary, they usually should be avoided as a matter of style, since they disrupt the implicit position change that gives string scanning much of its succinctness.

12.5 STRING ANALYSIS FUNCTIONS

All the string analysis functions can be used in string scanning. In this context, the trailing arguments that specify the string to be analyzed and the range are omitted. For example,

find(s)

is equivalent to

find(s, &subject, &pos, 0)

When used in string scanning, these string analysis functions have the forms

```
any(c)
bal(c1, c2, c3)
find(s)
many(c)
match(s)
upto(c)
```

Note that **bal(c)** is the form used for parenthesis-balanced strings (see §4.3.2).

Since these string analysis functions all produce positions in the subject, they usually are used with **tab,** as illustrated earlier. The argument of **move,** on the other hand, usually is a fixed value. For example,

```
text ? while tab(upto('aeiou')) do
    write(move(1))
```

writes all the lowercase vowels in **text.**

For convenience, **=s** is a synonym for **tab(match(s)),** which matches the string **s** and moves the position past it. For example,

="(" & tab(−1) & =")"

matches any string that begins with a left parenthesis and ends with a right parenthesis.

12.6 NESTED SCANNING

The values of **&subject** and **&pos** are saved when a scanning operation begins and are restored when it produces a result or fails. This allows nested scanning. For example, in

```
line ? while tab(upto(wchar)) do
    write(tab(many(wchar)) ? (tab(−1) & tab(0)))
```

the subject in

```
tab(many(wchar)) ? (tab(−1) & tab(0))
```

is produced by the outer scanning operation and is scanned in turn by

```
(tab(−1) & tab(0))
```

This example therefore writes the last character of every word.

12.7 RETURNING VALUES FROM SCANNING

A **suspend** expression can be used in a scanning operation to generate results that are produced during string scanning. An example is the following procedure, which generates the words from the input file:

```
procedure words()
    local wchar, line, word
    wchar := &lcase ++ &ucase ++ '\'−'
    while line := read() do
        line ? while tab(upto(wchar)) do {
            word := tab(many(wchar))
            suspend word
            }
    end
```

Since a **suspend** expression repeatedly resumes its argument, it is important that its argument not contain a matching function whose resumption would restore the previous position in the subject. For example,

```
    .
    .
    .
while tab(upto(wchar)) do
    suspend tab(many(wchar))
    .
    .
    .
```

suspends with a word, but when

tab(many(wchar))

is resumed, **tab** restores the position in the subject to its value prior to the match. When

tab(upto(wchar))

is resumed again, the position in the subject is the same as it was previously. The position is not changed, and

tab(many(wchar))

produces the same word again. The consequence is an endless loop that repeatedly produces the first word of the first line of the input file.

This problem can be avoided in two ways. One way is to use an auxiliary identifier such as the one used in the procedure at the beginning of this section. This effectively separates the matching function from the resumption in the **suspend** expression. Another way to avoid the problem is to limit the resumption of the argument of the **suspend** expression explicitly as in

suspend tab(many(wchar)) \ 1

The keywords **&subject** and **&pos** are global and accessible to all procedures. Procedure calls and returns have no effect on the values of **&subject** and **&pos**. The values of these keywords are saved when a scanning operation is evaluated as described in the last section. They are restored only when the evaluation of the scanning operation is completed. The values of **&subject** and **&pos** are not restored when a scanning operation is terminated by a **break next, return, fail**, or **suspend** expression.

Such termination of a scanning operation can be the cause of programming errors that are mysterious and difficult to locate. Except for suspension from a scanning operation to generate a sequence of results, it is good practice to write scanning expressions so that their evaluation is always completed.

Unlike global identifiers, **&subject** and **&pos** are dereferenced if they are used as arguments of **return** or **suspend** expressions. Similarly, an expression that subscripts **&subject** is dereferenced if it is the argument of a **return** or **suspend** expression.

EXERCISES

12.1.[*]   Redo Exercises 4.2 and 4.7 using string scanning.

12.2.[*]   Write a procedure **enrepl(s)** that abbreviates strings of repeated characters by replacing the repeated characters by one instance of the character followed by the number of times it occurs enclosed in parentheses. Assume that **s** does not contain parentheses. Do not replace a repeated string of characters that has a size of less than five. For example,

> enrepl("aaaaaabbbbbbbbcccccccdd")

should produce

> a(6)b(8)c(6)dd

Write a corresponding procedure **derepl(s)** that restores strings produced by **enrepl(s)** to their original form.

12.3. Write a procedure that writes a "snapshot" of the state of string scanning by writing the value of the subject with a vertical bar underneath the current position.

12.4. Write a procedure **selword(s)** that generates only those words in the input file that contain the substring **s**.

12.5.* Redo Exercise 11.10 using string scanning.

13

CO-EXPRESSIONS

The production of a sequence of results by an expression is limited to the place where that expression appears in the program. Furthermore, the results of an expression can be produced only by iteration or by goal-directed evaluation; there is no mechanism for explicitly resuming an expression to get a result. Consequently, the results produced by an expression are strictly constrained, both in location and in the sequence of program evaluation.

Co-expressions overcome these limitations. A co-expression "captures" an expression so that it can be explicitly resumed at any time and place.

13.1 CO-EXPRESSION OPERATIONS

13.1.1 Creating Co-Expressions

The expression

create *expr*

produces a co-expression for *expr*. This co-expression is a value that consists of the information that is necessary to evaluate *expr*: a reference to *expr* itself, the location in *expr* where it is to be resumed, and copies of any local identifiers that are referenced in *expr*. For example,

e := create find(s1, s2)

assigns to e a co-expression for the expression find(s1, s2). If s1 and s2 are local to the procedure in which this expression occurs, the co-expression contains copies of these identifiers with the values that s1 and s2 have when the **create** expression is evaluated. The expression find(s1, s2) is *not* evaluated when the **create** expression is evaluated.

The precedence of the **create** expression is lower than that of any infix operation, so

> create i + find(s1, s2)

groups as

> create (i + find(s1, s2))

13.1.2 Activating Co-Expressions

A co-expression is *activated* by the operation

> @e

When a co-expression is activated the first time, its expression is evaluated to produce its first result. When a co-expression is activated again, its expression is resumed to produce another result. For example,

> write(@e)

writes the first position at which s1 occurs as a substring of s2. The activation of a co-expression fails if its expression does not produce a result. Therefore,

> e := create find(s1, s2)
> while write(@e)

is equivalent to

> every write(find(s1, s2))

The activation operation dereferences the result produced by the expression; activation never produces a variable.

Since activation is an explicit operation, the results of an expression can be produced wherever or whenever they are needed. An example is a label generator that might be used at various places in an assembler. A co-expression can be created for the expression that generates the labels, and this co-expression then can be activated as needed:

```
labgen := create ("L" || (1 to 1000))
              :
              :
label := @labgen
              :
              :
label := @labgen
              :
              :
```

so that the labels L1, L2, L3, and so on are produced as they are needed.

Similarly,

```
e := create find(s1, s2)
while write(@e) do @e
```

writes every other result from the sequence for find(s1, s2). The result of each activation of e in the control expression is written, but the result of the subsequent activation of e in the **do** clause is not written.

13.1.3 The Size of Co-Expressions

The operation

```
*e
```

produces the number of results that have been produced by activating e, that is, its current "size". For example,

```
e := create find(s1, s2)
while @e
write(*e)
```

writes the number of positions at which s1 occurs as a substring of s2.

If a co-expression is activated after its expression has produced its last result, the activation fails and the size of the co-expression does not increase.

13.1.4 Refreshing Co-Expressions

The operation

```
^e
```

produces a copy of the co-expression e with its resumption location and the values of its local identifiers restored to the values they had when e was created. Therefore, the refresh operation provides a means of repeating the sequence of results for an expression. For example,

```
e := create find("th", "that theory is wrong")
write("The first position is ", @e)
write("The second position is ", @e)
e := ^e
write("The first position still is ", @e)
```

writes

```
The first position is 1
The second position is 6
The first position still is 1
```

The values of global identifiers are not affected by refreshing, nor are the values of local identifiers in the procedure in which the co-expression was created, since each co-expression has its own copies of its local identifiers.

13.2 USING CO-EXPRESSIONS

Most uses of co-expressions occur in situations where generators can be used to advantage but where neither iteration nor goal-directed evaluation can be used to produce results at the desired time or place.

Consider the problem of determining whether two expressions produce the same sequences of results. Neither iteration nor goal-directed evaluation allows the results of two sequences to be produced in parallel. One possible approach is to construct a list containing all the results for one of the expressions:

```
seq1 := []
every put(seq1, expr₁)
```

Once **seq1** is constructed, the values in it can be compared with the results from the second expression without constructing a second list:

```
i := 1
result := "yes"                    # presume success
every x := expr₂ do
    if x === seq1[i] then i +:= 1
    else {
        result := "no"             # note failure
        break
        }
if i ~= *seq1 + 1 then result := "no"
```

The final test is necessary, since a sequence may be an initial subsequence of a longer sequence.

This approach has several disadvantages. If the result sequence for *expr₁* is long, the space required for seq1, and the time necessary to construct it, may be prohibitive. Furthermore, the entire list must be constructed even if *expr₁* and *expr₂* differ in their first results. The coding is awkward also; it cannot be incorporated in a procedure that succeeds or fails depending on the equivalence of the two result sequences. That is, in a procedure call such as

equalseq(*expr₁, expr₂*)

expr₁ and *expr₂* are evaluated *before* equalseq is invoked; there is no way for a procedure to resume its arguments.

If a procedure whose arguments are co-expressions is used, the result sequences for two expressions can be compared by successive activations of the co-expressions. One method is

```
procedure equalseq(e1, e2)
   local x
   while x := @e1 do
      (x === @e2) | fail          # fail if different
      if @e2 then fail            # fail if longer
      else return
   end
```

Since the two result sequences may have different lengths, one co-expression, e1, is used to control the loop. If the sequence for e2 terminates first, or if two corresponding values are different, the procedure call fails. If the activation of e1 fails, a check is made to determine if e2 has additional results. If so, the procedure call also fails.

The structural asymmetry in the procedure arises from the need to check the lengths of the two result sequences; there is no way to determine the length of a result sequence without generating all the results. The same asymmetry exists in the list construction approach used earlier.

Note that equalseq may terminate (in failure) even if two result sequences are infinite in length.

The arguments of the procedure equalseq must be co-expressions. An example is

```
e1 := create upto('aeiou', line1)
e2 := create upto('aeiou', line2)
if equalseq(e1, e2) then write ("vowel match")
else write("vowel mismatch")
```

13.3 MODELING GENERATIVE CONTROL STRUCTURES

Generative control structures, such as alternation and iteration, can be modeled by more traditional control structures and co-expressions. Such models provide insight into generators. In these models, the results produced by successive evaluations of @e can be thought of much like the results produced by read(f), which produces a new line from the file f every time it is evaluated.

Consider a procedure that models alternation:

```
procedure Alt(e1, e2)
   local x
   while x := @e1 do suspend x
   while x := @e2 do suspend x
end
```

The order in which this procedure produces results shows how simple alternation really is. Similarly,

```
procedure Every(e1, e2)
   while @e1 do @^e2
end
```

illustrates how iteration is related to the more traditional **while** loop. Note that a refreshed copy of e2 is activated in the **do** clause; this corresponds to the successive *evaluations* of an expression as opposed to successive *resumptions*.

Control operations that are not built into Icon also can be formulated in this way. An example is the interleaved generation of the results of two expressions. A procedure that models this control operation is

```
procedure Inter(e1, e2)
   suspend |@(e1 | e2)
end
```

If the result sequence for one expression runs out before the other, the remaining results for the longer sequence are produced. Therefore, the result sequence for

```
Inter(create 1 to 3, create 6 to 10)
```

is {1, 6, 2, 7, 3, 8, 9, 10}.

Since each co-expression has its own copies of local identifiers, global identifiers must be used when modeling control operations that rely on side effects. For example, if

```
every i := 1 to 10 do p(i)
```

is modeled by

Every(create i := 1 to 10, create p(i))

the identifier i must be global so that the two co-expressions share the same identifier.

13.4 COROUTINE PROGRAMMING

Co-expressions have many of the properties of coroutines; in fact, the term co-expression indicates this similarity, while emphasizing that it applies to any expression, not just a procedure call. A few additional facilities are needed to support full coroutine programming.

13.4.1 Additional Co-Expression Facilities

In order for any co-expression to transfer control to any other co-expression, there must be a way to activate the co-expression that activated the expression that is currently being evaluated. It is also necessary to have a co-expression for the call of the procedure main that initiated program execution. These two co-expressions are built into Icon as the values of the keywords &source and &main. Therefore,

@&source

activates the co-expression from which current evaluation originated, allowing a "return" to this activating co-expression.

Communication among co-expressions can be accomplished by transmitting a value to a co-expression when it is activated. This is done by the operation

expr @ e

which activates e and supplies the result produced by *expr* to it. This result is ignored if e is being activated for its first result.

The transmission operation associates from left to right and has the same precedence as the limitation control structure. The use of the transmission operation is shown in the next section.

13.4.2 Using Co-Expressions as Coroutines

Most situations in which coroutines are really needed are quite complicated. Except for the "producer-consumer" type of problem, which is a useful special case, examples of coroutine programming are usually contrived. A typical producer-consumer problem is the following [12].

A filter A accepts characters from a source and puts them out, replacing all occurrences of aa by b. A similar filter B replaces all occurrences of bb by

C. Input is fed into A, the output of A is fed into B, and the output of B is written out.

An example of a stream of characters as they pass through these filters is

aabbx ... xabbax ... → bbbx ... xabbax ... → cbx ... xacax ...
             A   B

This filtering process can be programmed as follows:

```
global A, B

procedure main()
    A := create compact("a", "b", create |reads(), B)
    B := create compact("b", "c", A, &main)
    repeat writes(@B)
end

procedure compact(s1, s2, in, out)
    local s
    repeat {
        s := @in
        if s == s1 then {
            s := @in
            if s == s1 then s := s2
            else s1 @ out
            }
        s @ out
        }
end
```

The co-expression in provides the input for compact. In the case of A, this is a co-expression for a generator of characters from the input file, |reads(). In the case of B, it is A. The co-expression out provides the output for compact. In the case of A, it is B. In the case of B, it is the co-expression for the procedure main where B is activated and its results are written.

The identifier B must be global, since B has the null value when the co-expression that is assigned to A is created. If B were local, a copy of its value would be made at this point and the subsequent assignment to B would have no effect on the first co-expression. The identifier A need not be global, since its value is assigned before the second co-expression is created. Both are declared global here for uniformity.

EXERCISES

13.1. Write a procedure labgen(s) that produces a co-expression for a label sequence with the prefix s.

13.2. Write a procedure eqlseq(e1, e2) that succeeds if e1 and e2 have sequences of equal length but fails otherwise.

13.3.* Write a procedure Repalt(e) that models |*expr*.

13.4. Write a procedure Limit(e1, e2) that models $expr_1 \setminus expr_2$.

13.5.* Write a procedure Seqimage(e) that produces a string image of the result sequence produced by the expression in e. For example,

   Seqimage(create 1 to 5)

should produce

   {1, 2, 3, 4, 5}

13.6. Write a procedure evaltime(e, i) that evaluates the expression in e repeatedly i times and produces the average number of milliseconds required for the evaluation. Assume that the time required to activate e is insignificant, but compensate for the time spent in the evaluation loop and the time required to refresh e.

13.7.* The filtering program in §13.4.2 assumes an endless stream of input. Modify it to handle a finite stream.

13.8.* Generalize the filtering program to handle a list of filters, the first taking characters from the input file, the last writing characters to the output file, and intermediate filters connected in tandem. Test the program with filters that replace aa by b, bb by c, cc by d, and dd by e.

14

PROGRAMMING
WITH GENERATORS

Generators, used with iteration and goal-directed evaluation, allow many computations to be expressed in a concise and natural manner. In many cases they internalize computations that otherwise would require complex loops, auxiliary identifiers, and tedious comparisons.

Most programming languages do not have generators. Consequently, using the full capacity of generators requires new programming techniques and nontraditional ways of approaching problems. This chapter describes ways to use generators and gives a number of idioms for some kinds of computations that are natural in Icon.

14.1 THE APPLICABILITY OF GENERATORS

In order to take full advantage of generators, it is important to understand that all expressions in Icon are generators. Those expressions that produce only a single result and those that may fail are only special degenerate cases of generators. Furthermore, an operation that itself produces only a single result may produce a sequence of results if its arguments are generators.

Consider, for example, an operation as mundane as addition:

$$expr_1 + expr_2$$

The result sequence for this expression consists of all possible sums of numbers from the result sequences for its arguments. The length of the result sequence is the product of the length of the result sequences for the arguments. For example, the result sequence for

(1 to 5) + (1 to 3)

is {2, 3, 4, 3, 4, 5, 4, 5, 6, 5, 6, 7, 6, 7, 8}. Similarly, the result sequence for

!s1 || !s2 || !s3

consists of all the possible three-character strings with one character each from s1, s2, and s3.

The same situation exists for functions. For example,

every write(0 to 1, 0 to 7, 0 to 7)

writes the octal codes for the ASCII characters:

```
000
001
002
 .
 .
 .
175
176
177
```

The left-to-right order of argument evaluation and the last-in, first-out resumption of arguments to generate additional results are apparent in these examples and must be considered if the order of results is important.

Another unobvious situation in which generators may be useful is in selection control structures. For example, the control structure

if *expr₁* then *expr₂* else *expr₃*

can be thought of as being replaced by the selected expression, either $expr_2$ or $expr_3$. This selected expression can be a generator. An example is

if j > 0 then 1 to j else −1 to j by −1

which selects an increasing sequence if the value of j is positive, but a decreasing sequence otherwise. Such an expression may be used in any context where a **to-by** expression might be used. An example is

every i := if j > 0 then 1 to j else −1 to j by −1 do p(i)

14.2 CONDENSING EXPRESSIONS

Because of the way in which the argument evaluation mechanism in Icon works, it is often possible to condense expressions that would be more complicated if they were written in a conventional manner. The resulting expressions frequently are a more natural expression of the computation than the conventional counterparts, although any unconventional formulation may appear strange at first. With use, such formulations become idiomatic and natural in Icon.

Consider again the ways to check whether or not a file can be opened, as given in §9.1. The formulation

> if intext := open("shaw.txt") then *expr*
> else stop("cannot open input file")

places *expr* in an awkward place, especially if it is complicated. The alternative formulation

> if not (intext := open("shaw.txt"))
> then stop("cannot open input file")

contorts the meaning of the selection, much like a double negative in the English language. As described in §11.5.1, another approach is to consider the opening of the file and the error termination to be alternatives:

> (intext := open("shaw.txt")) | stop("cannot open input file")

This formulation corresponds to "either open the file or stop program execution" as opposed to "if the file cannot be opened, then stop program execution". Phrasing alternatives in terms of "either … or" instead of "if not … then …" frequently results in constructions that are clearer and more concise in Icon.

A similar situation occurs in procedures that may return one of several values, depending on which one of a number of computations succeeds. The traditional formulation is

> if x := *expr$_1$* then return x
> else if x := *expr$_2$* then return x
> $\vdots$
> else if x := *expr$_n$* then return x
> else fail

A considerably more concise formulation is possible:

> return *expr$_1$* | *expr$_2$* | … | *expr$_n$*

Note that the **fail** expression is not necessary, since if *expr$_1$*, *expr$_2$*, …, *expr$_n$* all fail, the outcome of the **return** expression is failure.

There are two situations in which the "distributivity" of alternation can be used to obtain concise formulations. Consider the following expression:

> compute(*expr$_1$*) | compute(*expr$_2$*)

This expression can be written more compactly as

compute(*expr₁* | *expr₂*)

The first formulation corresponds to "compute *expr₁* or compute *expr₂*", while the second corresponds to "compute *expr₁* or *expr₂*".

A somewhat less obvious possibility is illustrated by the following expression

compute(*expr*) | stop(*expr*)

which corresponds to "either compute *expr* or stop with *expr*". Here the function applied to *expr* can be factored out:

(compute | stop)(*expr*)

This construction may appear strange at first, but it becomes natural as a formulation for "either compute or stop with *expr*". This kind of construction is particularly useful for programs that apply different functions to input lines, depending on their values.

14.3 INFINITE RESULT SEQUENCES

An expression may have an infinite result sequence. Examples are

(i := 1) | (|(i +:= 1))

which generates the positive integers $\{1, 2, 3, \dots\}$ and fibseq() in §11.7.

Such expressions provide a natural and concise way of characterizing sequences, just as

i to j

does. The fact that a result sequence is infinite is not, in itself, a problem. The production of results from such sequences can be controlled in several ways.

One way to control a generator is by explicit limitation, as described in §11.7. For example, fibseq() might be tested by a main procedure of the form

```
procedure main()
    every write(fibseq()) \ 20
end
```

Another way of controlling generation is by loop exits. A slightly different form for the preceding test is

```
procedure main()
    local i
    every write(i := fibseq()) do
        if i > 5000 then break
end
```

Generation also can be controlled by returning or suspending from a procedure. For example, a procedure such as

```
procedure posint()
    local i
    i := 0
    suspend |(i +:= 1)
end
```

is just an *encapsulation* of the argument of the **suspend** expression. That is, the result sequence for **posint()** is the positive integers. The procedure call **posint()** can be used anywhere without the need for repeating the expression that it encapsulates.

The use of a procedure to encapsulate a generator allows recursive generators. Consider the problem of generating all the strings from a set of characters with the strings produced in the order of their length. For example, the result sequence for the cset 'abc' would be

{ "", "a", "b", "c", "aa", "ab", "ac", "ba", ... }

where the first value in the sequence is the empty string. A procedure that has the desired result sequence is

```
procedure star(chars)
    suspend "" | (star(chars) || !chars)
end
```

In order to understand the result sequence for this procedure, consider

star('abc')

The first result is the empty string, produced by suspending with "". Consequently, the result sequence begins as

{ "", ... }

The subsequent results consist of each result in the result sequence for **star('abc')** followed by each character in 'abc'. Since !chars is repeatedly resumed for each value produced by **star(chars)**, each character in chars (a, b, and c in this example) is appended to the first value in the result sequence of **star(chars)**. Therefore, the result sequence consists of

{ "", "a", "b", "c", ... }

When **star(chars)** is resumed for its second result, it produces **a**, onto which are appended **a**, **b**, and **c**, and so on.

   Understanding recursive generators and using them effectively is much the same as understanding recursive functions and using them effectively.

14.4 LIMITATIONS ON THE USE OF GENERATORS

As discussed in Chapter 13, the generation of the results of an expression is limited to the place in the program where the expression occurs. If the same expression is used elsewhere in the program, it generates the results from the beginning of its result sequence, not from where previous generation terminated. This is the difference between evaluation and resumption. For example, in

```
procedure main()
   .
   .
   .
every write(fibseq()) \ 20
   .
   .
   .
every write(fibseq()) \ 20
   .
   .
   .
end
```

the first 20 Fibonacci numbers are written twice; the second iteration does not produce the next 20 results in the sequence.

   Co-expressions provide the most natural way of overcoming these limitations of generators. An alternative approach to the preceding is to use the original procedure for **fibseq** and to resume it through the activation of a co-expression:

```
procedure main()
   fseq := create fibseq()
   .
   .
   .
every write(|@fseq) \ 20
   .
   .
   .
every write(|@fseq) \ 20
   .
   .
   .
end
```

14.5 NESTED ITERATION

Many problems that require the production of all possible solutions can be formulated using nested iteration. For example, many word puzzles depend on the intersection of two words in a common character. In constructing or solving such puzzles, all the places that two words intersect may be of interest.

Given two words word1 and word2,

```
i := upto(word2, word1)
```

produces the position in word1 of one intersection. In this expression the string value of word2 is automatically converted to a cset consisting of the possible characters at which an intersection in word1 can occur. While i gives the position of such an intersection in word1, the position in word2 is needed also. The pair of positions can be determined by

```
if i := upto(word2, word1)
then j := upto(word1[i], word2)
```

This computation can be cast in terms of a procedure that locates the positions and displays the intersection:

```
procedure cross(word1, word2)
    local i, j
    if i := upto(word2, word1)
    then {
        j := upto(word1[i], word2)
        every write(right(word2[1 to j − 1],i))
        write(word1)
        every write(right(word2[j + 1 to *word2], i))
        write()
        }
    return
end
```

For example, cross("lottery", "boat") produces

```
    b
lottery
    a
    t
```

This approach produces at most one intersection. All intersections can be produced by using nested iteration:

```
procedure cross(word1, word2)
    local i, j
    every i := upto(word2, word1) do
        every j := upto(word1[i], word2) do {
            every write(right(word2[1 to j - 1],i))
            write(word1)
            every write(right(word2[j + 1 to *word2], i))
            write()
            }
    return
end
```

In this procedure, i iterates over the positions in **word1** at which there is a character in **word2**, while j iterates over the positions in **word2** at which this character occurs. The results written for **cross("lottery", "boat")** are

```
    b
l o t t e r y
    a
    t

    b
    o
    a
l o t t e r y

    b
    o
    a
l o t t e r y
```

14.6 BACKTRACKING

Backtracking is one of the more powerful programming techniques for solving problems that involve searching through many possible combinations of values. Control backtracking is implicit in Icon, but data backtracking is not, except in string scanning. The reversible assignment operation, however, provides a means for performing explicit data backtracking.

A classical search problem that can be solved elegantly with backtracking techniques consists of placing eight queens on a chessboard so that no two queens are on the same column, row, or diagonal. One solution of this problem is

Since there can be only one queen on the same column, a natural approach to solving this problem is to assign one queen to each column. The queens then can be placed consecutively, starting with the first queen in column one.

The first queen can be placed in any row, since there are no other queens on the board yet. The natural place to put the first queen is in row one. The second queen cannot be placed in row one, since the first queen is in this row, nor in row two, since the first queen is on a diagonal through this position. Row three is an acceptable place for the second queen, however. Continuing this process, each successive queen is placed on the first free row. When an attempt is made to place the sixth queen, however, there are no free rows:

Some previously placed queen must be moved to another position. This is

accomplished by backtracking to the previous queen, which can be placed in
row eight instead of row four:

Another attempt is now made to place the sixth queen. No row is free, however, and backtracking takes place to the fifth queen again. There are no more
free rows for the fifth queen, so backtracking takes place to the fourth queen,
which is now placed in row seven:

Now placement of the fifth queen is attempted anew. Eventually, through
backtracking, the positions are finally adjusted so that all eight queens are
placed, as shown on the board at the beginning of this section. Notice that it is
not necessary to try all queens in all positions; a queen is moved only when it

position cannot lead to a final solution.

This informal description of the placement process clearly corresponds to the way that arguments are evaluated in Icon: left-to-right evaluation with last-in, first-out resumption to obtain alternative results. The solution of the eight queens problem therefore can be formulated in terms of functions that place the queens according to the method described. A way of representing the chessboard and of determining free positions is needed, however.

The geometrical representation of the chessboard as an eight-by-eight array is not particularly useful. Instead, the occupancy of columns, rows, and diagonals is important. The columns are taken care of by the assignment of one queen to each column. A list provides a natural way of representing the rows:

row := list(8, 0)

where row i is zero if there is no queen on it and nonzero otherwise.

The diagonals are slightly more difficult, since there are 30 of them in all. One approach is to divide the diagonals into two groups [13]. Fifteen of the diagonals are downward facing, with their left ends lower than their right ends:

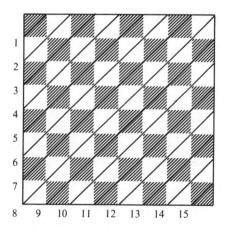

The other 15 diagonals are upward facing:

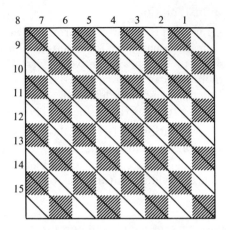

In each case, the diagonals can be represented by lists:

down := list(15, 0)
up := list(15, 0)

with zero or nonzero values as for the rows.

In placing a queen c on row r, it is necessary to assure that row, down, and up for that position are zero. The expression

$$r + c - 1$$

selects the correct downward facing diagonal, while

$$8 + r - c$$

selects the correct upward facing diagonal. A queen c can be placed on row r if the following comparison succeeds:

row[r] = down[r + c − 1] = up[8 + r − c] = 0

To place a queen, a nonzero value is assigned to the corresponding positions in row, down, and up. The row number is a convenient value to use, since it records the row on which the queen is placed and can be used in displaying the resulting solution:

row[r] <− down[r + c − 1] <− up[8 + r − c] <− r

Reversible assignment is used so that the queen can be removed automatically during backtracking. The complete program is

```
procedure main()
    write(q(1), q(2), q(3), q(4), q(5), q(6), q(7), q(8))
end

procedure q(c)
    suspend place(1 to 8, c)        # look for a row
end

procedure place(r, c)
    static up, down, row
    initial {
        up := list(15, 0)
        down := list(15, 0)
        row := list(8, 0)
        }
    if row[r] = down[r + c − 1] = up[8 + r − c] = 0
    then suspend row[r] <− down[r + c − 1] <−
        up[8 + r − c] <− r         # place if free
end
```

The procedure q(c) corresponds to the queen on column c. The procedure place(r, c) places queen c on row r if that position is free. If place(r, c) is successful, it suspends so that if it is resumed because the next queen cannot be placed, the queen is removed by reversing the assignment.

The expression

write(q(1), q(2), q(3), q(4), q(5), q(6), q(7), q(8))

serves to place the queens. When all the queens are successfully placed, the row positions are written:

15863724

All possible solutions can be obtained by iteration:

every write(q(1), q(2), q(3), q(4), q(5), q(6), q(7), q(8))

There are 92 solutions in all, although only 12 are unique because of symmetries.

EXERCISES

14.1.[*] Write a procedure **gensubstr(s)** that generates all the nonempty substrings of **s**. Do not generate the same substring in the same position
more than once, but generate all substrings even if there are duplicates.
For example, **gensubstr("aaa")** should produce the result sequence

{ *"a"*, *"aa"*, *"aaa"*, *"a"*, *"aa"*, *"a"* }

or the same results in a different order.

14.2. Trace the call of **star('abc')** as given in §14.3 and observe the interac-
tion between generation and recursion.

14.3. Extend the procedure **cross** in §14.5 so that it finds all the intersections of three words in a common character. Devise a way to display
the results.

14.4. Trace the solution of the eight queens problem given in §14.6 and
observe the backtracking process.

14.5.[*] Modify the solution of the eight queens problem to display the placement of the queens in a visually attractive way.

14.6. Modify the solution of the eight queens problem to keep track of how
many times a queen is placed at each position. Display the results in a
way that is easily understood.

14.7. Write a program that determines all the ways that eight rooks can be
placed on a chessboard so that no two rooks are on the same column
or row.

15

HIGH-LEVEL
STRING PROCESSING

Although only a few operations are related to string scanning, their apparent simplicity is deceptive. Except for generators, string scanning adds more to the power of Icon and influences programming techniques more than any other feature. Furthermore, the ways that string scanning can be used are not all obvious. This chapter explores string scanning, concentrating on techniques that exploit its potential and lead to good programming style.

Since string scanning resembles pattern matching in SNOBOL4, SNO-BOL4 programmers are likely to use its programming style in Icon. This often leads to frustration and poor Icon programs. This chapter mentions some differences and similarities between the two languages. The reader who is unfamiliar with SNOBOL4 can disregard such remarks.

15.1 THE GENERALITY OF STRING SCANNING

15.1.1 Integrating Scanning with Other Operations

The pattern-matching facilities of SNOBOL4 are largely separate from the rest of the SNOBOL4 language. Pattern matching has its own repertoire of control structures and operations, and most of the operations in the rest of the SNOBOL4 language cannot be used directly in pattern matching. The opposite is true in Icon: String scanning is integrated into the rest of the language, and all operations can be used in string scanning. This includes control structures. For example,

```
text ? if tab(upto('aeiou'))
    then write(move(1)) else write("no vowel")
```

writes the first vowel in text, if there is one, but writes no vowel otherwise. The SNOBOL4-style approach to this would be

```
text ? (tab(upto('aeiou')) & write(move(1))) |
    write("no vowel")
```

While both formulations do the same thing, the former is more natural in Icon.

As illustrated, the values produced by matching functions can be used as arguments in other computations, which in turn can be integrated into string scanning. As another example, suppose that an input file, consisting of lines in which two items are separated by a colon, is to be converted to a file in which the two items are left-adjusted in columns that are 10 characters wide. This can be done by

```
while line := read() do {
    if line ? {
        first := tab(upto(':')) &
        move(1) &
        second := tab(0)
        }
    then write(left(first, 10), left(second, 10))
    }
```

The conjunctions are used to prevent writing an erroneous line if an input line is not in the correct format. If this happens, the scanning expression fails. This situation can be handled in an **else** clause.

The preceding program can be reformulated in a more compact way by using the values produced by the matching functions directly as arguments to write. The move(1) also can be combined with the tab(0):

```
while line := read() do
    line ? write(
        left(tab(upto(':')), 10),
        (move(1) & left(tab(0), 10))
        )
```

15.1.2 The Order of Matched Substrings

Matching functions usually produce substrings of the subject from left to right. While this left-to-right order is not mandatory, since either tab or move can move to the left in the subject, string analysis functions like find inherently operate from left to right. If the order in which substrings of the subject is produced corresponds to the order in which they are needed in a computation, they can be used directly as arguments in the computation as illustrated by the preceding examples. Sometimes the order is not even important. Consider counting words:

```
    ⋮
while line := read() do
    line ? while tab(upto(wchar)) do
        words[tab(many(wchar))] +:= 1
    ⋮
```

In this computation the order in which the entry values for **words** are produced is unimportant. The resulting table is the same, regardless of the order in which the words occur.

Sometimes, however, the order in which substrings occur in the subject is not the order in which they are needed in a computation. Suppose that a file consists of lines that contain a word, its grammatical category, and a count, with colons for separators, as in

```
    ⋮
the:article:20
they:pronoun:10
three:adjective:4
    ⋮
```

and a file is needed with the order of the items on a line reversed:

```
    ⋮
20:article:the
10:pronoun:they
4:adjective:three
    ⋮
```

Here the substrings in the input lines are in the wrong order. The most obvious way to solve this problem is to use auxiliary identifiers:

```
while line := read() do
    if line ? {
        first := tab(upto(':')) & move(1) &
        second := tab(upto(':')) & move(1) &
        third := tab(0)
        }
    then write(third, ":", second, ":", first)
```

A less obvious approach is to use a procedure to reorder the strings when they are written:

```
procedure xwrite(first, second, third)
   write(third, ":", second, ":", first)
   return
end
         :
         :
while line := read() do
   line ? xwrite(
      tab(upto(':')),
      (move(1) & tab(upto(':'))),
      (move(1) & tab(0))
      )
```

The parameters of **xwrite** provide the necessary auxiliary identifiers. The advantage of a procedure in such a situation is that it abstracts the desired order of processing from the order in which the strings are actually produced. In fact, the order and format in which the output is written can be changed by revising **xwrite** without having to rewrite the scanning expression.

One way to conceptualize such a formulation is to consider the *pattern* of substrings in the subject and what computations are to be performed on them. For the previous example, the desired transformation has the schematic form

$$first:second:third \quad \rightarrow \quad \textbf{write}(third:second:first)$$

15.2 PATTERN MATCHING

15.2.1 Matching Expressions

The functions **tab**(i) and **move**(i) are called matching functions because they change the position in the subject and produce the substring of the subject between the old and new positions. While the value of i in **tab**(i) can be computed in many ways using string analysis functions, actual matching is only done by **tab**(i) and **move**(i).

Matching expressions that extend the repertoire of matching functions provide a way of expressing more complicated matching operations. Matching expressions must obey a *protocol* that allows them to be used like matching functions. The protocol for a matching expression *expr* is as follows:

1. The evaluation of *expr* does not change the value of **&subject**.

2. If *expr* succeeds, it produces the substring of **&subject** between the values of **&pos** before and after its evaluation.

3. If *expr* fails, it does not change the value of **&pos**.

4. If *expr* is resumed but does not produce another result, it restores **&pos** to the value it had prior to the time *expr* was evaluated.

For example,

> tab(upto(', ')) || move(1)

is a matching expression, while

> tab(upto(', ')) & move(1)

is not, since it does not produce the substring of **&subject** between the values of **&pos** before **tab(upto(', '))** is evaluated and after **move(1)** is evaluated. Similarly,

> &subject[.&pos:&pos := upto(', ')]

is not a matching expression. If it is resumed, it does not restore the previous value of **&pos**. On the other hand,

> &subject[.&pos:&pos <- upto(', ')]

is a matching expression, since, if it is resumed, the reversible assignment operation restores the previous value of **&pos**. Note that in both cases the first occurrence of **&pos** in the range specification must be dereferenced before a new value is assigned to **&pos**.

Matching expressions are useful in the same way that matching functions are: They produce the substring of **&subject** that they match, and they perform data backtracking so that alternative matches are attempted at the same position in **&subject**.

When doing pattern matching on strings, it is generally good practice to use matching expressions. Most pattern matching is done from left to right. In such cases,

> $expr_1$ || $expr_2$

should be used in preference to

> $expr_1$ & $expr_2$

since the former expression produces the matched substring, while the latter does not. Both operations perform data backtracking, however. If production of matched substrings is not important, conjunction may be used in place of concatenation.

15.2.2 Matching Procedures

A *matching procedure* is a procedure the call of which is a matching expression. As an example, consider a procedure that does what the function tab(i) does.

```
procedure tab(i)
    suspend &subject[.&pos:&pos <- i]
end
```

Such a procedure is merely an encapsulation of a matching expression (see §14.3) and satisfies all the rules of protocol for matching expressions. The matching function move(i) can be written as a procedure in an analogous manner.

Using this technique, a variety of matching procedures can be written. For example,

```
procedure arb()
    suspend &subject[.&pos:&pos <- &pos to *&subject + 1]
end
```

matches any string from the current position through the end of the subject and is analogous to the SNOBOL4 pattern ARB. Note that arb() may generate more than one value. Therefore,

```
arb() || ="load" || arb() || ="r6"
```

matches any string that contains the substring load followed by the substring r6; load need not appear at the beginning of the subject, and load and r6 need not be consecutive substrings.

Matching procedures only need to obey the four rules of protocol; they do not have to obey the constraints that apply to patterns in SNOBOL4. An example is

```
procedure rarb()
    suspend &subject[.&pos:
        &pos <- ((*&subject + 1) to &pos by -1)]
end
```

which matches any string, but starts with the longest possible string and matches progressively shorter ones each time it is resumed. For example,

```
text ? (arb() & =" " & (exp := rarb())) & =" ")
```

assigns to exp the string between the first and last spaces in text.

Another instance is a matching procedure that matches any one of several strings in a list:

```
procedure lmatch(slist)
    suspend =!slist
end
```

For example,

```
lmatch(["black", "white", "gray"])
```

matches black, white, or gray.

One advantage of using a matching procedure for high-level string processing is that a procedure is a value. As such, it can be used as an argument to other matching procedures. An example of such a use is given by

```
procedure arbno(p)
    suspend "" | (p() || arbno(p))
end
```

The procedure arbno(p) matches zero or more instances of whatever p() matches. The first alternative, the empty string, corresponds to zero matches of p(). The second alternative matches whatever p() matches, concatenated with whatever arbno(p) matches: zero or more instances of whatever p() matches. For example, given

```
procedure shades()
    suspend arb() || lmatch(["black", "white", "gray"])
end
```

then

```
arbno(shades)
```

matches strings that contain zero or more occurrences of black, white, or gray.

Note that the argument of arbno must be a matching procedure. It cannot be a matching expression, since the argument is called in the body of the procedure for arbno. For example, in

```
arbno(lmatch(["black", "white", "gray"]))
```

the call of lmatch is evaluated before arbno is called. Not only is this order of evaluation incorrect, but also the value assigned to the parameter p is a string, not a procedure.

15.3 GRAMMARS AND LANGUAGES

A pattern characterizes a set of strings: the strings that it matches. A set of strings is a language. The strings in a language (its "sentences") are derived or described according to grammatical rules.

Natural languages, such as English, are very complex. The grammatical rules of such a language (its syntax) describe the language only superficially. In fact, there are many aspects of natural languages that defy precise description. There are many interesting languages, including programming languages, whose structure can be defined by precise and comparatively simple grammatical rules.

There is a close relationship between patterns and the grammars for languages. For some kinds of grammars, there is a direct mapping from the rules of the grammar to patterns that match strings in the corresponding language.

In §7.6 a language for a simple class of arithmetic expressions was introduced informally in terms of mutually recursive definitions:

1. An *expression* is a *term* or a *term* followed by a + followed by an *expression*.

2. A *term* is an *element* or an *element* followed by a * followed by a *term*.

3. An *element* is one of the characters x, y, z or an *expression* enclosed in parentheses.

These definitions can be expressed more formally in terms of a grammar as follows: Let X, T, and E stand for *expression*, *term*, and *element*, respectively. Then a grammar corresponding to the preceding definitions is

$$X \;::=\; T\,|\,T{+}X$$
$$T \;::=\; E\,|\,E{*}T$$
$$E \;::=\; x\,|\,y\,|\,z\,|\,(X)$$

Uppercase letters are used here to denote nonterminal symbols, while other characters, including parentheses, stand for themselves. The symbol ::= stands for "is defined to be". The concatenation of characters replaces "followed by" in the informal definition, and the vertical bar replaces "or". Note the similarity of this use of the vertical bar to the alternation control structure in Icon. In grammars, the vertical bar has lower precedence than concatenation.

Each nonterminal symbol defines its own language. There is a language for expressions defined by X, a language for terms defined by T, and a language for elements defined by E. One nonterminal symbol is designated as a "goal" for the language of interest. X is the goal in the examples that follow.

In deriving the strings for the language defined by a nonterminal symbol, the symbol ::= in the grammar means that an instance of the nonterminal symbol on its left can be replaced by any one of the alternatives on the right. For example, T can be replaced by E*T. Starting with the goal symbol X, some possible sequences of symbols that that can be derived are

X	goal
T+X	second alternative for X
T+T	first alternative for X
E+T	first alternative for first instance of T
x+T	first alternative for E
x+E	first alternative for T
x+(X)	fourth alternative for E
x+(T)	first alternative for X
x+(E∗T)	second alternative for T
x+(y∗T)	second alternative for E
x+(y∗E)	first alternative for T
x+(y∗z)	third alternative for E

Since there are no more nonterminal symbols in this string, x+(y∗z) is a string in the language defined by X.

The alternatives in the preceding derivation were chosen at random, as they were in the random selection procedures given in §7.6. Application of all the rules in all possible ways produces all strings in the language. There are an infinite number of strings in the language for X, as there are in most interesting languages.

15.3.1 Recognizers

Recognition is the process of determining whether or not a string belongs to a language and is the converse of derivation. In the present context, this amounts to matching the strings that are in a language and only those strings.

In the case of grammars like the preceding, there is a straightforward and mechanical way of producing patterns that match the strings in the language.

1. Terminal symbols are matched by corresponding matching expressions for the specific strings. For example, x is matched by ="x".

2. Nonterminal symbols are matched by matching procedures. For example, X is matched by X(). The form of such matching procedures is given later.

3. A sequence of symbols is matched by the concatenation of the matching expressions for the individual symbols. For example, T+X is matched by

$$T() \ || \ ="+" \ || \ X()$$

4. Alternatives are matched by the alternation of matching expressions. For example,

$$E \ | \ E∗T$$

is matched by

E() | (E() || ="*" || T())

5. A matching procedure encapsulates the matching expression for the corresponding nonterminal symbol. For example, the matching procedure for

X ::= T | T+X

is

```
procedure X()
    suspend T() | (T() || ="+" || X())
end
```

These rules can be used to convert any context-free grammar of the kind given previously directly into matching procedures.

The procedure for the nonterminal goal symbol is called in a scanning operation. Since recognition requires that the entire string be matched, not just an initial substring of it, the scanning operation takes the form

line ? (X() & pos(0))

A program to recognize strings in the language defined by X is

```
procedure main()
    while writes(line := read()) do
        if line ? (X() & pos(0)) then write(" accepted")
        else write(" rejected")
end
```

The kind of recognizer given here is called a top-down, recursive-descent recognizer with backtracking. There are two problems with this kind of recognizer: It is inefficient, and it cannot handle left recursion in the grammar. Left recursion occurs when the definition of a nonterminal symbol has an alternative that begins with a nonterminal symbol leading back to itself. For example, in a rule such as

X ::= X+T | T

the matching procedure

```
procedure X()
    suspend (X() || ="+" || T()) | T()
end
```

calls itself indefinitely, which causes internal stack overflow and program termination with an error message.

Despite these problems, this approach to recognizing strings is sometimes useful, and in any event it provides insights into the relationship between grammars and pattern matching.

There are other possibilities also. The previous matching procedures have no arguments. By adding arguments, recognizers can be constructed for classes of languages that are more general than context-free languages. Consider, for example, the program

```
procedure main()
    while writes(line := read()) do
        if line ? (ABC("") & pos(0)) then write(" accepted")
        else write(" rejected")
end

procedure ABC(X)
    suspend =X | (="a" || ABC("b" || X) || ="c")
end
```

This program matches strings in the language $a^n b^n c^n$ for $n = 0, 1, \ldots$: the empty string, **abc, aabbcc, aaabbbccc,** ... . This is a well-known context-sensitive language, which cannot be derived from any context-free grammar. While there are much more obvious ways of recognizing such strings than the procedure given, it is representative of a general class of recognizers for context-sensitive languages.

Tracing provides insight into the matching process. For the input line **aaabbbccc,** the trace output is

```
abc.icn: 7    | ABC("")
abc.icn: 2    | ABC suspended ""
abc.icn: 7    | ABC resumed
abc.icn: 2    | | ABC("b")
abc.icn: 2    | | | ABC("bb")
abc.icn: 2    | | | | ABC("bbb")
abc.icn: 2    | | | | ABC suspended "bbb"
abc.icn: 2    | | | ABC suspended "abbbc"
abc.icn: 2    | | ABC suspended "aabbbcc"
abc.icn: 2    | ABC suspended "aaabbbccc"
```

For the input line **aaabbbcccc,** however, the trace output is

```
abc.icn: 7     | ABC("")
abc.icn: 2     | ABC suspended ""
abc.icn: 7     | ABC resumed
abc.icn: 2     | | ABC("b")
abc.icn: 2     | | | ABC("bb")
abc.icn: 2     | | | | ABC("bbb")
abc.icn: 2     | | | | ABC suspended "bbb"
abc.icn: 2     | | | ABC suspended "abbbc"
abc.icn: 2     | | ABC suspended "aabbbcc"
abc.icn: 2     | ABC suspended "aaabbbccc"
abc.icn: 7     | ABC resumed
abc.icn: 2     | | ABC resumed
abc.icn: 2     | | | ABC resumed
abc.icn: 2     | | | | ABC resumed
abc.icn: 3     | | | | ABC failed
abc.icn: 3     | | | ABC failed
abc.icn: 3     | | ABC failed
abc.icn: 3     | ABC failed
```

15.3.2 Parsers

Recognizing strings in a language has limited usefulness. For one thing, recognition produces only a yes or a no, but no information on how the string is matched or how its structure is related to the grammar.

It is relatively easy to convert matching procedures like those given previously into parsing procedures that produce a "parse tree" which retains the structure of the match. The technique is to produce lists of matched strings rather than concatenations of matched strings. A matching procedure such as

```
procedure X()
    suspend T() | (T() || ="+" || X())
end
```

can be rewritten as a parsing procedure:

```
procedure X()
    suspend [T()] | [T(), ="+", X()]
end
```

Since parsing procedures produce lists, the result is a list of lists, or a tree, that shows the details of the parse. For example, the value produced for the string x+(y*z) is

$$[[["x"]], "+", [[["(", [[["y"], "*", [["z"]]]], ")"]]]]$$

Such a list is more easily understood if it is drawn as a tree:

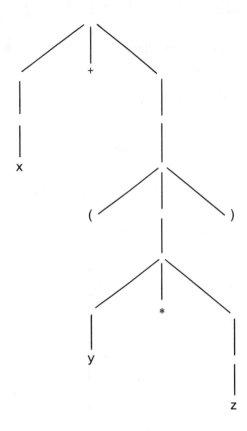

It is useful to provide a tag as the first value in each list to identify the nonterminal symbol. With this addition, the parsing procedures for the grammar in the preceding section are

```
procedure T()
    suspend ["T", E()] | ["T", E(), ="*", T()]
end

procedure E()
    suspend ["E", =("x" | "y" | "z")] | ["E", ="(", X(), =")"]
end
```

```
procedure X()
    suspend ["X", T()] | ["X", T(), ="+", X()]
end
```

Note that the more compact formulation

=("x" | "y" | "z")

is used in place of the direct translation

="x" | ="y" | ="z"

The tree produced for the preceding example is:

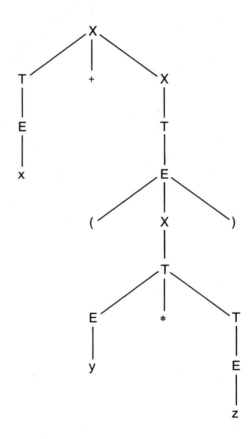

EXERCISES

15.1. Write a matching procedure that does what the function move(i) does.

15.2.* Redo Exercise 11.10 using arb as described in §15.2.2.

15.3.* Write a matching procedure limit(p, i) that matches at most the first i strings matched by the matching procedure p.

15.4. Write a matching procedure select(p, i) that matches only the ith string matched by p.

15.5. Consider the following procedure:

```
procedure ABC(A, B, C)
    suspend (=A || =B || =C) |
        ABC("a" || A, "b" || B, "c" || C)
end
```

The expression

```
line ? (ABC("", "", "") & pos(0))
```

matches strings of the form $a^n b^n c^n$ for $n = 0, 1, 2, \ldots$. It is not a recognizer, however. Explain the problem.

15.6.* Write a recognizer for strings of the form $a^n b^n c^n d^n$ for $n = 0, 1, 2, \ldots$.

15.7. Write a program that reads a context-free production grammar and produces an Icon program that recognizes strings in the language described by this grammar. Provide a means of specifying the goal symbol.

5.8. Write a program as specified in the preceding exercise that produces a parser instead of a recognizer.

16

LIST PROCESSING

Icon is not primarily a list-processing language. It provides the facilities, however, that are needed for processing structures in conjunction with string processing, such as the parse trees that were developed in §15.3.2. This chapter describes how lists can be used for representing and manipulating trees, graphs, and other structures.

16.1 TREES

A tree is a directed graph without cycles (loops) and with additional constraints on how arcs can be directed to nodes. In a tree, there can be at most one arc directed into any node, although there may be many arcs directed out of a node. One node, the *root*, has no arcs directed into it. Nodes that have no arcs directed out of them are *leaves*. Usually a value is associated with each node. The parse tree given at the end of Chapter 15 is an example.

A common way to represent trees with strings corresponds to the way that arithmetic expressions are given in prefix form. For example, the arithmetic expression

$$(a*b)+(c-d)$$

has the prefix form

$$+(*(a,b),-(c,d))$$

and corresponds to the tree

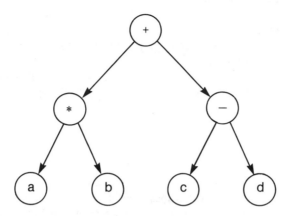

When a tree is represented by a string, the parentheses and commas indicate structural relationships. The string representation of a tree is compact, but it is awkward to process for many purposes. There are a variety of ways that a tree can be represented with structures. A natural way uses lists. For the previous example, a possible representation is

["+", ["*", ["a"], ["b"]], ["−", ["c"], ["d"]]]

In this representation each node of the tree is represented by a list. The first value in each list is the value that is associated with the node. Subsequent values in a list correspond to arcs to other nodes. Note that this representation is somewhat different from the one used for parse trees in Chapter 15. In that representation, leaves are represented by strings, not lists. The representation here is more general.

Input and output are restricted to strings. In order to process trees, procedures are needed to convert from the string representation of a tree to its list representation, and conversely. The string representation of a tree is a value followed by a parenthesized string of trees separated by commas. The conversion of the string representation of a tree, indicated by *stree*, to the list representation, indicated by *ltree*, has the form

value (*stree, stree,* ...)   →   [*value, ltree, ltree,* ...]

A procedure to do this is naturally recursive, since the structure of the string representation of a tree is recursive.

The string must be analyzed and a corresponding list must be constructed. One approach is

```
procedure Itree(stree)
    local a
    stree ?
        if a := [tab(upto('('))] then { # start with value
            move(1)
                                        # add subtrees
            while put(a, Itree(tab(bal(',', )')))) do
                move(1)
            }
        else a := [tab(0)]              # leaf
    return a
end
```

The **if-then-else** expression determines whether or not the *stree* has arcs from it (that is, whether it contains a value followed by a parenthesis). If it does, these *subtrees* are processed iteratively and appended to **a**. Note that

tab(bal(',',)'))

matches a parenthesis-balanced string (an *stree*) up to a comma or right parenthesis that terminates the string of subtrees. In each case, Itree is applied to convert the *stree* to an *ltree* before it is appended to the list. If stree does not contain a left parenthesis, then it must be a leaf, which is the list

[tab(0)]

It is instructive to trace the recursive processing:

```
Itree.icn: 15   | Itree("+(*(a, b), −(c, d))")
Itree.icn: 7    | | Itree("*(a, b)")
Itree.icn: 7    | | | Itree("a")
Itree.icn: 11   | | | Itree returned ["a"]
Itree.icn: 7    | | | Itree("b")
Itree.icn: 11   | | | Itree returned ["b"]
Itree.icn: 11   | | Itree returned ["*", list(1), list(1)]
Itree.icn: 7    | | Itree("−(c, d)")
Itree.icn: 7    | | | Itree("c")
Itree.icn: 11   | | | Itree returned ["c"]
Itree.icn: 7    | | | Itree("d")
Itree.icn: 11   | | | Itree returned ["d"]
Itree.icn: 11   | | Itree returned ["−", list(1), list(1)]
Itree.icn: 11   | Itree returned ["+", list(3), list(3)]
```

Line 15 is in the main procedure, which calls Itree. Note that tracing shows only one level of detail for lists.

Conversion from the list representation to the string representation is similar:

```
procedure stree(ltree)
    local s
    if *ltree = 1 then return ltree[1]   # start with leaf
    s := ltree[1] || "("                 # append value
                                         # append stree
    every s ||:= stree(ltree[2 to *ltree]) || ","
    return s[1:-1] || ")"
end
```

Note that the last comma produced in the **every** loop is replaced by a right parenthesis in the value that is returned.

Frequently, it is useful to be able to visit all the nodes (subtrees) of a tree. This can be done easily with a generator:

```
procedure visit(ltree)
    suspend ltree | visit(ltree[2 to *ltree])
end
```

Again, the recursive definition of the structure of a tree is reflected in the processing. The tree itself is produced first. Then its subtrees are produced, skipping the first value in each list, which corresponds to the value of that node.

The procedure visit(ltree) can be used in a variety of ways. For example,

```
every write(stree(visit(ltree)))
```

writes all the subtrees in **ltree**, while

```
every write(visit(ltree)[1])
```

writes the values of all nodes in the tree. Similarly,

```
every a := visit(ltree) do
    if *a = 1 then write(a[1])
```

writes the values of all leaves in **ltree**.

Sometimes it is necessary to know whether or not two trees have the same structure and the same node values, that is, if they are equivalent. The operation

```
a1 === a2
```

does not determine whether or not two trees are equivalent, but only if they are identical; that is, if **a1** and **a2** are the same list (see §10.1). A procedure to compare two trees for equivalence is

```
procedure teq(a1, a2)
   local i
   if *a1 ~= *a2 then fail          # check sizes
   if a1[1] ~== a2[1] then fail     # check values
   every i := 2 to *a1 do           # check subtrees
      if not teq(a1[i], a2[i]) then fail
   return a2
end
```

The sizes of the two lists are checked first to avoid unnecessary computation. Next the values of the root nodes are compared. If they are the same, corresponding subtrees are compared, calling **teq** recursively. If all subtrees are the same, **a2** is returned, conforming to the convention for built-in comparison operations.

A more general operation for comparing list structures is useful:

```
procedure eq(x, y)
   local i
   if x === y then return y         # succeed if identical
   if type(x) == type(y) == "list" then {
      if *x ~= *y then fail         # check sizes
      every i := 1 to *x do         # check subtrees
         if not eq(x[i], y[i]) then fail
      return y
      }
end
```

This procedure does not require that the first value in a list be a string. Since the operation

```
x === y
```

compares any two values of the same type, this procedure works properly for equivalent values in lists, regardless of where they are located. For example, it works properly for the more specialized form of parse trees given in §15.3.2.

16.2 DAGS

A directed acyclic graph, or *dag*, is a graph in which there are no loops leading from a node back to itself. A *rooted* dag is like a tree except that there may be several arcs directed into any node, except the root. Dags typically occur as the result of common subexpression elimination, where a subtree that is the same as another is eliminated and the two arcs are directed to one of the subtrees. For example, the expression

$$(a*b)+((a*b)-c)$$

has the tree

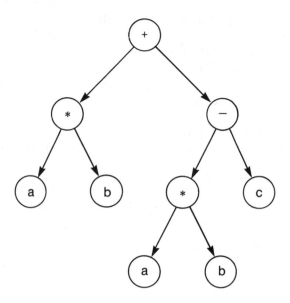

The duplicate subtree can be eliminated by converting this tree to a dag:

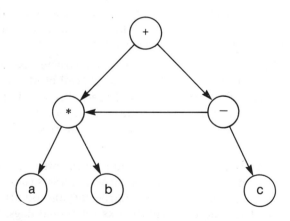

Instead of converting a tree to a dag, it is easier to construct the dag in the first place. The technique used here is to tabulate the parts of the structure that have been built already and to direct arcs to them rather than to construct equivalent parts:

```
procedure ldag(stree, done)
    local a
    /done := table()                    # start table
                                        # return list if done
    if a := \done[stree] then return a
    stree ?                             # build like a tree
        if a := [tab(upto('('))] then {
            move(1)
            while put(a, ldag(tab(bal(',', )'))), done)) do
                move(1)
            }
        else a := [tab(0)]
    return done[stree] := a             # put in table
end
```

When **ldag** is called to construct a dag for **stree**, the second argument is omitted, since there are no parts already formed. An example corresponding to the infix expression given previously is

```
ldag("+(*(a,b),−(*(a,b),c))")
```

The expression

```
/done := table()
```

assigns an empty table to **done** on this call. In general, **stree** is looked up in **done** to see if a dag has already been constructed for this string. If it has, that value is returned. Otherwise, **stree** is processed in the same way as it is in **ltree**. Note that the recursive call of **ldag** includes the table **done** as its second argument, passing the parts that have been constructed. Finally, the newly constructed dag is added as the assigned value for the entry value **stree**.

The method of handling the table of constructed parts deserves note. Since the table is constructed at the "top-level" call of **ldag** and subsequently passed as an argument to recursive calls of **ldag**, it is local to the processing of a particular *stree*. If it were global instead, independent uses of **ldag** might interfere with each other. The table cannot be constructed in an initial clause for the same reason.

Note that the tree-processing functions in the preceding section all work properly on rooted dags. The procedure **stree** processes rooted dags as well as trees, effectively "unfolding" them. Similarly, **teq** and **eq** also work properly on rooted dags. The procedure **visit** works on rooted dags, although nodes with more than one arc into them are visited once for each arc.

16.3 GRAPHS WITH CYCLES

General directed graphs, or *digraphs,* allow cycles in which there can be a series of arcs from a node back to that node. Such digraphs can be constructed using the preceding list representation. For example,

g := ["a"]
put(g, g)

constructs a digraph with a single node that has an arc to itself:

A general digraph cannot be represented by a simple linear sequence of node values and punctuation to indicate its structure like the string representation of trees. Some method is needed to identify the nodes and to indicate the arcs to them. There are various notational schemes for representing digraphs with strings. One scheme is to provide a name for each node and to give its value along with a list of the names of the nodes to which it has arcs. For example,

n1:+, n2, n1

describes a node named n1 with the value + and arcs to nodes n2 and n1. The colon separates the name of the node from its value and the arcs.

Several nodes for the same graph can be described using one string if another separator, say a semicolon, is used. An example is

n1:+, n2, n1; n2:a, n3; n3:−, n1

which describes the graph

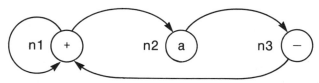

A digraph has no root that can serve as a designated starting point for processing. In fact, a digraph need not be connected; it can consist of several parts that are not connected by arcs. For example,

n1:a, n2; n2:b, n1; n3:c, n4; n4:d, n3, n4

represents the digraph

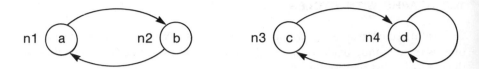

A string, or *sgraph*, such as the one shown, is awkward to process. A corresponding list representation, or *lgraph*, is more complex than it is for trees, since there is no root and the arcs are not constrained in any way. One approach to the representation of a graph as a structure is to have a list for each node in which the first list value is the value of the node, and subsequent values are the lists for which there are arcs. This is the same representation as that used for trees, but it cannot be constructed so easily. One way to start is to put the names of the nodes in the lists first and then replace them by their lists once all the lists are created. For the preceding digraph, the lists are

```
a1 := ["a", "n2"]
a2 := ["b", "n1"]
a3 := ["c", "n4"]
a4 := ["d", "n3", "n4"]
```

The arcs can now be inserted by replacing the node names by their corresponding lists:

```
a1[2] := a2
a2[2] := a1
a3[2] := a4
a4[2] := a3
a4[3] := a4
```

Note that the arc from **a2** to **a1** could have been been inserted at the time that **a2** was created, but the arc from **a1** to **a2** could not have been, since **a2** did not exist when **a1** was created. The insertion of arcs in a digraph is a two-pass process in general.

In order to keep track of the nodes, the graph itself can be represented by a table in which the entries are the node names and the corresponding assigned values are the lists:

```
g := table()
g["n1"] := a1
g["n2"] := a2
g["n3"] := a3
g["n4"] := a4
```

The preceding sections of program illustrate the step-by-step construction of a specific graph. A procedure to form a table for a graph from its string representation is somewhat more complicated than the procedure to form the list representation of a tree, but it illustrates string scanning techniques in combination with list processing:

```
procedure lgraph(sgraph)
    local nodes, ndescr, nlist, a, name, i
    nodes := table()                    # table of nodes
    sgraph ?
        while ndescr := tab(many(~';')) do {
            move(1)
            ndescr ? {                  # process one node
                a := []                 # new list goes in table
                nodes[tab(upto(':'))] := a
                move(1)
                                        # add value and names
                while put(a, tab(many(~', '))) do
                    move(1)
            }
        }
    every name := !nodes do             # change names to lists
        every i := 2 to *name do
            name[i] := nodes[name[i]]
    return nodes
end
```

Note that many(~';') and many(~', ') are used to identify items with separating punctuation but without terminating punctuation. The use of upto(';'), for example, will not work, since there is no semicolon after the last node specification in the notation used here.

EXERCISES

16.1.[*]   Write a procedure that determines the maximum depth of an *ltree*, that is, the longest series of arcs from the root to a leaf.

16.2.   Write a procedure that prints an *ltree*, indenting according to the depth in the tree.

16.3.[*]   Write a procedure that copies an *ltree*.

16.4.[*]   A binary tree is a tree in which there are exactly two arcs out of every node that is not a leaf. Design a representation for binary trees using records. Write procedures that convert the string representation of a binary tree to the record representation, and vice versa.

16.5. Write a procedure **gimage(x)** that generalizes the function **image(x)** by producing an understandable representation of any structure, including lists, tables, and so forth.

16.6. Write a procedure that converts an *lgraph* to an *sgraph*.

17

MAPPINGS AND LABELINGS

17.1 MAPPING TECHNIQUES

Ordinarily the function map(s1, s2, s3) is used to perform a character substitution on s1 by replacing characters in s1 that occur in s2 by the characters of s3 that are in corresponding positions to those in s2. In this kind of use, s2 and s3 are parameters that characterize the substitution, and s1 varies, as in

map(line, "aeiou", "*****")

which replaces all lowercase vowels in line by stars.

If s1 and s2 are considered to be parameters and s3 is allowed to vary, some surprising results are possible.

17.1.1 Transpositions

If the value of labels is a string of distinct characters (that is, containing no duplicates), and the value of trans is a rearrangement, or *transposition*, of the value of labels, then

map(trans, labels, s3)

produces the corresponding transposition of s3. For example,

map("654321", "123456", s3)

produces the reversal of the value of s3. Suppose the value of s3 is quotas as in map("654321", "123456", "quotas")

Then the **6** in the first argument is replaced by the character corresponding to the **6** in the second argument, that is, **s**. Similarly, the character **5** in the first argument is replaced by the character corresponding to the **5** in the second argument, that is, **a**, and so on:

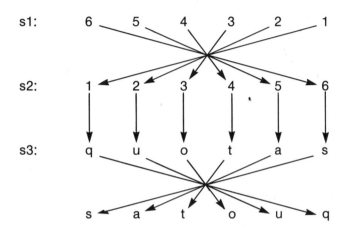

The value produced is **satouq**, the reversal of **quotas**, since the specified transposition, **654321**, is the reversal of the labeling string, **123456**. If the transposition is different, as in

map("561234", "123456", s3)

the result produced is correspondingly different: In this case it is the rotation of **s3** two characters to the right (or four to the left).

Any characters can be used for the labeling as long as there are no duplicates. This limits the maximum size of a transposition to 256. The more important restriction is that the sizes of **labels** and **s3** must be the same. Therefore,

map("654321", "123456", s3)

only can be used to reverse six-character strings. In many cases, however, the transposition can be performed piece by piece. That is,

reverse(s1 || s2) == reverse(s2) || reverse(s1)

Although there is a built-in function **reverse(s)**, a corresponding procedure using mapping techniques provides a model for a variety of transpositions. A procedure is

```
procedure reverse(s)
    static labels, trans, max
    initial {
        labels := "abcdefghijklmnopqrstuvwxyz"
        trans := "zyxwvutsrqponmlkjihgfedcba"
        max := *labels
        }
    if *s <= max then
        return map(right(trans, *s), left(labels, *s), s)
    else return reverse(right(s, *s − max)) ||
        map(trans, labels, left(s, max))
end
```

The values chosen for **labels** and **trans** are two strings of reasonable size that are easy to write. If the size of **s** is not too large, it can be reversed by one application of **map**. The expression

```
left(labels, *s)
```

truncates **s** at the right and produces a labeling of the correct length. The expression

```
right(trans, *s)
```

produces the corresponding transposition from the other end of **trans**.

If **s** is too long to be reversed by one application of **map**, recursion is used. Piece-by-piece reversal of long strings can be done iteratively, of course; recursion simply provides a more compact solution for the purposes of illustration.

The reversal process is more efficient for larger values of **labels** and **trans**. The longest possible labeling is 256, as mentioned earlier. Strings of all 256 characters are impractical to write out literally, but they can be computed by

```
labels := string(&cset)
trans := ""
every trans := !labels || trans
```

A more sophisticated approach is to obtain the longest labeling and transposition strings by bootstrapping, starting with short labeling and transposition strings. For example,

```
labels := "12"
trans := "21"
```

characterizes reversal. The procedure **reverse** can be modified to perform the bootstrapping in its **initial** clause:

```
procedure reverse(s)
    static labels, trans, max
    initial {
        labels := "12"                         # short label
        trans := "21"                          # short transposition
        max := *labels
        trans := reverse(string(&cset))        # long transposition
        labels := string(&cset)                # long label
        max := *labels                         # new size
    }
        .
        .
        .
```

When **reverse** is called the first time, it calls itself to change short values of **labels** and **trans** to the longest possible values. Note that **labels, trans,** and **max** must be defined consistently when **reverse** calls itself in its **initial** clause.

The two strings

```
labels := "12"
trans := "21"
```

characterize the reversal of two-character strings. The extension of this transposition to the reversal of strings of arbitrary length occurs in the way substrings of **labels** and **trans** are selected and the handling of the case in which **s** is too long to be transposed by a single use of **map**. Consider a transposition in which every odd-numbered character is swapped with its even-numbered neighbor. For six-character strings, this has the form

```
map("123456", "214365", s3)
```

This transposition is also characterized by

```
labels := "12"
trans := "21"
```

which is the same transposition used for reversal. The procedure to swap characters is very similar to **reverse**. The two procedures differ in the way that substrings of **labels** and **trans** are selected and in the handling of strings that are too long to be transposed by a single use of **map**, which is based on

```
swap(s1 || s2) == swap(s1) || swap(s2)
```

The complete procedure for swapping adjacent characters is

```
procedure swap(s)
    static labels, trans, max
    initial {
        labels := "12"
        trans := "21"
        max := *labels
        trans := swap(string(&cset))
        labels := string(&cset)
        max := *labels
        }
    if *s <= max then
        return map(left(trans, *s), left(labels, *s), s)
    else return swap(left(s, *s - max)) ||
        map(trans, labels, right(s, max))
end
```

This procedure only works properly if the size of s is even; see Exercise 17.2.

It is reasonable to question the use of mapping techniques for transpositions of this kind, since the procedures are relatively complicated and many transpositions can be written concisely using more conventional techniques. Mapping techniques have two advantages: First they are fast, especially when the same transposition is performed many times, overcoming the initialization overhead for procedures. Second, mapping techniques also provide a clear characterization of the transposition process.

17.1.2 Positional Transformations

For transpositions like

map(trans, labels, s3)

labels cannot contain duplicate characters and trans must be a transposition of labels. If these two constraints are relaxed, other kinds of *positional transformations* are possible [14].

The strings trans and labels do not have to be the same size. If some characters in labels are omitted from trans, the corresponding characters in s3 are omitted from the result. For example,

map("124578", "12345678", s3)

deletes the third and sixth characters of an eight-character string, s3. Therefore,

map("124578", "12345678", "03:56:42")

produces 035642. In cases like this, labels that are more mnemonic make the intent clearer. Furthermore, the labels that correspond to deleted characters can be anything; they need not be distinct. An equivalent positional transformation is

map("hxmysz", "hx:my:sz", s3)

If characters occur in trans that do not occur in labels, these characters are added to the result. Consequently,

map("hx:my:sz", "hxmysz", "035642")

produces 03:56:42.

If labels contains duplicate characters, the rightmost correspondence with characters in s applies. For example,

map("be", "beeeeee", s3)

produces the first and last characters of strings s3 of size seven.

Characters in labels can also be duplicated in trans. For instance,

map("123321", "123", s3)

produces the three-character string s3 followed by its reversal. An example is

map("123321", "123", "−∗|")

which produces

−∗||∗−

17.2 LABELINGS

In the preceding sections, characters are used as labels to identify positions of characters in strings. Characters can also be used to stand for objects. Since there are only 256 different characters, their use as labels for objects is limited, but where they can be used they often allow a compact representation and efficient manipulation. Two examples follow.

17.2.1 Manipulating Decks of Cards

Since a standard deck of playing cards consists of 52 different cards, it is a natural candidate for representation by characters, such as

deck := &ucase || &lcase

Note that concatenation produces a string. In this string, the correspondence of individual playing cards is arbitrary. For example, A might correspond to the ace of clubs, B to the two of clubs, N to the ace of diamonds, and so on.

To illustrate the ease of performing computations on such a representation, consider shuffling a deck of cards. One method of shuffling is given in §10.3. A slightly different approach is

```
procedure shuffle(deck)
    every !deck :=: ?deck
    return deck
end
```

In order to display a shuffled deck or any hand of cards, the implied correspondence between characters and cards must be converted to a readable format. Suppose that in a "fresh" deck the first 13 characters are clubs, the second 13 are diamonds, and so on. Then if

```
fresh := &ucase || &lcase
```

and

```
suits := repl("C",13) || repl("D",13) || repl("H",13) ||
    repl("S",13)
```

the mapping

```
map(deck, fresh, suits)
```

produces a string showing the suit of each card in **deck**. Similarly, if the denominations in each suit of a fresh deck are arranged with the ace first, followed by the two, and so on through the jack, queen, and king, then

```
denoms := repl("A23456789TJQK",4)
```

used in the mapping

```
map(deck, fresh, denoms)
```

produces a string showing the denomination of each card in **deck**. A complete procedure for displaying the cards with suits on one line and denominations below is

```
procedure disp(deck)
    static fresh, suits, denoms
    initial {
        fresh := &ucase || &lcase
        suits := repl("C",13) || repl("D",13) || repl("H",13) ||
            repl("S",13)
        denoms := repl("A23456789TJQK",4)
        }
    write(map(deck, fresh, suits))   # suits
    write(map(deck, fresh, denoms))# denominations
end
```

A typical display might be:

CDCHSS...
5 3 K T Q8 ...

While such a display is understandable, it is not attractive. Consider the problem of displaying a bridge hand in the conventional way, with each suit given separately.

One way to extract all the cards of a given suit from a hand is to map all characters that are not in that suit into a single character. A space provides a convenient representation for all cards in the suits that are not of interest. If the first 13 cards in a fresh deck are clubs, then

clubs := "abcdefghijklm" || repl(" ",39)

characterizes the clubs. If hand contains characters from fresh, then

map(hand, fresh, clubs)

maps all clubs in hand into distinct characters and all other characters in hand into spaces. Characters that do not correspond to clubs are "filtered out". Diamonds can be obtained by using

diamonds := repl(" ",13) || "abcdefghijklm" || repl(" ",26)

in a similar manner. Since the same string is used to label the characters in both suits, corresponding clubs and diamonds are mapped into the same characters. These characters correspond to the ranks of the card in the suit: Cards of the same rank in different suits are mapped into the same character. Furthermore

string(cset(map(hand, fresh, clubs)))

places the clubs in order. Any spaces are condensed into a single space which, because of the order of the ASCII characters, is at the beginning of the resulting string. This space is essentially "invisible".

17.2.2 Manipulating Graphs

In §16.3 a general way of representing graphs is presented. In many cases, a considerably more concise representation is possible. If the number of nodes in a graph is small and only the structural properties of graphs are of interest, a graph can be represented by a distinct identifying character corresponding to each node. An arc from one node to another can be represented by the two characters for the nodes in order according to the direction of the arc. For example, the graph

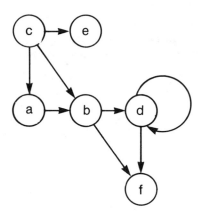

can be represented by the string

    g := "abbdbfcacbcedddf"

where **ab** represents the arc from **a** to **b**, **bd** represents the arc from **b** to **d**, and so on.

Many computations are particularly simple if such a representation is used. For example the number of arcs in a graph **g** is given by

    *g/2

and the number of nodes is given by

    *cset(g)

This representation assumes there is no isolated node that has no arc into it or out of it. If such a node exists, a separate list of nodes is necessary.

An example of a structural manipulation is the determination of the *transitive closure* of a node in a graph, that is, all the nodes in a graph that can be reached from a given node by a series of arcs, including the given node itself. For example, the transitive closure of **a** in the preceding graph is **a**, **b**, **d**, and **f**. The first step in determining transitive closure is obtaining the immediate successors of a set of nodes, those to which there is an arc from any of the nodes in the set:

```
procedure successors(graph, nodes)
   local snodes
   snodes := ''                    # start with none
   graph ? repeat {
      if tab(any(nodes)) then snodes ++:= move(1)
      else move(2) | break        # exit at end of string
      }
   return snodes
end
```

The successor of every odd-numbered character in graphs that is contained in nodes is added to snodes by the augmented assignment operation.

Transitive closure starts with the single node of interest and successively expands the set of nodes that can be reached from it until no new nodes are added:

```
procedure closure(graph, nodes)
   local snodes
   snodes := nodes                 # start with given nodes
   while snodes ~===
      (nodes ++:= successors(graph, nodes)) do
         snodes := nodes           # update if change
   return nodes
end
```

Note that at each step all the successors that can be reached from any node currently in the closure are added to the closure.

The comparison expression that controls the **while** loop can be combined with the assignment in the **do** clause, making the loop more compact:

```
while snodes ~===:= (nodes ++:= successors(graph, nodes))
```

EXERCISES

17.1. One simple form of cipher transposes characters in fixed-length blocks of a message. Design a transposition cipher and write programs that encipher and decipher messages using this cipher.

17.2. Determine the result that is produced by swap(s) if the size of s is odd. Modify the procedure so that the last character of s is not transposed if the size of s is odd.

17.3.   Write a procedure that interleaves the characters of two strings. For example, the result of interleaving **abc** and **xyz** should be **axbycz**. Decide what to do if the two strings are not the same size.

17.4.[*]   One way to underscore printed text is to precede each character of the text by an underscore and a backspace. For example,

> write("_\bt_\be_\bx_\bt")

produces <u>text</u>. Write a procedure that produces underscored text.

17.5.[*]   One way to print boldface text is to overstrike each character of the text several times (four overstrikes are usually sufficient to produce the appearance of boldface text on typewriter-like devices). Write a procedure that produces boldface text.

17.6.   Write a procedure that reverses strings using character-by-character concatenation. Compare timings of this procedure with those for the procedure **reverse** given in §17.1.1. Plot the times versus the size of the string that is reversed.

17.7.   Write a procedure that displays hands of cards with each suit sorted in the manner that is conventional for the game of bridge. Such a display might be

```
S   7
H   A J 2
D   A J 9 7 4 3
C   K Q 2
```

17.8.   Write a program that shuffles, deals, and displays bridge hands.

17.9.   Write a procedure that produces the nodes of a graph in topological order so that if there is an arc from node **a** to node **b**, **a** appears before **b**. Note that not all graphs can be topologically sorted.

17.10.   The representation of the arcs of a graph by character pairs is hard to prepare and difficult to read. A more natural representation uses arrows and punctuation. For example, the graph given in §17.2.2 could be represented by

> a−>b;b−>d;b−>f;c−>a;c−>b;c−>e;d−>d;d−>f;

Write a procedure that converts this representation for input to the pair representation and a procedure that converts the pair representation to this representation for output.

18

LARGE INTEGERS

The maximum value that an integer can have in Icon is limited by the architecture of the computer on which it is implemented. See Appendix B for details. This limit is adequate for most ordinary computations, but there are situations in which very large integers are needed and in which no specific maximum size can be specified.

This chapter describes several ways of representing large integers and contrasts techniques for processing different types of data. The procedures given here are intended to illustrate aspects of programming in Icon and are not intended for extensive computations with large integers; there are highly efficient application packages for that purpose.

18.1 REPRESENTING LARGE INTEGERS

Consider the integer 3,793,234,045. This base-10 notation represents the coefficients of a polynomial:

$$3*10^9+7*10^8+9*10^7+3*10^6+2*10^5+3*10^4+4*10^3+0*10^2+4*10^1+5*10^0$$

This number also can be represented using a larger base, for example 10,000:

$$37*10,000^2+9,323*10,000^1+4,045*10,000^0$$

Therefore, the coefficients in base-10,000 notation are 37, 9323, and 4045. Numerical computations can be performed on integers using the base 10,000 in the same manner as using the base 10. This allows numerical computations on large integers to be performed on segments of manageable size.

There are several ways that segmented large integers can be represented. Strings and lists are the obvious ways. The representation of a large integer as a string of digits is straightforward and makes input and output of large integers trivial. For example, the integer 3,793,234,045 is represented by the string **3793234045**.

A list of coefficients, such as

[37, 9323, 4045]

is nearly as straightforward as the string representation, but it requires conversion on input and output.

18.2 ADDITION OF LARGE INTEGERS

Addition illustrates the basic problems involved in performing numerical computation on large integers. A string representation of large integers is given first, followed by two other contrasting representations.

18.2.1 A String Representation

There are two kinds of addition in the numerical computations that follow: base-10 addition, which corresponds to

i1 + i2

and base-n addition, for which a procedure call such as

add(x1, x2)

is needed. To avoid confusion, the term *sum* is used for base-10 addition, while the term *addition* is used for base-n addition. The value 10,000 is used for n for purposes of illustration.

Consider adding 213,504,961,785 and 581,465,035,213. In the string representation, this amounts to

("2135" + "5814") || ("0496" + "6503") || ("1785" + "5213")

Note that in such an expression, strings are automatically converted to integers, and vice versa. This case is simple, since both integers are of the same length, there are no carries, and all sums produce four digits. If any of these conditions do not hold, there are complications that must be handled.

As with longhand addition, the general approach is to start with the rightmost coefficients (segments), performing a sum with a possible carry to the left. Since the base is a power of 10, the size of a segment is just the number of digits in the base less 1. Two global identifiers are needed for these values:

global base, segsize

which can be initialized in the main procedure as

```
base := 10000
segsize := *base − 1
```

The addition procedure begins as follows:

```
procedure add(s1, s2, carry)
    local size, sum
    if *s1 > *s2 then s1 :=: s2
    size := *s2
    if size <= segsize then return s1 + s2 + carry
        .
        .
        .
```

Since s1 and s2 may be of different sizes, their values are exchanged, if necessary, so that s2 always is at least as long as s1. If the size of the longest is less than or equal to the size of a segment, an ordinary sum is returned. This value is one digit longer than the length of a segment if there is a carry; it merely is the beginning of a new segment on the left.

In the general case, the two strings must be segmented. To make processing easier, leading zeros are added to s1, if necessary, to make it the same length as s2:

```
s1 := right(s1, size, "0")
```

the sum of the rightmost segments is:

```
sum := right(s1, segsize) + right(s2, segsize) + carry
```

This computation makes use of the fact that right truncates its argument on the left if the string is longer than the specified size. The resulting sum may be larger than the base. The segment for the sum and the carry are the remainder and quotient of division by the base, respectively:

```
seg := sum % base
carry := sum / base
```

The process then is applied to the next segment to the left, and so on. This process is simplest to formulate recursively:

```
add(left(s1, size − segsize), left(s2, size − segsize), carry) ||
    right(seg, segsize, "0")
```

Here left is used to truncate s1 and s2 at the right, while right is used to provide leading zeros for seg that may be deleted in its computation.

There is one remaining problem. A carry ordinarily is specified only when add calls itself recursively. If the third argument is omitted in the call, carry has the null value. This possibility is taken care of by

/carry := 0

The complete procedure is

```
procedure add(s1, s2, carry)
    local size, sum
    /carry := 0                          # default carry
    if *s1 > *s2 then s1 :=: s2
    size := *s2
    if size <= segsize then return s1 + s2 + carry
    s1 := right(s1, size, "0")
    sum := right(s1, segsize) + right(s2, segsize) + carry
    return add(left(s1, size − segsize),
        left(s2, size − segsize), sum / base) ||
        right(sum % base, segsize, "0")
end
```

18.2.2 A List Representation

There are several problems with the string representation. The strings representing large integers are constantly broken down and reconstructed during addition. Furthermore, string-to-integer conversion is required when sums are formed, and integer-to-string conversion is required when the sums are concatenated. All of these computations are expensive. Finally, addition begins with the least significant digits, which are at the right end of the strings. While right(s, segsize) extracts these digits, the process is conceptually awkward, since string processing normally proceeds from left to right.

Some of these problems can be overcome (or exchanged for other problems) by using a list representation. Here it is more convenient to place the least significant digits first, so that 3,793,234,045 is represented by

[4045, 9323, 37]

rather than with the coefficients in the opposite order suggested earlier.

Now the sum of two coefficients can be computed directly by an expression such as

a1[i] + a2[i]

No string-to-integer or integer-to-string conversion is required, but procedures are needed to convert strings to lists on input and to perform the converse conversion on output.

To produce a list of coefficients, the least significant coefficient is needed first, since the sizes of the strings generally are not even multiples of the segment length. This provides a good example of the usefulness of being able to move from the right toward the left in string scanning.

```
procedure large(s)
   local a
   a := []
   s ? {
      &pos := 0                          # start at right end
      while put(a, integer(move(−segsize)))
                                         # add remaining digits
      if &pos ~= 1 then put(a, integer(tab(1)))
      }
   return a
end
```

Note that the segments are converted to integers as they are put in the list.

The procedure to add two large integers in the list representation is similar to that for the string representation, except for a number of details and special cases that must be handled differently. In the procedure that follows, the carry is represented as a list with one value, either 0 or 1. The process is recursive, with the first values in the two lists being summed and pushed onto the list that results from adding the remaining sections of the lists. Special cases occur when the remaining sections are empty; an empty list is equivalent to zero in this representation.

```
procedure add(a1, a2, carry)
   local sum
   /carry := [0]                         # default carry
   if *a1 = *a2 = 0 then
      return if carry[1] ~= 0 then carry else []
   if *a1 > *a2 then a1 :=: a2
   if *a1 = 0 then return add(carry, a2)
   sum := a1[1] + a2[1] + carry[1]
   carry := [sum / base]
   return push(add(a1[2:0], a2[2:0], carry), sum % base)
end
```

The function **push** produces the list produced by **add** (see §5.1.5). Note that **add** eventually gets called with an argument that is an empty list, which terminates the recursion.

In order to write a long integer represented by a list, it must be converted to a string. One approach is

```
procedure lstring(a)
   local s
   s := ""
   every s := right(!a, segsize, "0") || s
   s ?:= (tab(upto(~'0') | −1) & tab(0))
   return s
end
```

This procedure iterates through the list, padding the segments to the required size. If this were not done, a small coefficient such as 0 would produce an erroneous string representation. However, appending the leading zeros to the segments may produce leading zeros on the final result. Removing leading zeros is somewhat tricky, since if the result is composed entirely of zeros, a single zero should be produced. The scanning expression in the procedure does this by tabbing to the first nonzero character if possible, but otherwise tabbing to the next-to-last character. The desired result is the remainder of the string.

18.2.3 A Linked-List Representation

The list representation used in the preceding section relies on Icon's ability to increase the size of a list by pushing values onto it. Another representation that allows an automatic increase in size is a linked list. Such a linked list is composed of records with two fields, one field for the coefficient and the other field for the next record (a link to it). While lists of size two can be used instead of records, records allow processing in a more mnemonic manner. The declaration

record largint(coeff, link)

provides a **largint** type with the two fields coeff and link.

The linked-list representation of a large integer such as 3,793,234,045 can be pictured as

As for the list representation, there are special cases to be handled in dealing with the linked-list representation. For example, the null value for a link indicates the end of a linked list. In this representation, the null value is equivalent to zero. The addition procedure otherwise is similar to the one for the list representation.

```
procedure add(g1, g2, carry)
   local sum
   /carry := largint(0)                    # default carry
   if /g1 & /g2 then return if carry.coeff ~= 0 then carry
   else &null
   if /g1 then return add(carry, g2)
   if /g2 then return add(g1, carry)
   sum := g1.coeff + g2.coeff + carry.coeff
   carry := largint(sum / base)
   return largint(sum % base, add(g1.link, g2.link, carry))
end
```

As for the list representation, conversion on input and output are required. In both cases, recursion provides compact solutions:

```
procedure large(s)
   if *s <= segsize then return largint(integer(s))
   else return largint(right(s, segsize),
         large(left(s, *s − segsize)))
end
```

```
procedure lstring(g)
   local s
   if /g.link then s := g.coeff
   else s := lstring(g.link) || right(g.coeff, segsize, "0")
   s ?:= (tab(upto(~'0') | −1) & tab(0))
   return s
end
```

18.3 MULTIPLYING LARGE INTEGERS

The multiplication of large integers is formulated easily by following the long-hand method. The least significant coefficient of the first large integer, is multiplied by the second large integer and this result is added to the result of multiplying the remaining portion of the first large integer by the second large integer.

A procedure for multiplying large integers in the linked-list representation is

```
procedure mpy(g1, g2)
    local prod
    if /(g1 | g2) then return &null    # zero product
    prod := g1.coeff * g2.coeff
    return largint(prod % base,
        add(mpy(largint(g1.coeff), g2.link), mpy(g1.link, g2),
        largint(prod / base)))
end
```

Note that if either g1 or g2 has the null value, which is equivalent to zero, the procedure returns the null value.

Procedures for multiplying large integers in the string and list representations are similar.

EXERCISES

18.1.   What determines the maximum value that can be used for the base in large integer computations?

18.2.* Write a procedure that verifies that a string is a valid large integer.

18.3.* Write a procedure that inserts commas to separate three-digit groups in the string representation of large integers.

18.4.   Write procedures that compare the magnitudes of large integers in each of the three representations given in this chapter.

18.5.   Write a procedure that copies large integers in the linked-list representation.

18.6.   Write procedures that perform large integer addition iteratively for each of the representations.

18.7.   Write procedures that subtract and divide large integers in each of the representations.

18.8.   Modify the procedure fibseq in §11.7 that generates the Fibonacci sequence to add large integers. Generate the first 100 Fibonacci numbers.

18.9.* Take any positive integer, reverse the order of its digits, and add it to itself. Repeat the process until the result is palindromic, that is, until the sum reads the same backward and forward. For example, starting with 37, the sums are 37 + 73 = 110, and 110 + 011 = 121, which is a palindrome. There is a conjecture that all such sequences eventually terminate in palindromes. Write a generator palseq(i) that generates the sequence of sums as described. For example, the result sequence for palseq(37) should be {110, 121}. Test your solution on the integers from 1 to 100. *Caution:* The conjecture may be false. Some integers, such as 196, are not known to produce sequences that terminate.

19

SYMBOLIC ALGEBRA

Many string processing problems involve the transformation of strings from one form to another. In symbolic algebra, where strings represent arithmetic expressions or similar data, the problems involve recognizing various patterns and converting them to others.

19.1 INFIX-TO-PREFIX CONVERSION

Arithmetic expressions are usually written in infix form with operators between the arguments and with parentheses used for grouping as illustrated in §7.6. Rules of precedence and associativity for operators are used to avoid excessive numbers of parentheses. Icon itself is typical in this respect. Such a syntax is designed for human use. In computer processing, it is more convenient to dispense with precedence and associativity rules and to use parentheses to group all arguments with their operators or to use some other equivalent representation. Furthermore, it often is convenient to have operators appear before their arguments, that is, to have operations in prefix form rather than the infix form that is easier for human beings to read.

Some typical infix operators with their relative precedences and associativities are

operator	precedence	associativity
∧	3	right to left
*	2	left to right
/	2	left to right
+	1	left to right
−	1	left to right

For example,

    x−y−z*delta

is equivalent to

    ((x−y)−(z*delta))

and

    u+v/n∧e∧2

is equivalent to

    (u+(v/(n∧(e∧2))))

The prefix forms of these two expressions are:

    −(−(x, y), *(z, delta))
    +(u, /(v, ∧(n, ∧(e, 2))))

Note that the variables and constants have the same form in both infix and prefix notation.

The general problem is to convert infix expressions with the preceding operators into prefix form. There may be superfluous parentheses, but the infix expressions otherwise are assumed to be well formed (that is, syntactically correct).

The general approach to the problem is recursive, with a procedure fix(exp) that converts an infix expression exp into prefix form. Therefore, the transformation has the form

$$expr_1 \; oper \; expr_2 \; \rightarrow \; oper \; (\, \text{fix}(expr_1), \text{fix}(expr_2)\,)$$

The first problem is to remove any outer parentheses that may occur around the argument of fix. Since superfluous parentheses are allowed, this process must be repeated. One approach is:

    while exp ?:= 2(="("", tab(bal(')')), pos(−1))

As long as exp begins with a left parenthesis, the balanced string up to a right parenthesis is matched, and pos(−1) checks that this parenthesis is the last character of the string being scanned. If the right parenthesis is the last character of the string being scanned, the scanning expression succeeds. The value produced by

   tab(bal(')'))

is assigned to exp, and the **while** loop continues with exp being scanned again. The next step is to analyze exp to get the proper operator for the pattern

   $expr_1$ $oper$ $expr_2$

This pattern may occur in an infix expression in many ways. For example, in

   x—y*2
   ↑ ↑

there are two ways the pattern occurs, as indicated by the arrows beneath the operators. Precedence is used to select the correct operator. The first occurrence of the pattern is the correct one in this example, since multiplication has higher precedence than subtraction, and hence y is an argument of the multiplication, not the subtraction. The correct pattern therefore is obtained by looking for the operators of lowest precedence first.

A similar problem occurs in selecting among several operators of equal precedence. Therefore, in

   x—y—z

there are two ways the pattern could be applied. Since subtraction is left-associative, this expression is equivalent to

   (x—y)—z

and the rightmost left-associative operator is the correct one. On the other hand, the opposite is true of right-associative operators. For example,

   x∧e∧2

is equivalent to

   x∧(e∧2)

In summary, there are two rules:

1. Look for the operator of lowest precedence first and then for operators with increasingly higher precedence.
2. Locate the rightmost left-associative operator but the leftmost right-associative operator.

Since string scanning operates from left to right, it is easiest to handle right-associative operators. A procedure is:

```
procedure rassoc(exp, op)
   return exp ? form(tab(bal(op)), move(1), tab(0))
end
```

where form(arg1, op, arg2) constructs the desired prefix expression:

```
procedure form(arg1, op, arg2)
   return op || "(" || fix(arg1) || "," || fix(arg2) || ")"
end
```

The rightmost left-associative operator can be located by iterating over the result sequence for the positions of all such operators:

```
procedure lassoc(exp, op)
   local j
   return exp? {
      every j := bal(op)
      form(tab(\j), move(1), tab(0))
      }
end
```

The expression \j tests whether or not any value was assigned to j in the **every** loop. If the result sequence for bal(op) is empty, the initial null value of j is not changed,

```
tab(\j)
```

fails, and lassoc fails, indicating that op does not occur in exp. Note that form(arg1, op, arg2) performs the necessary rearrangement of the strings produced by scanning (see §15.1.2).

The functions rassoc and lassoc must be applied in the correct order. The obvious approach is

```
if exp := lassoc(exp, '+−') then return exp
else if exp := lassoc(exp, '*/') then return exp
else if exp := rassoc(exp, '∧') then return exp
else return exp
```

Note that the second arguments of lassoc and rassoc are character sets, allowing all operators in a class to be processed at the same time. The final component of this expression returns exp unchanged if it contains no operators, that is, if it is an identifier or a constant. This presumes, of course, that exp is well formed.

The preceding program segment can be made considerably more concise by using goal-directed evaluation in the **return** expression:

```
    return lassoc('+−' | '*/') | rassoc('∧') | exp
```

The argument of the **return** expression consists of the possible alternatives, which are evaluated from left to right. Notice that the argument of lassoc also contains two alternatives, an application of the fact that

$$p(expr_1) \mid p(expr_2)$$

and

$$p(expr_1 \mid expr_2)$$

are equivalent.

The procedure to convert infix expressions into prefix form first removes outer parentheses and then applies lassoc and rassoc, as shown previously:

```
procedure fix(exp)
    while exp ?:= 2(="(", tab(bal(')')), pos(−1))
    return lassoc(exp, '+−' | '*/') | rassoc(exp, '∧') | exp
end
```

The rest of the program for infix-to-prefix conversion is

```
procedure main()
    while write(fix(read()))
end

procedure lassoc(exp, op)
    local j
    return exp ? {
        every j := bal(op)
        form(tab(\j), move(1), tab(0))
        }
end

procedure rassoc(exp, op)
    return exp ? form(tab(bal(op)), move(1), tab(0))
end

procedure form(arg1, op, arg2)
    return op || "(" || fix(arg1) || "," || fix(arg2) || ")"
end
```

Note that the prefix form is determined in form; suffix or fully parenthesized infix forms can be produced by rearranging the concatenation. A tree can be produced just as easily:

```
procedure form(arg1, op, arg2)
    return [op, fix(arg1), fix(arg2)]
end
```

provided that an identifier or constant is returned in a list in fix(exp):

return lassoc(exp, '+−' | '∗/') | rassoc(exp, '∧') | [exp]

19.2 SYMBOLIC EVALUATION

In the transformation of expressions in §19.1, the operators are passive and devoid of meaning, except for their precedence and associativity. Therefore, an expression such as

1+0

is transformed into

+(1, 0)

even though it is equivalent to 1.

In situations where symbolic expressions are produced by algebraic manipulation, simplifications are often possible. In fact, if simplifications are not performed, expressions may become unmanageably large and complex.

One approach to simplification is to associate procedures with the arithmetic operators and apply these procedures when the expressions are formed. The procedure form(arg1, op, arg2) can be changed as follows:

```
procedure form(arg1, op, arg2)
    arg1 := fix(arg1)
    arg2 := fix(arg2)
    return case op of {
        "+" :   add(arg1, arg2)
        "−" :   sub(arg1, arg2)
        "∗" :   mpy(arg1, arg2)
        "/" :   div(arg1, arg2)
        "∧" :   rse(arg1, arg2)
    }
end
```

Simplifications are now performed in the procedures corresponding to the operators. For addition, some of the possibilities are given in the following procedure:

```
procedure add(arg1, arg2)
   return {
      (integer(arg1) + integer(arg2)) |
      (if arg1 == "0" then arg2) |
      (if arg2 == "0" then arg1) |
      (if arg1 == arg2 then symop("2", "*", arg2)) |
      symop(arg1, "+", arg2)
      }
end
```

The procedure symop(arg1, op, arg2) performs the purely symbolic operation:

```
procedure symop(arg1, op, arg2)
   return op || "(" || arg1 || "," || arg2 || ")"
end
```

In add(arg1, arg2), the first alternative in the **return** expression performs integer addition, if that is possible. The next two alternatives correspond to

$$0 + expr \rightarrow expr$$
$$expr + 0 \rightarrow expr$$

while the fourth alternative corresponds to

$$expr + expr \rightarrow 2 * expr$$

which is generally considered to be a simplification. The final alternative in the **return** expression in add provides for pure symbolic addition, which is performed in case no simplification is possible.

If similar procedures are written for the other arithmetic operations, the result is simplified to an extent that depends on the expressions that are processed and on the sophistication of the procedures.

19.3 SYMBOLIC DIFFERENTIATION

The classical example of symbolic algebra is symbolic differentiation. Using the notation given previously for infix operations, the familiar derivatives are

$$\frac{d}{dx}(c) = 0$$
$$\frac{d}{dx}(x) = 1$$

$$\frac{d}{dx}(u+v) = \frac{du}{dx} + \frac{dv}{dx}$$

$$\frac{d}{dx}(u-v) = \frac{du}{dx} - \frac{dv}{dx}$$

$$\frac{d}{dx}(u*v) = u*\frac{dv}{dx} + v*\frac{du}{dx}$$

$$\frac{d}{dx}(u/v) = (v*\frac{du}{dx} - u*\frac{dv}{dx})/(v \wedge 2)$$

$$\frac{d}{dx}(u \wedge n) = n*(u \wedge (n-1))*\frac{du}{dx}$$

where u and v are expressions possibly containing x, while c and n are constants.

The operation of differentiating an expression with respect to a variable can be considered to be just another binary operation and can be cast in infix form. If the character ~ is used to indicate the operation of differentiation, the derivative of (x+y) with respect to x is written

(x+y)~x

in infix form, or

~(+(x, y), x)

in prefix form. Since differentiation normally is not represented as an operator, its precedence and associativity must be specified. A reasonable choice is to make the operator ~ left associative and to make its precedence higher than any other operator. Therefore,

u+v~x

groups as

u+(v~x)

and corresponds to

$$u + \frac{d}{dx}(v)$$

while

v~x~x

groups as

(v~x)~x

and corresponds to

$$\frac{d^2}{dx^2}(v)$$

The last line in fix then is replaced by

```
return lassoc(exp,'+−' | '*/') | rassoc(exp, '∧') |
    lassoc(exp, '~') | exp
```

Differentiation can be added to the repertoire of symbolic operations by adding

$$"\!\sim\!" \; : \;\; drv(arg1, arg2)$$

to the **case** expression in **form**.

A procedure for producing the derivatives for the familiar cases given previously is

```
procedure drv(exp, var)
    local arg1, op, arg2
    if exp ? {
        op := tab(upto('(')) &
        move(1) &
        arg1 := tab(bal(',')) &
        move(1) &
        arg2 := tab(bal(')'))
    }
    then return case op of {
        "+" :  add(drv(arg1, var), drv(arg2, var))
        "−" :  sub(drv(arg1, var), drv(arg2, var))
        "*" :  add(mpy(arg1, drv(arg2, var)),
                   mpy(arg2, drv(arg1, var)))
        "/" :  div(sub(mpy(arg2, drv(arg1, var)),
                   mpy(arg1, drv(arg2, var))), rse(arg2, "2"))
        "∧" :  mpy(mpy(arg2, rse(arg1, sub(arg2, "1"))),
                   drv(arg1, var))
    }
    else return if exp == var then "1" else "0"
end
```

This procedure assumes that var is a variable and that the second argument in exponentiation is a constant. Note that exp is a prefix expression that is re-analyzed in order to determine which computation to perform. This is necessary because exp is evaluated before the derivative is performed and because the derivative depends on the primary operator in exp. This suggests that a representation of expressions that does not require repeated string analysis would be more efficient. See Exercise 19.3.

EXERCISES

19.1.[*]   Write a program that converts expressions from prefix to infix form.

19.2.[*]   Provide symbolic evaluation procedures similar to add in §19.2 for the other arithmetic operations.

19.3.   Revise the symbolic evaluation and differentiation procedures to operate on expressions represented by trees.

19.4.[*]   Adapt the procedures for infix-to-prefix conversion and symbolic evaluation to allow functions such as sin(x).

19.5.   Add prefix operations to the repertoire of the symbolic evaluation procedures, using functional notation.

19.6.[*]   Modify the version of form used in symbolic evaluation in §19.2 so that an operation for which there is no simplification procedure is returned in symbolic form.

19.7.   Add the common trigonometric functions to the symbolic evaluation and differentiation repertoire.

19.8.   Generalize the symbolic differentiation of exponential expressions to allow the power to be any expression, not just a constant.

19.9.   Add an integration operation to the symbolic evaluation procedures and provide symbolic integration for a few simple cases.

20

RANDOM STRINGS

In §7.6 random strings are generated by a program in which each procedure corresponds directly to the definition of a nonterminal symbol. This approach requires a different program for every set of definitions. A more general approach is to read the definitions into a program and generate random strings from the definitions. This allows the same program to be used for different languages and permits extensions and refinements to the way that languages are defined. This chapter develops such a program.

20.1 REPRESENTING GRAMMARS

Since the program reads grammatical definitions and processes them, there are two problems to be considered: the form in which the definitions are provided to the program and the form in which they are represented internally.

20.1.1 Grammar Input

A notation for grammars was introduced in §15.3. The advantage of such a formal notation over the informal description of languages given in §7.6 is that the formal notation is unambiguous and can be analyzed easily. The notation used in §15.3, in which uppercase letters stand for nonterminal symbols, is not general enough to represent many languages of interest. One problem is that many languages contain the uppercase letters as terminal symbols. Another problem is that a single letter is inadequate for representing nonterminal symbols; longer, more mnemonic names are needed.

An alternative notation for grammars encloses nonterminal names in angular brackets. The grammar in §15.3 can be rephrased in this notation as

```
<expr>::=<term>|<term>+<expr>
<term>::=<element>|<element>*<term>
<element>::=x|y|z|(<expr>)
```

Any character to the right of a ::= that is not a vertical bar or enclosed in angular brackets is a terminal symbol. In particular, spaces are valid terminal symbols. This notation is used for grammars in this chapter.

20.1.2 Internal Representation of Grammars

The random generation process involves selecting alternatives for nonterminal symbols from their definitions. A grammar could be represented in a program by strings such as

```
expr := "<term>|<term>+<expr>"
```

Such a representation is not easy to use for the random generation of strings. For example, the determination of nonterminal symbols requires repeated analysis of the string. Selection of a random alternative requires counting the number of alternatives (the number of vertical bars plus 1) and then analyzing the string to select an alternative at random. Since such operations are performed repeatedly during generation, it is better to analyze the definitions once and put them in a form in which the desired operations can be performed easily and quickly.

One way to distinguish terminal symbols from nonterminal symbols is to use strings for terminal symbols and records for nonterminal symbols. With the declaration

```
record nonterm(name)
```

an instance of the nonterminal symbol <expr> is represented by

```
nonterm("expr")
```

A natural way to represent a definition is to use lists; a list of the alternatives in which each value is a list of the terminal and nonterminal symbols for that alternative. For the preceding grammar, this amounts to

```
expr1 := [nonterm("term")]
expr2 := [nonterm("term"), "+", nonterm("expr")]
expr := [expr1, expr2]
term1 := [nonterm("element")]
term2 := [nonterm("element"), "*", nonterm("term")]
term := [term1, term2]
element1 := ["x"]
element2 := ["y"]
element3 := ["z"]
element4 := ["(", nonterm("expr"), ")"]
element := [element1, element2, element3, element4]
```

These definitions are in a form that can be accessed readily. For example, ?**expr** produces a randomly selected alternative for <**expr**>.

Given a nonterminal symbol, there must be a way to obtain its definition. This can be accomplished if the definitions are put in a table rather than assigned to identifiers:

```
defs := table()
defs["expr"] := [expr1, expr2]
defs["term"] := [term1, term2]
defs["element"] := [element1, element2, element3, element4]
```

Now the definition for a goal symbol is produced by

```
definition := defs[goal]
```

20.2 PROCESSING GRAMMARS

In the previous example, the table and lists for the grammar are part of the program. A program for generating random strings must read in the grammar and construct the table and lists. This is primarily a string scanning problem.

The general form of a line is

<name> ::= definition

where the definition has the form

alternative | alternative | ... | alternative

and each alternative is a sequence of symbols. A line of input first must be analyzed to identify the name and the corresponding definition. The desired transformation is

<name> ::= definition → defs[name] := alts(definition)

where **alts** produces a list of alternatives from the definition. This transformation can be performed directly by

```
procedure define(line)
   return line ?
       defs[(="<", tab(find(">::=")))] := (move(4), alts(tab(0)))
   end
```

That is, the entry value for **defs** is the second expression in

```
(="<", tab(find(">::=")))
```

which is

```
tab(find(">::="))
```

and the assigned value is the remainder of the line after the ::=, once it has been processed:

```
alts(tab(0))
```

Note that **define** fails if **line** is not a syntactically valid definition.

The procedure **alts** constructs the list of alternatives for the definition. If it is assumed that an alternative may not be empty, an alternative is simply a string of characters that does not include a vertical bar:

```
tab(many(~'|'))
```

To construct the list, it is easiest to start with an empty list and add values on the right, using the queue access method:

```
procedure alts(defn)
   local alist
   alist := []
   defn ? while put(alist, syms(tab(many(~'|')))) do move(1)
   return alist
   end
```

where **syms** is a procedure that produces a list of symbols. It is similar to **alts**, except that it is necessary to distinguish terminal symbols from nonterminal symbols.

```
procedure syms(alt)
   local slist
   slist := []
   alt ? while put(slist, tab(many(~'<')) |
         nonterm(2(="<", tab(upto('>')), move(1))))
   return slist
   end
```

Note that **nonterm** records are added to the list for nonterminal symbols and that a string of terminal symbols is treated as a single symbol.

20.3 THE GENERATION PROCESS

Generating random strings from a grammar involves starting with a goal, such as <expr>. As illustrated in §15.3, a nonterminal symbol can be replaced by any one of the alternatives in its definition. If this process is repeated, a string of terminal symbols may result. If the alternatives are selected at random, the string is a "randomly selected" string in the language.

It is easiest always to make the replacement for the leftmost nonterminal symbol. A possible sequence of steps leading from <expr> to a terminal string is

<expr>
↑
<term>
↑
<element>
↑
(<expr>)
↑
(<term>+<expr>)
↑
(<element>+<expr>)
↑
(x+<expr>)
↑
(x+<term>)
↑
(x+<element>)
↑
(x+y)
↑

The arrows indicate the division between terminal symbols on the left and the next nonterminal symbol to be processed on the right. When there are no more nonterminal symbols to be processed, the generation is complete.

In summary, the process is as follows:

1. Start with the nonterminal goal symbol.

2. Working from left to right, replace the leftmost nonterminal symbol by a randomly chosen alternative for it.

Note that a recursive definition may get out of hand. In fact, there is no guarantee that the process will terminate: The sequence of symbols may become longer and longer with more and more nonterminal symbols. The probability of the random selection process "converging" to a string, as opposed to continuing indefinitely, can be computed from the structure of the grammar; it depends on the amount and nature of recursion in the definitions. This problem is not considered here, but see Exercise 20.6.

The actual generation process operates on the internal structures given in §20.1.2. It is convenient to separate the symbols between the terminal symbols on the left and those on the right that remain to be processed. A procedure for generating strings is

```
procedure gener(goal)
    local pending, genstr, symbol
    repeat {
        pending := [nonterm(goal)]
        genstr := ""
        while symbol := get(pending) do
            if type(symbol) == "string" then genstr ||:= symbol
            else pending := ?defs[symbol.name] ||| pending
        suspend genstr
        }
    end
```

The pending list initially consists of the nonterminal goal symbol, while **genstr** initially is empty. Symbols are removed from the left of the pending list. A terminal symbol is appended to the end of the evolving string, while a nonterminal symbol is replaced by a randomly selected alternative from its definition. The process terminates when the pending list is empty.

20.4 GENERATION SPECIFICATIONS

Some method is needed to specify the generation of strings from a nonterminal goal symbol. One way is to choose a syntax for specifying generation that is different from the syntax for definition and let the program determine whether to generate or define. For example, a nonterminal symbol followed by an integer could specify how many strings are to be generated from the language defined by the nonterminal symbol. Therefore,

<expr>10

specifies the generation of 10 <expr>s. A procedure to process generation specifications is

```
procedure generate(line)
    local goal, count
    line ? {
        ="<" &
        goal := tab(upto('>')) &
        move(1) &
        count := tab(0)
        }
        every write(gener(goal)) \ count
    return
end
```

The main processing loop can be written as

```
while line := read() do
    (define | generate)(line)
```

Note that define is applied to a line of input first; if define fails, indicating an invalid definition, generate is applied to the line.

20.5 THE COMPLETE PROGRAM

The main procedure must create the global table defs. The complete program follows.

```
global defs

record nonterm(name)

procedure main()
    local line
    defs := table()
    while line := read() do
        (define | generate)(line)
end

procedure define(line)
    return line ?
        defs[(="<", tab(find(">::=")))] := (move(4), alts(tab(0)))
end
```

```
procedure alts(defn)
    local alist
    alist := []
    defn ? while put(alist, syms(tab(many(~'|')))) do move(1)
    return alist
end

procedure syms(alt)
    local slist
    slist := []
    alt ? while put(slist, tab(many(~'<')) |
        nonterm(2(="<", tab(upto('>')), move(1))))
    return slist
end

procedure generate(line)
    local goal, count
    line ? {
        ="<" &
        goal := tab(upto('>')) &
        move(1) &
        count := tab(0)
        }
        every write(gener(goal)) \ count
    return
end

procedure gener(goal)
    local pending, genstr, symbol
    repeat {
        pending := [nonterm(goal)]
        genstr := ""
        while symbol := get(pending) do
            if type(symbol) == "string" then genstr ||:= symbol
            else pending := ?defs[symbol.name] ||| pending
        suspend genstr
        }
end
```

Note that this program allows nonterminal symbols to be redefined. Definitions also can be interspersed with generation specifications. Therefore, a grammar can be built, tested, and modified incrementally.

EXERCISES

20.1. What happens if an undefined nonterminal symbol is encountered during the generation process? Modify the program so that it issues a diagnostic message in this case but continues processing.

20.2.* What happens if the string that follows the nonterminal symbol in a generation specification is not a positive integer? Modify the procedure **generate** to fail in this case.

20.3.* What happens if an input line is neither a valid definition nor a valid generation specification? Modify the program so that it produces a diagnostic message if an input line is not valid but continues processing subsequent lines.

20.4. Write a program that produces parse trees for randomly generated strings.

20.5.* Provide a means whereby the characters <, >, and | can be included in randomly generated strings.

20.6. As mentioned in §20.3, the random generation process may fail to terminate. See Reference 15 for a discussion of this problem. One way to circumvent the termination problem is to provide a means of biasing the selection process toward alternatives that are more likely to lead to terminal symbols. Provide a mechanism that allows the specification of biases in grammars.

A

ICON SYNTAX

The description of the syntax of Icon that follows uses the italic typeface to denote syntactic classes, such as *program*, and the sans-serif typeface to denote literal program text, such as global. An optional symbol is denoted by the subscript *opt*, so that

(*expression*$_{opt}$)

denotes an optional expression that is enclosed in parentheses.

Alternatives are denoted by vertical stacking. For example,

program:
    declaration
    declaration program

defines a *program* to be a *declaration* or a *declaration* followed by a *program*.

Program syntax.   A program consists of a sequence of declarations.

program:
    declaration
    declaration program

declaration:
    global-declaration
    record-declaration
    procedure-declaration

global-declaration:
   global *identifier-list*
   external *identifier-list*

identifier-list:
   identifier
   identifier , identifier-list

record-declaration:
   record *identifier* (*field-list$_{opt}$*)

field-list:
   field-name
   field-name , field-list

procedure-declaration:
   header locals$_{opt}$ initial-clause$_{opt}$ body **end**

header:
   procedure *identifier* (*identifier-list$_{opt}$*) ;

locals:
   local-specification identifier-list
   local-specification identifier-list ; *locals*

local-specification:
   local
   static
   dynamic

initial-clause:
   initial *expression*

body:
   expression$_{opt}$
   expression$_{opt}$; *body*

Expression syntax.   There are several classes of expressions that are distinguished by their precedence and associativity. To the extent that precedence is meaningful, these expressions are given in the order of their precedence, starting at the highest precedence.

expression:
   parenthesized-expression
   compound-expression
   list-expression
   field-reference-expression
   subscripting-expression
   invocation-expression
   prefix-expression
   limitation-expression
   transmission-expression
   exponentiation-expression *
   multiplicative-expression
   additive-expression
   concatenation-expression
   comparison-expression
   alternation-expression
   to-by-expression
   assignment-expression
   scanning-expression
   conjunction-expression
   create-expression
   return-expression
   break-expression
   next-expression
   case-expression
   if-then-else-expression
   loop-expression
   identifier
   field-name
   keyword
   literal

Parentheses around an expression prevent its components from grouping with expressions outside the parentheses.

parenthesized-expression:
   (*expression*)

The braces around a sequence of expressions prevent components of the expressions within the braces from grouping with expressions outside the braces.

compound-expression:
　　{ *expression-sequence* }

expression-sequence:
　　expression$_{opt}$
　　expression$_{opt}$; *expression-sequence*

Considered as an operator, the semicolon has the lowest possible precedence.

The brackets around a list expression prevent components of expressions within the braces from grouping with expressions outside the braces.

list-expression:
　　[*expression-list*]

expression-list:
　　expression$_{opt}$
　　expression$_{opt}$, *expression-list*

Considered as an operator, the comma has the same precedence as the semicolon, which is the lowest possible precedence.

Field reference expressions necessarily group from left to right.

field-reference-expression:
　　expression . *field-name*

Subscripting expressions necessarily group from left to right.

subscripting-expression:
　　expression [*expression*]
　　expression [*range-specification*]

range-specification:
　　expression : *expression*
　　expression +: *expression*
　　expression −: *expression*

Range specifications are valid only in the context of subscripting expressions.

Invocation expressions group from left to right.

invocation-expression:
  *expression*_{*opt*} (*expression-list*)

Prefix expressions necessarily group from right to left.

prefix-expression:
  not *expression*
  | *expression*
  ! *expression*
  * *expression*
  + *expression*
  − *expression*
  . *expression*
  / *expression*
  = *expression*
  ? *expression*
  \ *expression*
  ~ *expression*
  @ *expression*
  ∧ *expression*

Limitation and transmission expressions group from left to right and have the same precedence.

limitation-expression:
  expression \ *expression*

transmission-expression:
  expression @ *expression*

Exponentiation expressions group from right to left.

exponentiation-expression:
  expression ∧ *expression*

Multiplicative expressions group from left to right.

multiplicative-expression:
    expression ***** *expression*
    expression **/** *expression*
    expression **%** *expression*
    expression ****** *expression*

Additive expressions group from left to right.

additive-expression:
    expression **+** *expression*
    expression **−** *expression*
    expression **++** *expression*
    expression **−−** *expression*

Concatenation expressions group from left to right.

concatenation-expression:
    expression **||** *expression*
    expression **|||** *expression*

Comparison expressions group from left to right.

comparison-expression:
    expression **<** *expression*
    expression **<=** *expression*
    expression **=** *expression*
    expression **>=** *expression*
    expression **>** *expression*
    expression **~=** *expression*
    expression **<<** *expression*
    expression **<<=** *expression*
    expression **==** *expression*
    expression **>>=** *expression*
    expression **>>** *expression*
    expression **~==** *expression*
    expression **===** *expression*
    expression **~===** *expression*

Alternation expressions group from left to right.

alternation-expression:
    expression | *expression*

To-by expressions are indicated by reserved words, not operator symbols.

to-by-expression:
    expression **to** *expression* *by-clause*$_{opt}$

by-clause:
    by *expression*

A dangling **by** is associated with the nearest previous **to**.

Assignment expressions group from right to left.

assignment-expression:
    expression := *expression*
    expression <− *expression*
    expression :=: *expression*
    expression <−> *expression*
    expression +:= *expression*
    expression −:= *expression*
    expression *:= *expression*
    expression /:= *expression*
    expression %:= *expression*
    expression ∧:= *expression*
    expression <:= *expression*
    expression <=:= *expression*
    expression =:= *expression*
    expression >=:= *expression*
    expression >:= *expression*
    expression ~=:= *expression*
    expression ++:= *expression*
    expression −−:= *expression*
    expression **:= *expression*
    expression ||:= *expression*

expression <<:= *expression*
expression <<=:= *expression*
expression ==:= *expression*
expression >>=:= *expression*
expression >>:= *expression*
expression ~==:= *expression*
expression ?:= *expression*
expression |||:= *expression*
expression ===:= *expression*
expression ~===:= *expression*
expression &:= *expression*
expression @:= *expression*

Scanning expressions group from left to right.

scanning-expression:
  expression ? *expression*

Conjunction expressions group from left to right.

conjunction-expression:
  expression & *expression*

The remaining expressions all have low precedence.

create-expression:
  create *expression*

---

return-expression
  return *expression*$_{opt}$
  suspend *expression*$_{opt}$
  fail

---

break-expression:
  break *expression*$_{opt}$

---

next-expression:
  next

case-expression:
    case *expression* **of** { *case-list* }

case-list:
    case-clause
    case-clause ; *case-list*

case-clause:
    expression : *expression*
    default : *expression*

There may be only one **default** clause in a **case** expression.

---

if-then-else-expression:
    if *expression* **then** *expression* *else-clause*$_{opt}$

else-clause:
    else *expression*

A dangling **else** is associated with the nearest previous **if**.

---

loop-expression:
    repeat *expression*
    while *expression* *do-clause*$_{opt}$
    until *expression* *do-clause*$_{opt}$
    every *expression* *do-clause*$_{opt}$

do-clause:
    do *expression*

A dangling **do** is associated with the nearest previous **while**, **until**, or **every**.

Identifiers, field names, keywords, and literals.   The most elementary components of an Icon program are identifiers, field names, keywords, and literals.

An identifier must begin with a letter or an underscore, which may be followed by any number of letters, underscores, and digits. Upper- and lowercase letters are different. The syntax for field names is the same as the syntax for identifiers. Reserved words may not be used as identifiers or field names. Reserved words are all lowercase. The following are reserved words

break	external	record
by	fail	repeat
case	global	return
create	if	static
default	initial	suspend
do	local	then
dynamic	next	to
else	not	until
end	of	while
every	procedure	

Keywords consist of an ampersand followed by one of a selected number of identifiers. The keywords, which are lowercase, are as follows:

&ascii	&input	&source
&clock	&lcase	&subject
&cset	&level	&time
&date	&main	&trace
&dateline	&null	&ucase
&errout	&output	&version
&fail	&pos	
&host	&random	

There are two categories of literals.

literal:
  numeric-literal
  quoted-literal

Numeric literals, in turn, are divided into two categories.

numeric-literal:
  integer-literal
  real-literal

Integer literals have two forms.

integer-literal:
    digit-literal
    radix-literal

Digit literals consist of one or more digits. Radix literals allow the radix for digits to be specified.

radix-literal:
    digit-literal **r** *digit-specification*

Either **r** or **R** may be used to indicate a radix literal.

The value of the integer literal specifies the radix and must be between 2 and 36, inclusive. The digit specification consists of a sequence of digits and letters, where **a** stands for 10, **b** stands for 11, and so forth though **z**. Upper- and lowercase letters in digit specifications are equivalent. The characters in digit specifications must stand for values that are less than the radix.

Real literals have two forms.

real-literal:
    decimal-literal
    exponent-literal

decimal-literal:
    digit-literal **.** *digit-literal*$_{opt}$

exponent-literal:
    digit-literal **e** digit-literal
    decimal-literal **e** digit-literal

Either **e** or **E** may be used to indicate an exponent literal.

Quoted literals are divided into two categories.

quoted-literal:
    cset-literal
    string-literal

Cset literals consist of a string of characters enclosed in single quotes. A single quote cannot appear within the enclosing quotes unless it is escaped. Escape sequences are described later.

String literals consist of a string of characters enclosed in double quotes. A double quote cannot appear within the enclosing quotes unless it is escaped.

Escape sequences allow characters to be included in string literals that otherwise would be awkward or impossible to include. An escape sequence consists of a backslash followed by one or more characters that are given special meanings. The escape sequences and the characters that they stand for are as follows:

\b	backspace
\d	delete (rubout)
\e	escape (altmode)
\f	formfeed
\l	linefeed (newline)
\n	newline (linefeed)
\r	carriage return
\t	horizontal tab
\v	vertical tab
\'	single quote
\"	double quote
\\	backslash
\ddd	*octal code*
\x*dd*	*hexadecimal code*
\∧*c*	*control code*

The linefeed and newline characters are the same; both are included to accommodate the different terminologies of ASCII and UNIX.

The sequence *ddd* stands for the character with octal code *ddd*, where *d* is an octal digit 0, 1, ..., 7. The sequence \x*dd* stands for the character with hexadecimal code *dd*, where *d* is a hexadecimal digit 0, 1, ..., A, ... F. Upper- and lowercase hexadecimal digits, such as a and A, are equivalent. Only enough digits need to be given to specify the desired octal or hexadecimal number, provided the characters that follow cannot be considered as part of the escape sequence. For example, \43 specifies the character #, and \xA is equivalent to \x0A.

The control code sequence \∧*c* stands for the ASCII character control-*c*. For example, \∧A stands for control-A. In general, \∧*c* stands for the character corresponding to the five low-order bits of *c*.

If the character following a backslash is not one of those in the preceding list, the backslash is ignored. Therefore, \a stands for a.

White space.   Program text that has no meaning in itself is collectively called "white space". Except in quoted literals, spaces and tabs serve as syntactic separators. They are needed to separate tokens that otherwise could be construed as a single token. For example, ifnot $expr_1$ then $expr_2$

is syntactically erroneous, since **ifnot** is interpreted as an identifier rather than two reserved words.

Spaces otherwise have no significance. For example, spaces can appear between a prefix operator and its argument. Spaces can also be used as optional separators to improve the visual appearance of a program. Spaces are necessary to separate infix operators from prefix operators in situations that could be ambiguous. For example,

$expr_1 || expr_2$

might be interpreted in two ways, as concatenation or as alternation followed by repeated alternation of the second expression. The Icon translator resolves such potential ambiguities by taking the longest legal sequence of operator symbols to be a single token, so this example is interpreted as concatenation. A space between the two bars would cause the expression to be interpreted as alternation followed by repeated alternation.

A #, except in a quoted literal, introduces a comment, which terminates at the end of the line. A comment is considered to be white space by the Icon translator.

Semicolons and line breaks.   The Icon translator generally is indifferent to program layout, but it automatically inserts a semicolon at the end of a line if that line ends an expression and the next line begins another expression. Therefore,

```
x := 1
y := 2
z := 0
```

is equivalent to

```
x := 1; y := 2; z := 0
```

Because the translator inserts semicolons at the ends of lines where possible, care must be taken in splitting an expression between two lines. In the case of an infix operation, the operator should be placed at the end of the first line, not the beginning of the second. Therefore,

$expr_1 || expr_2$

should be split as

$expr_1 ||$
$\quad expr_2$

The translator does not insert a semicolon at the end of the first line, since the expression on that line is not complete. However, in

$$expr_1$$
$$|| \ expr_2$$

a semicolon is inserted at the end of the first line, since

$$expr_1; \ || \ expr_2$$

is syntactically correct. Here || is two prefix repeated alternation operators.

Identifiers may be arbitrarily long, but they must be contained on one line. A quoted literal may be continued from one line to the next by placing an underscore as the last character of the literal and omitting the closing quote. If a quoted literal is continued in this way, the underscore as well as any spaces or tabs at the beginning of the next line are ignored. For example,

```
cons := "bcdfghjklmn_
pqrstvwxyz"
```

is equivalent to

```
cons := "bcdfghjklmnpqrstvwxyz"
```

The ASCII character set. Icon uses the ASCII character set, extended to 256 characters, for programs and data. Except as noted in this appendix, all characters are distinct. The ASCII character set is listed next with corresponding decimal, octal, hexadecimal, and binary codes. Different computer terminals have different keyboard entry combinations for some control characters. The most common entry sequences are listed here. Some computer terminals have alternative entry combinations.

decimal	octal	hex	binary	graphic	keyboard entry
000	000	00	00000000		null (control-@)
001	001	01	00000001		control-A
002	002	02	00000010		control-B
003	003	03	00000011		control-C
004	004	04	00000100		control-D
005	005	05	00000101		control-E
006	006	06	00000110		control-F
007	007	07	00000111		bell (control-G)
008	010	08	00001000		backspace (control-H)
009	011	09	00001001		tab (control-I)
010	012	0A	00001010		linefeed (newline, control-J)
011	013	0B	00001011		vertical tab (control-K)
012	014	0C	00001100		formfeed (control-L)
013	015	0D	00001101		carriage return (control-M)
014	016	0E	00001110		control-N

015	017	0F	00001111		control-O
016	020	10	00010000		control-P
017	021	11	00010001		control-Q
018	022	12	00010010		control-R
019	023	13	00010011		control-S
020	024	14	00010100		control-T
021	025	15	00010101		control-U
022	026	16	00010110		control-V
023	027	17	00010111		control-W
024	030	18	00011000		control-X
025	031	19	00011001		control-Y
026	032	1A	00011010		control-Z
027	033	1B	00011011		escape (altmode, control-[)
028	034	1C	00011100		quit (control-\)
029	035	1D	00011101		control-]
030	036	1E	00011110		control-^
031	037	1F	00011111		control-_
032	040	20	00100000		space
033	041	21	00100001	!	!
034	042	22	00100010	"	"
035	043	23	00100011	#	#
036	044	24	00100100	$	$
037	045	25	00100101	%	%
038	046	26	00100110	&	&
039	047	27	00100111	'	'
040	050	28	00101000	(	(
041	051	29	00101001	)	)
042	052	2A	00101010	*	*
043	053	2B	00101011	+	+
044	054	2C	00101100	,	,
045	055	2D	00101101	−	−
046	056	2E	00101110	.	.
047	057	2F	00101111	/	/
048	060	30	00110000	0	0
049	061	31	00110001	1	1
050	062	32	00110010	2	2
051	063	33	00110011	3	3
052	064	34	00110100	4	4
053	065	35	00110101	5	5
054	066	36	00110110	6	6
055	067	37	00110111	7	7
056	070	38	00111000	8	8
057	071	39	00111001	9	9
058	072	3A	00111010	:	:

059	073	3B	00111011	;	;
060	074	3C	00111100	<	<
061	075	3D	00111101	=	=
062	076	3E	00111110	>	>
063	077	3F	00111111	?	?
064	100	40	01000000	@	@
065	101	41	01000001	A	A
066	102	42	01000010	B	B
067	103	43	01000011	C	C
068	104	44	01000100	D	D
069	105	45	01000101	E	E
070	106	46	01000110	F	F
071	107	47	01000111	G	G
072	110	48	01001000	H	H
073	111	49	01001001	I	I
074	112	4A	01001010	J	J
075	113	4B	01001011	K	K
076	114	4C	01001100	L	L
077	115	4D	01001101	M	M
078	116	4E	01001110	N	N
079	117	4F	01001111	O	O
080	120	50	01010000	P	P
081	121	51	01010001	Q	Q
082	122	52	01010010	R	R
083	123	53	01010011	S	S
084	124	54	01010100	T	T
085	125	55	01010101	U	U
086	126	56	01010110	V	V
087	127	57	01010111	W	W
088	130	58	01011000	X	X
089	131	59	01011001	Y	Y
090	132	5A	01011010	Z	Z
091	133	5B	01011011	[	[
092	134	5C	01011100	\	\
093	135	5D	01011101	]	]
094	136	5E	01011110	^	^
095	137	5F	01011111	_	_
096	140	60	01100000	`	`
097	141	61	01100001	a	a
098	142	62	01100010	b	b
099	143	63	01100011	c	c
100	144	64	01100100	d	d
101	145	65	01100101	e	e
102	146	66	01100110	f	f

103	147	67	01100111	g	g
104	150	68	01101000	h	h
105	151	69	01101001	i	i
106	152	6A	01101010	j	j
107	153	6B	01101011	k	k
108	154	6C	01101100	l	l
109	155	6D	01101101	m	m
110	156	6E	01101110	n	n
111	157	6F	01101111	o	o
112	160	70	01110000	p	p
113	161	71	01110001	q	q
114	162	72	01110010	r	r
115	163	73	01110011	s	s
116	164	74	01110100	t	t
117	165	75	01110101	u	u
118	166	76	01110110	v	v
119	167	77	01110111	w	w
120	170	78	01111000	x	x
121	171	79	01111001	y	y
122	172	7A	01111010	z	z
123	173	7B	01111011	{	{
124	174	7C	01111100	|	|
125	175	7D	01111101	}	}
126	176	7E	01111110	~	~
127	177	7F	01111111		rubout (delete)

B

MACHINE DEPENDENCIES
AND LIMITS

Size limitations. The limits on the sizes of values in Icon are determined in part by the architecture of the computer on which Icon is implemented and in part by the way that it is implemented.

The implementation uses both short integers and long integers. On a 16-bit computer with two's-complement arithmetic, short integers occupy one word and have values in the range -2^{15} to $2^{15}-1$, while long integers occupy two words and have values in the range -2^{31} to $2^{31}-1$. On a 32-bit computer with two's-complement arithmetic, short and long integers are the same and have values in the range -2^{31} to $2^{31}-1$. Since short and long integers may or may not be the same, depending on the particular computer, the terms *minshort* and *maxshort* are used subsequently to designate the smallest and largest short integers.

The maximum sizes of strings and lists are limited by *maxshort*. Numerical computation, on the other hand, uses long integers. Therefore, on a 16-bit computer, an Icon integer can be as large as $2^{31}-1$, but a string can be at most $2^{15}-1$ characters long.

In some cases, integer values are limited to *minshort* or *maxshort*. For example, the value of i in ?i cannot exceed *maxshort*. In an assignment to &trace, if the value assigned is greater than *maxshort* or less than *minshort*, the actual value that is assigned is −1.

On 16-bit computers, real numbers are represented by double-precision floating-point numbers. The range and precision of floating-point values depends on the specific computer architecture. For example, on a typical 16-bit computer, real numbers occupy 64 bits, have 8-bit exponents, and have values in the range $\pm10^{\pm38}$.

Input and output.   As mentioned in Chapter 9, input and output in Icon are dependent in many respects on the operating system under which Icon runs. Icon is designed to run under UNIX and delegates the handling of input and output to UNIX. For example, file names are interpreted by UNIX, not Icon.

The options for opening files under UNIX are

r	open for reading
w	open for writing
b	open for reading and writing (bidirectional)
a	open for writing in append mode
c	create and open for writing
p	pipe to/from a command

The b option usually applies to interactive input and output at a terminal that behaves like a file that is both written and read. With the p option, the first argument is passed to /bin/sh [7]. If a file is opened for writing but not for reading, c is implied. The c and a options have no effect on pipes. The p option only can be used with r or w but not both. Upper- and lowercase letters are equivalent in option specifications.

UNIX allows only 20 files to be open at one time. This limit includes standard input, standard output, and standard error output.

The maximum input line length for read(f) varies from implementation to implementation. If an input line is longer than the maximum, only the maximum number of characters are read. Subsequent characters are read on subsequent reads. The maximum input line length for reads(f, i) is *maxshort*. There is no limit to the length of a line that can be written.

C

RUNNING AN ICON PROGRAM

The way that an Icon program is run depends on many factors, including the particular implementation, the computer and operating system used, and local installation conventions. Local information for users often is available. This chapter describes the usual way that Version 5 of Icon is run under Version 7 of the UNIX operating system.

There are two forms of the Version 5 implementation, an interpreter and a compiler. Source programs for both must be on files that end with the suffix **.icn**. When the program is translated, the file name is recorded for use in trace and error messages.

The interpreter.   The Icon interpreter translates a source program into an intermediate form that is suitable for interpretation. The command to translate a program such as **rsg.icn** is

>   icont rsg.icn

The result is a file **rsg**, which can be executed by the interpreter by

>   iconx rsg

On some systems, **rsg** is directly executable and **iconx** is not needed. Translation and interpretation can be combined in one step by adding the —x option *after* the source program name. That is,

>   icont rsg.icn —x

translates and executes **rsg.icn**. It also leaves the file **rsg**, which can be executed subsequently by **iconx**. The placement of the —x option after the name of the source program allows options and command arguments to be provided to the executing program.

If − appears in place of a source program name, input is taken from standard input. In this case, the file name is recorded as stdin. For example,

icont − −x

translates and executes a source program from standard input.

Several source program files can be translated at the same time to produce a single output file, as in

icont part1.icn part2.icn

The name of the output file is taken from the first .icn file given, part1 in this case.

Translation actually consists of two phases: translation proper and linking. The translator produces two intermediate files for each .icn file, with suffixes .u1 and .u2. The linker combines the .u1 and .u2 files to form the final output file. The process is shown schematically as follows:

The .u1 and .u2 files normally are deleted, but they are saved if the linking phase is suppressed by the −c option, as in

icont −c rsg.icn

Similarly, if a .u1 file name is provided to icont, the corresponding .u1 and .u2 files are linked, as in

icont rsg.u1

The separation of the translation and linking phases allows portions of a program to be translated separately and combined during linking. For example, a frequently used library of utility procedures can be translated but not linked. Later the .u1 and .u2 files for this library can be linked with other programs that use the utilities. For example, if lib.icn is such a library,

icont −c lib.icn

produces lib.u1 and lib.u2. If deriv.icn uses procedures in lib.icn, these procedures need not be contained in deriv.icn but can be added during linking by icont deriv.icn lib.u1

The name of the output file is deriv.

When a program is divided into parts this way, each procedure must, of course, be contained entirely in one file. Record declarations may be in any of the files, but a record declaration cannot be duplicated. Global declarations can be duplicated.

The compiler. The compiler resembles the interpreter in that it contains a translator and linker, but the output of the linker is assembly language code, which is then assembled and loaded with run-time routines to produce an executable binary file. The last three phases of the process are shown, where *as* and *ld* are the UNIX assembler and loader, respectively.

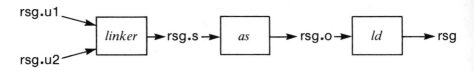

The command to compile a file rsg.icn is

iconc rsg.icn

The result is a file rsg that can be executed directly by

rsg

Another name for the output file may be specified by using the −o option followed by the desired file name. For example,

iconc −o rsg.out rsg.icn

produces an output file named rsg.out.

The −c option can be used to suppress linking (as well as assembling and loading) in the same way it is used in the interpreter so that parts of a program can be compiled separately.

External procedures. In addition to the repertoire of built-in procedures (functions) and procedures that are declared in a program, procedures written in C also can be incorporated in Icon programs that are processed by the Icon compiler (but not the interpreter).

Such *external* procedures must be written using specific coding conventions so that they interface the Icon system properly. See Reference 16 for a description of these conventions.

External procedures are declared in an Icon program by

external *identifier-list*

which declares the identifiers in the list to be global. External procedures are used just like functions.

When an Icon program is loaded, **.o** files for the external procedures must be provided. For example,

iconc deriv.icn gcd.o

specifies that the object file **gcd.o**, corresponding to a C file **gcd.c**, is to be loaded with the rest of the run-time system needed by **deriv.icn**. If **deriv.icn** contains the declaration

external gcd

then this external procedure can be used when the resulting output file is executed. C files can be compiled automatically by providing their names to the compiler, as in

iconc deriv.icn gcd.c

The object file **gcd.o** is left as a result, in addition to being incorporated in the output file.

Additional options.   There are several options in addition to those mentioned in the preceding sections. These options apply both to the interpreter and the compiler.

The −m option causes each **.icn** file to be preprocessed by the *m4* macro processor before it is translated. This provides a convenient way of including sections of source program, since *m4* has the capability to include other files.

The −s option suppresses informative messages, including error messages, that are produced by the translator and linker. Such messages normally are sent to standard error output.

The −t option causes **&trace** to be set to −1 at the beginning of execution. This makes it possible to specify tracing when a program is translated, even if the value of **&trace** is not set in the program. If **&trace** is set in the program, this overrides the −t option.

The −u option causes warning messages to be produced if undeclared identifiers are found during linking.

Environment variables.   There are several UNIX environment variables that can be used to set execution parameters.

The environment variable TRACE determines the initial value of &trace. For example, using the "Bourne" shell, [7]

> TRACE=−1 iconx rsg

causes rsg to be interpreted with &trace being set to −1 initially. This allows tracing to be specified when the program is executed, even if it is not specified in the program or during translation. The value of TRACE overrides the value set by the −t option during translation.

The environment variable NBUFS sets the number of input/output buffers. When a file is opened, it is assigned a buffer if one is available. If no buffer is available, input and output to that file are not buffered. Normally, three buffers are available. Standard input and standard output are buffered unless they are terminals. Standard error output is never buffered.

The environment variable STRSIZE sets the initial size, in bytes, of space used for storing strings. String space grows if necessary, but it never shrinks.

The environment variable HEAPSIZE sets the initial size, in bytes, of heap storage. The heap grows if necessary, but it never shrinks.

The environment variable NSTACKS sets the number of stacks available for co-expressions.

The environment variable STKSIZE sets the initial size, in words, of each co-expression stack. Co-expression stacks grow in size, but never shrink.

Choosing between the interpreter and compiler.   Since the interpreter avoids the assembly and loading phases of the compiler, it gets to program execution much more quickly than the compiler. In addition, output files produced by the interpreter are quite small and are roughly proportional to the size of the corresponding .icn program. On the other hand, output files produced by the compiler are large, since they contain all the run-time system routines needed to execute the program. Such files are more nearly proportional in size to the number of different language *features* used by a program than they are to the size of the program itself.

When the interpreter is executed, the entire Icon run-time system is loaded into memory, while for the compiler, only the routines contained in output files are loaded. Consequently, interpreted programs typically require more memory to *run* than compiled programs.

During execution, compiled programs run slightly faster than interpreted programs. A difference of 5% to 10% is typical.

With the exception of external procedures, the interpreter and compiler are completely compatible in the language features that they accept. The run-time behavior is the same for the compiler and interpreter (except for possible timing differences). In the absence of other concerns, it usually is convenient to develop a program using the interpreter and then to compile a final version.

Program execution. Program execution starts with an implicit call of the procedure main. If there are arguments on the UNIX command line that initiates program execution, or after the −x on the icont command, main is called with one argument that consists of a list of strings. Each string corresponds to an argument on the command line (not including the "zeroth" argument). Typical uses of such arguments are to pass options, file names, or parameters to the program. For example,

```
procedure main(x)
    every expr \ x[1] do
        .
        .
```

limits the number of times *expr* is resumed to the value given as the first argument on the command line.

Program execution terminates with the return from the initial call of main. The exit status is 0.

Executing UNIX commands. The function system(s) calls the UNIX subroutine *system* to execute the string s. For example,

```
system("ls")
```

lists the current directory. The function system(s) produces the exit status returned by the shell. The size of s is limited to 256.

Program termination. Program execution may terminate for a number of reasons. Normal termination occurs upon return from the initial call of the main procedure. This return may be either explicit or implicit. The exit status is 0 whether the main procedure succeeds or fails.

Sometimes it is useful to be able to terminate execution at an arbitrary point in the program. For example, a situation may occur that prevents normal completion of a processing loop. When this happens, it is not always easy to effect a return from the main procedure. Two functions terminate program execution directly: stop(s), described earlier, and exit(i). The function stop(s) returns an exit status of 1, while exit(i) terminates program execution without comment and returns the value of i as exit status.

Program execution may also be terminated because of an error detected by the Icon system. When this happens, an explanatory message is written by the Icon system, as described in Appendix D.

D

ERRORS

Errors during translation. Incorrect syntax causes errors that are detected during program translation. Such an error produces an error message that indicates the location in the program at which the translator detected the error and an explanation of the error.

Messages that may occur during translation because of syntax errors in the program are listed next. Translation continues following detection of an error, but the translated program cannot be executed.

```
end of file expected
global, record, or procedure declaration expected
inconsistent redeclaration
invalid argument list
invalid by clause
invalid case clause
invalid case control expression
invalid character
invalid context for break
invalid context for next
invalid context for return or fail
invalid context for suspend
invalid create expression
invalid declaration
invalid default clause
invalid digit in integer literal
invalid do clause
```

invalid else clause
invalid every control expression
invalid field name
invalid global declaration
invalid if control expression
invalid initial expression
invalid integer literal
invalid keyword
invalid keyword construction
invalid local declaration
invalid argument
invalid argument for unary operator
invalid argument in alternation
invalid argument in assignment
invalid argument in augmented assignment
invalid radix for integer literal
invalid real literal
invalid reference or subscript
invalid repeat expression
invalid section
invalid then clause
invalid to clause
invalid until control expression
invalid while control expression
missing parameter list in procedure declaration
missing colon
missing end
missing field list in record declaration
missing identifier
missing left brace
missing of
missing procedure name
missing record name
missing right brace
missing right bracket
missing right parenthesis
missing semicolon
missing semicolon or operator
missing then
more than one default clause
unclosed quote
unexpected end of file

Some syntactic errors are not detected until after the location of the actual error. An example is an extra left brace, which is not detected until some construction occurs that requires a matching, but missing, right brace. As the result of this phenomenon, the error message may not indicate the correct location of the error or its true nature.

Translation may be terminated because of various kinds of overflow:

out of global symbol table space
out of local symbol table space
out of string space
out of constant table space
out of tree space
yacc stack overflow

There is one warning message issued by the translator:

redeclared identifier

Unlike the preceding messages, this warning does not prevent the use of the translated program.

Errors during linking.   Two programming errors are detected by the linker:

inconsistent redeclaration
invalid field name

These errors prevent the program from being executed.

If the −u option is used, the linker produces the message

undeclared identifier

for identifiers that are not declared. This message is only a warning; it does not prevent the use of the linked program.

In the interpreter version of Icon the error message

out of buffer space

may occur during linking if the program is too large. This error prevents the program from being executed.

Errors during loading.   Errors that occur during loading in the compiler version of Icon are issued by the loader, which is not part of the Icon system itself. Errors may occur because insufficient memory is available or because of errors in external procedures (for example, unresolved references). In the case of loader errors, the resulting program may malfunction if an attempt is made to execute it.

Errors during program execution.   If an error occurs during program execution, a diagnostic message is produced indicating the nature of the error, where in the program the error occurred, and, when possible, an indication of the offending value.

Program errors are divided into three major categories, depending on the nature of the error.

Category 1: Invalid Type or Form

101	integer expected
102	numeric expected
103	string expected
104	cset expected
105	file expected
106	procedure or integer expected
107	record expected
108	list expected
109	string or file expected
110	string or list expected
111	variable expected
112	invalid type to size operation
113	invalid type to random operation
114	invalid type to subscript operation
115	list or table expected
116	invalid type to element generator
117	missing main procedure
118	co-expression expected

Category 2: Invalid Argument or Computation

201	division by zero
202	remaindering by zero
203	integer overflow
204	real overflow, underflow, or division by zero
205	value out of range
206	negative first argument to real exponentiation
207	invalid field name
208	second and third arguments to map of unequal length
209	invalid second argument to open
210	argument to system function too long
211	by clause equal to zero
212	attempt to read file not open for reading
213	attempt to write file not open for writing

Category 3: Capacity Exceeded

301	insufficient storage in heap
302	insufficient storage in string space
303	insufficient storage for garbage collection
304	insufficient storage for system stack
305	insufficient storage for co-expressions

An example of an error message is

Run-time error 102 at line 2 in copyl.icn
numeric expected
offending value: "a"

An error in Category 1 or 2 usually indicates a programming mistake, while an error in Category 3 occurs if there is not enough space to perform a computation.

Storage space in Icon is divided into a number of regions. Space for structures is allocated in a heap storage region. There are separate storage regions for strings and co-expressions. Garbage collection is performed automatically when more storage is needed.

The system stack region is used for saving values during procedure calls. Error 304 usually indicates excessive recursion.

E

SUMMARY OF
BUILT-IN OPERATIONS

This appendix summarizes the built-in operations of Icon. The operations are divided into six categories: functions, prefix operations, infix operations, control structures, keywords, and other operations. The descriptions of operations here are brief and are intended for quick reference only. References to sections where the operations are described in more detail are given to the right of the operation prototypes.

The expected types of the arguments are given by letters as described in §1.6 and §6.2. Type conversion is performed automatically, where possible, for types other than the expected types as described in §6.2. The phrase "s not **string**" means s is neither a string nor a type that can be converted to a string. Operations that perform significantly different computations, depending on the types of their arguments, are listed separately under the different types with cross references.

Defaults for omitted or null-valued arguments are listed, followed by the numbers of program errors that may occur as a result of improper usage of the operation. See Appendix D for the error messages. Errors that may occur because of storage overflow are not listed here.

In several cases nonpositive position specifications are allowed. The expression **poseq**(i, x) stands for the positive equivalent of i with respect to x.

Functions. The arguments of a function are evaluated from left to right. All the arguments are evaluated before the function is called. All arguments are evaluated before any argument is dereferenced. A function fails if any one of its arguments fails. A function may generate a sequence of results if any of its arguments generates a sequence of results.

The functions are listed in alphabetical order.

---

abs(n) §3.2

Produces the absolute value of n.

Error:

102   n not **integer** or **real**

---

any(c, s, i, j) §4.3.2, 4.3.3, 12.5

Produces i + 1 if s[i] is contained in c, but fails otherwise.

Defaults:

s   **&subject**
i   **&pos** if s is defaulted, otherwise 1
j   0

Errors:

101   i or j not **integer**
103   s not **string**
104   c not **cset**

---

bal(c1, c2, c3, s, i, j) §4.3.2, 4.3.3, 11.6, 12.5

Generates the sequence of integer positions in s up to a character of c1 in s[i:j] that is balanced with respect to characters in c2 and c3, but fails if there is no such position.

Defaults:

c1   **&cset**
c2   '('
c3   ')'
s   **&subject**
i   **&pos** if s is defaulted, otherwise 1
j   0

Errors:

101   i or j not **integer**
103   s not **string**
104   c1, c2, or c3 not **cset**

---

center(s1, i, s2)   §4.2.6
Produces a string of size i in which s1 is centered, with s2 used for padding at left and right as necessary.

Defaults:

i	1
s2	" "

Errors:

101	i not **integer**
103	s1 or s2 not **string**
205	i < 0 or i > *maxshort*

---

close(f)   §9.1
Produces f after closing it.

Error:

105	f not **file**

---

copy(x)   §10.2
Produces a copy of x if x is a list, table, or record; otherwise it produces x.

---

cset(x)   §6.2.2
Produces a cset resulting from the type conversion of x, but fails if the conversion is not possible.

---

display(i, f)   §10.6
Writes to f the identifiers and their values for i levels of procedure call and produces the null value.

Defaults:

i	&level
f	&errout

Errors:

101	i not **integer**
105	f not **file**
205	i < 0
213	f not open for writing

---

exit(i)   Appendix C
Terminates program execution with exit status i.

Default:
i   0

Errors:
101   i not **integer**
205   i < *minshort* or i > *maxshort*

---

find(s1, s2, i, j)   §1.2, 4.3.1, 4.3.3, 11.1, 11.6, 12.5
Generates the sequence of integer positions in s2 at which s1 occurs as a substring in s2[i:j], but fails if there is no such position.

Defaults:
s2   &subject
i   &pos if s2 is defaulted, otherwise 1
j   0

Errors:
101   i or j not **integer**
103   s1 or s2 not **string**

---

get(a)   §5.1.5
Produces the leftmost element of a and removes it from a, but fails if a is empty; synonym for pop(a).

Error:
108   a not **list**

---

image(x)   §10.4
Produces a string image of x.

---

integer(x)   §6.2.2
Produces the integer resulting from type conversion of x, but fails if the conversion is not possible.

---

left(s1, i, s2)   §4.2.6
Produces a string of size i in which s1 is positioned at the left, with s2 used for padding at the right as necessary.

Defaults:
i   1
s2   " "

Errors:
101   i not **integer**
103   s1 or s2 not **string**
205   i < 0 or i > *maxshort*

---

list(i, x)   §5.1.1
Produces a list of size i in which each value is x.

Default:
i   0

Errors:
101   i not **integer**
205   i < 0 or i > *maxshort*

---

many(c, s, i, j)   §4.3.2, 4.3.3, 12.5
Produces the integer position in s after the longest initial sequence of characters in c in s[i:j], but fails if there is no such position.

Defaults:
s   &subject
i   &pos if s is defaulted, otherwise 1
j   0

Errors:
101   i or j not **integer**
103   s not **string**
104   c not **cset**

---

map(s1, s2, s3)   §4.2.6
Produces a string of size *s1 obtained by mapping characters of s1 that occur in s2 into corresponding characters in s3.

Defaults:
s2   string(&ucase)
s3   string(&lcase)

Errors:
103   s1, s2, or s3 not **string**
208   *s2 ~= *s3

---

match(s1, s2, i, j)   §4.3.1, 4.3.3, 12.5
Produces i + *s1 if s1 == s2[i+:*s1], but fails otherwise.

Defaults:
s2   &subject
i   &pos if s2 is defaulted, otherwise 1
j   0

Errors:
101   i or j not **integer**
103   s1 or s2 not **string**

---

move(i)   §12.3
Produces &subject[&pos:&pos + i] and assigns i + &pos to &pos, but fails
if i is out of range; reverses assignment if resumed.

Error:
101   i not **integer**

---

numeric(x)   §6.2.2
Produces an integer or real number resulting from the type conversion of x,
but fails if the conversion is not possible.

---

open(s1, s2)   §9.1, Appendix B
Produces a file resulting from opening s1 according to options s2, but fails
if the file cannot be opened according to options.

Default:
s2   "r"

Errors:
103   s1 or s2 not **string**
209   a character in s2 is not an option or is in an improper combination

---

pop(a)   §5.1.5
Produces the leftmost element of a and removes it from a, but fails if a is
empty; synonym for **get(a)**.

Error:
108   a not **list**

---

pos(i)   §12.4
Produces &pos if &pos = poseq(i, &subject), but fails otherwise.

Error:
101   i not **integer**

---

pull(a)   §5.1.5
Produces the rightmost element of **a** and removes it from **a**, but fails if **a** is empty.

Error:
108   **a** not **list**

---

push(a, x)   §5.1.5
Produces **a** and adds **x** to the left end of **a**.

Error:
108   **a** not **list**

---

put(a, x)   §5.1.5
Produces **a** and adds **x** to the right end of **a**.

Error:
108   **a** not **list**

---

read(f)   §1.2, 9.2
Produces a string consisting of the next line from **f**, but fails on end of file.

Default:
f   &input

Errors:
105   **f** not **file**
212   **f** not open for reading

---

reads(f, i)   §9.2
Produces a string consisting of next **i** characters from **f**, or the remaining characters of **f** if fewer remain on **f**, but fails on end of file.

Defaults:
f   &input
i   1

Errors:
101   **i** not **integer**
105   **f** not **file**
205   **i** $<= 0$ or **i** $>$ *maxshort*
212   **f** not open for reading

real(x)   §6.2.2

Produces a real number resulting from type conversion of x, but fails if the conversion is not possible.

---

repl(s, i)   §4.2.6

Produces a string consisting of i concatenations of s.

Errors:
101   i not **integer**
103   s not **string**
205   i < 0 or i > *maxshort*

---

reverse(s)   §4.2.6

Produces a string consisting of the reversal of s.

Error:
103   s not **string**

---

right(s1, i, s2)   §4.2.6

Produces a string of size i in which s1 is positioned at the right, with s2 used for padding at the left as necessary.

Defaults:
i   1
s2   " "

Errors:
101   i not **integer**
103   s1 or s2 not **string**
205   i < 0 or i > *maxshort*

---

sort(a)   §5.1.6, 6.4

Produces a list with values of a in sorted order.

Error:
115   a not **list** (see sort(t, i) following)

---

sort(t, i)   §5.1.6, 6.4

Produces a list of two-element lists of entries and assigned values from t; ordered by entries for i = 1, by values for i = 2.

Default:
i   1

Errors:
101   i not **integer**
115   t not **table** (see sort(a) preceding)
205   i not 1 or 2

---

stop(x1, x2, ..., xn)   §2.1, 9.3, Appendix C
Terminates program execution with exit status 1 after writing x1, x2, ...,
xn.

Default:
xi   ""

Errors:
109   xi not **string** or **file**
213   xi file not open for writing

---

string(x)   §6.2.2
Produces a string resulting from the type conversion of x, but fails if the
conversion is not possible.

---

system(s)   Appendix C
Produces the integer exit status resulting from calling the UNIX subroutine
system to execute s.

Errors:
103   s not **string**
210   *s > 256

---

tab(i)   §12.2, 12.3
Produces &subject[&pos:i] and assigns poseq(i, &subject) to &pos, but
fails if i is out of range; reverses assignment if resumed.

Error:
101   i not **integer**

---

table(x)   §5.2.1
Produces a table with an initial assigned value x.

trim(s, c)   §4.2.6

Produces a string consisting of the characters of s up to the trailing characters contained in c.

Default:

c   ' '

Errors:

103   s not **string**
104   c not **cset**

---

type(x)   §6.1

Produces a string consisting of the type of x.

---

upto(c, s, i, j)   §4.3.2, 4.3.3, 11.1, 11.6, 12.5

Generates the sequence of integer positions in s up to a character in c in s[i:j], but fails if there is no such position.

Defaults:

s   &subject
i   &pos if s is defaulted, otherwise 1
j   0

Errors:

101   i or j not **integer**
103   s not **string**
104   c not **cset**

---

write(x1, x2, ..., xn)   §1.1, 9.3

Writes x1, x2, ..., xn with a newline added and produces the last string written.

Default:

xi   ""

Errors:

109   xi not **string** or **file**
213   xi **file** not open for writing

---

writes(x1, x2, ..., xn)   §9.3

Writes x1, x2, ..., xn without a newline added and produces the last string written.

Default:
xi   """"

Errors:
109   xi not **string** or **file**
213   xi **file** not open for writing

Prefix operations. Prefix operations are distinguished from control structures that have prefix syntax by the fact that the arguments of prefix operations are evaluated before the operation is performed. A prefix operation fails if its argument fails. A prefix operation may generate a sequence of results if its argument generates a sequence of results.

The prefix operations are arranged in groups according to the expected type of the argument.

+**n**   §3.2
Produces the numeric value of **n**.

Error:
102   n not **integer** or **real**

−**n**   §3.2
Produces the negative of **n**.

Errors:
102   n not **integer** or **real**
203   integer overflow

?**i**   §3.5
Produces a number from a pseudo-random sequence: an integer in range 1 to i inclusive if i > 0, a real number in range 0.0 to 1.0 if i = 0.

Errors:
113   i not **integer** (see ?x following)
205   i < 0 or i > *maxshort*

~**c**   §4.1.3
Produces the cset complement of **c** with respect to **&cset**.

Error:
104   c not **cset**

=s   §12.5

Equivalent to **tab(match(s))**.

Error:

103   s not **string**

!f   §11.5.5

Produces a string consisting of the next line from **f**, but fails on end of file.

Errors:

116   f not **file** (see !x following)
212   f not open for reading

@e   §13.1.2

Produces the outcome of activating **e**.

Error:

118   e not **co-expression**

---

^e   §13.1.4

Produces a refreshed copy of **e**.

Error:

118   e not **co-expression**

∗x   §4.1.3, 4.2.2, 5.1.1, 5.2.1, 5.3, 13.1.3

Produces the size of **x** if **x** is a cset, string, list, table, record, or co-expression.

Error:

112   x not **cset, string, list, table, co-expression**, or a record type

---

!x   §11.5.5

Generates the sequence of elements of **x** if **x** is a string, list, table, or record, but fails if **x** is empty; produces a variable if **x** is a variable.

Errors:

103   x originally **string**, but type changed between resumptions
116   x not **string, list, table**, or a record type (see !f preceding)

?x   §4.2.4, 5.1.2, 5.2.1, 5.3
Produces a randomly selected element from x if x is a string, list, table, or record, but fails if x is empty; produces a variable if x is a variable.

Error:
113   x not **string, list, table,** or a record type (see **?i** preceding)

.x   §8.3
Produces the value of x.

/x   §6.3
Produces x if the value of x is the null value, but fails otherwise; produces a variable if x is a variable.

\x   §6.3
Produces x if the value of x is not the null value, but fails otherwise; produces a variable if x is a variable.

Infix operations. Infix operations are distinguished from control structures that have infix syntax by the fact that the arguments of infix operations are evaluated before the operation is performed. An infix operation fails if either of its arguments fails. An infix operation may generate a sequence of results if either of its arguments generates a sequence of results. The arguments of infix operations are not dereferenced until they both are evaluated.

The infix operations are arranged according to the expected types of their arguments. Augmented assignment operations are listed last.

---

n + m   §3.2
Produces the sum of n and m.

Errors:
102   n or m not **integer** or **real**
203   integer overflow
204   real overflow or underflow

---

n − m   §3.2
Produces the difference of n and m.

Errors:
102   n or m not **integer** or **real**
203   integer overflow
204   real overflow or underflow

---

n * m   §3.2
Produces the product of n and m.

Errors:
102   n or m not **integer** or **real**
203   integer overflow
204   real overflow or underflow

---

n / m   §3.2
Produces the quotient of n and m.

Errors:
102   n or m not **integer** or **real**
201   m = 0
204   real overflow or underflow

---

n % m   §3.2
Produces the remainder of n divided by m.

Errors:
102   n or m not **integer** or **real**
202   m = 0
204   real overflow or underflow

---

n ∧ m   §3.2
Produces n raised to the power m.

Errors:
102   n or m not **integer** or **real**
204   real overflow, underflow, or n = 0 and m <= 0
206   n < 0 and m real

---

n < m   §3.3
Produces the numeric value of m if n is numerically less than m, but fails otherwise.

Error:
102   n or m not **integer** or **real**

---

n <= m   §3.3
Produces the numeric value of m if n is numerically less than or equal to
m, but fails otherwise.

Error:
102   n or m not **integer** or **real**

---

n = m   §3.3
Produces the numeric value of m if n is numerically equal to m, but fails
otherwise.

Error:
102   n or m not **integer** or **real**

---

n >= m   §3.3
Produces the numeric value of m if n is numerically greater than or equal
to m, but fails otherwise.

Error:
102   n or m not **integer** or **real**

---

n > m   §3.3
Produces the numeric value of m if n is numerically greater than m, but
fails otherwise.

Error:
102   n or m not **integer** or **real**

---

n ~= m   §3.3
Produces the numeric value of m if n is not numerically equal to m, but
fails otherwise.

Error:
102   n or m not **integer** or **real**

---

c1 ++ c2   §4.1.3
Produces the cset union of c1 and c2.

Error:
104   c1 or c2 not **cset**

---

c1 —— c2   §4.1.3
Produces the cset difference of **c1** and **c2**.

Error:
104   **c1** or **c2** not **cset**

---

c1 ∗∗ c2   §4.1.3
Produces the cset intersection of **c1** and **c2**.

Error:
104   **c1** or **c2** not **cset**

---

s1 || s2   §4.2.3
Produces a string consisting of **s1** followed by **s2**.

Error:
103   **s1** or **s2** not **string**

---

s1 << s2   §4.2.5
Produces the string value of **s2** if **s1** is lexically less than **s2**, but fails otherwise.

Error:
103   **s1** or **s2** not **string**

---

s1 <<= s2   §4.2.5
Produces the string value of **s2** if **s1** is lexically less than or equal to **s2**, but fails otherwise.

Error:
103   **s1** or **s2** not **string**

---

s1 == s2   §4.2.5
Produces the string value of **s2** if **s1** is lexically equal to **s2**, but fails otherwise.

Error:
103   **s1** or **s2** not **string**

---

s1 >>= s2   §4.2.5
Produces the string value of **s2** if **s1** is lexically greater than or equal to **s2** but fails otherwise.

Error:
103   s1 or s2 not **string**

---

s1 >> s2   §4.2.5
Produces the string value of s2 if s1 is lexically greater than s2, but fails otherwise.

Error:
103   s1 or s2 not **string**

---

s1 ~== s2   §4.2.5
Produces the string value of s2 if s1 is not lexically equal to s2, but fails otherwise.

Error:
103   s1 or s2 not **string**

---

a1 ||| a2   §5.1.3
Produces a list containing the values of a1 followed by the values of a2.

Error:
108   a1 or a2 not **list**

---

x @ e   §13.4.1
Activates e, transmitting the value of x to it; produces the outcome of activating e.

Error:
118   e not **co-expression**

---

x := y   §1.1, 1.5
Assigns the value of y to x and produces the variable x.

Errors:
101   x is **&pos, &random**, or **&trace**, but y not **integer**
103   x is subscripted **string** or **&subject**, but y not **string**
111   x not a variable

---

x <- y   §11.8.2
Assigns the value of y to x and produces the variable x; reverses assignment if resumed.

Errors:

101	x is **&pos**, **&random**, or **&trace**, but y not **integer**
103	x is subscripted **string** or **&subject**, but y not **string**
111	x not a variable

---

x := y   §10.3

Exchanges the values of x and y and produces the variable x.

Errors:

101	x or y is **&pos**, **&random**, or **&trace**, but other argument not **integer**
103	x or y is subscripted **string** or **&subject**, but other argument not **string**
111	x or y not a variable

---

x <-> y   §11.8.2

Exchanges the values of x and y and produces the variable x; reverses exchange if resumed.

Errors:

101	x or y is **&pos**, **&random**, or **&trace**, but other argument not **integer**
103	x or y is subscripted **string** or **&subject**, but other argument not **string**
111	x or y not a variable

---

x === y   §10.1

Produces the value of y if x and y have the same value, but fails otherwise.

---

x ~=== y   §10.1

Produces the value of y if x and y do not have the same value, but fails otherwise.

---

x & y   §8.4

Produces y; produces a variable if y is a variable.

---

x . y   §5.3

Produces a variable for the y field of record x.

Errors:

| 107 | x not a record type |
| 207 | x does not have field y |

---

n +:= m   §3.2, 3.4

Assigns the sum of n and m to n and produces the variable n.

Errors:

102	n or m not **integer** or **real**
111	n not a variable
203	integer overflow
204	real overflow or underflow

---

n −:= m   §3.2, 3.4

Assigns the difference of n and m to n and produces the variable n.

Errors:

102	n or m not **integer** or **real**
111	n not a variable
203	integer overflow
204	real overflow or underflow

---

n *:= m   §3.2, 3.4

Assigns the product of n and m to n and produces the variable n.

Errors:

102	n or m not **integer** or **real**
111	n not a variable
203	integer overflow
204	real overflow and underflow

---

n /:= m   §3.2, 3.4

Assigns the quotient of n divided by m to n and produces the variable n.

Errors:

102	n or m not **integer** or **real**
111	n not a variable
201	m = 0
204	real underflow or underflow

---

n %:= m   §3.2, 3.4

Assigns the remainder of n divided by m to n and produces the variable n.

Errors:

102	n or m not **integer** or **real**
111	n not a variable
202	m = 0
204	real overflow or underflow

---

n ^:= m   §3.2, 3.4

Assigns n raised to the power m to n and produces the variable n.

Errors:

102   n or m not **integer** or **real**
111   n not a variable
204   real underflow, underflow, or n = 0 and m <= 0
206   n < 0 and m real

---

n <:= m   §3.3, 3.4

Assigns the numeric value of m to n if n is numerically less than m, but fails otherwise; produces the variable n.

Errors:

102   n or m not **integer** or **real**
111   n not a variable

---

n <=:= m   §3.3, 3.4

Assigns the numeric value of m to n if n is numerically less than or equal to m, but fails otherwise; produces the variable n.

Errors:

102   n or m not **integer** or **real**
111   n not a variable

---

n =:= m   §3.3, 3.4

Assigns the numeric value of m to n if n is numerically equal to m, but fails otherwise; produces the variable n.

Errors:

102   n or m not **integer** or **real**
111   n not a variable

---

n >=:= m   §3.3, 3.4

Assigns the numeric value of m to n if n is numerically greater than or equal to m, but fails otherwise; produces the variable n.

Errors:

102   n or m not **integer** or **real**
111   n not a variable

n >:= m   §3.3, 3.4

Assigns the numeric value of m to n if n is numerically greater than m, but fails otherwise; produces the variable n.

Errors:

102   n or m not **integer** or **real**

111   n not a variable

---

n ~=:= m   §3.3, 3.4

Assigns the numeric value of m to n if n is not numerically equal to m, but fails otherwise; produces the variable n.

Errors:

102   n or m not **integer** or **real**

111   n not a variable

---

c1 ++:= c2   §4.1.3, 4.1.4

Assigns the cset union of c1 and c2 to c1 and produces the variable c1.

Errors:

104   c1 or c2 not **cset**

111   c1 not a variable

---

c1 −−:= c2   §4.1.3, 4.1.4

Assigns the cset difference of c1 and c2 to c1 and produces the variable c1.

Errors:

104   c1 or c2 not **cset**

111   c1 not a variable

---

c1 **:= c2   §4.1.3, 4.1.4

Assigns the cset intersection of c1 and c2 to c1 and produces the variable c1.

Errors:

104   c1 or c2 not **cset**

111   c1 not a variable

---

s1 ||:= s2   §4.2.3

Assigns a string consisting of s1 followed by s2 to s1 and produces the variable s1.

Errors:
103   s1 or s2 not **string**
111   s1 not a variable

---

s1 <<:= s2   §4.2.5

Assigns the string value of s2 to s1 if s1 is lexically less than s2, but fails otherwise; produces the variable s1.

Errors:
103   s1 or s2 not **string**
111   s1 not a variable

---

s1 <<=:= s2   §4.2.5

Assigns the string value of s2 to s1 if s1 is lexically less than or equal to s2, but fails otherwise; produces the variable s1.

Errors:
103   s1 or s2 not **string**
111   s1 not a variable

---

s1 ==:= s2   §4.2.5

Assigns the string value of s2 to s1 if s1 is lexically equal to s2, but fails otherwise; produces the variable s1.

Errors:
103   s1 or s2 not **string**
111   s1 not a variable

---

s1 >>=:= s2   §4.2.5

Assigns the string value of s2 to s1 if s1 is lexically greater than or equal to s2, but fails otherwise; produces the variable s1.

Errors:
103   s1 or s2 not **string**
111   s1 not a variable

---

s1 >>:= s2   §4.2.5

Assigns the string value of s2 to s1 if s1 is lexically greater than s2, but fails otherwise; produces the variable s1.

Errors:
103   s1 or s2 not **string**
111   s1 not a variable

---

s1 ~==:= s2   §4.2.5

Assigns the string value of s2 to s1 if s1 is not lexically equal to s2, but fails otherwise; produces the variable s1.

Errors:
103   s1 or s2 not **string**
111   s1 not a variable

---

a1 |||:= a2   §5.1.3

Assigns to a1 a list consisting of the values of a1 followed by the values of a2 and produces the variable a1.

Errors:
108   a1 or a2 not **list**
111   a1 not a variable

---

x @:= e   §3.4, 13.4.1

Activates e, transmitting the value of x to it; assigns the value produced by activating e to x; produces the variable x.

Errors:
111   x not a variable
118   e not **co-expression**

---

x ===:= y   §3.4, 10.1

Assigns the value of y to x if x and y have the same value, but fails otherwise; produces the variable x.

Error:
111   x not a variable

---

x ~===:= y   §3.4, 10.1

Assigns the value of y to x if x and y do not have the same value, but fails otherwise; produces the variable x.

Error:
111   x not a variable

---

x &:= y   §3.4, 8.4

Assigns the value of y to x and produces the variable x.

Errors:

101   x is &pos, &random, or &trace, but y not **integer**
103   x is subscripted **string** or &subject, but y not **string**
111   x not a variable

Control structures.   The order of evaluation of arguments in control structures depends on the particular control structure. The term outcome in the following descriptions is used in its extended sense to apply to result sequences. Some portions of these control structures may be omitted; see Appendix A.

---

break *expr*   §2.1, 8.1
Exits from the enclosing loop and produces the outcome of *expr*.

---

case *expr* **of** { ... }   §2.2, 8.1
Produces the outcome of the **case** clause that is selected by the value of *expr*; *expr* is limited to at most one result.

---

create x   §13.1.1
Produces a co-expression for x.

---

every *expr₁* **do** *expr₂*   §11.3.1
Evaluates *expr₂* for each result produced by resuming *expr₁*; fails when the resumption of *expr₁* does not produce a result.

---

fail   §7.4
Returns from the current procedure, producing failure.

---

if *expr₁* **then** *expr₂* **else** *expr₃*   §1.3, 2.2, 8.1
Produces the outcome of *expr₂* if *expr₁* succeeds, otherwise the outcome of *expr₃*; *expr₁* is limited to at most one result.

---

next   §2.1
Transfers control to the beginning of the enclosing loop.

---

not *expr*   §2.1
Produces the null value if *expr* fails, but fails if *expr* succeeds.

---

repeat *expr*   §2.1
Evaluates *expr* repeatedly.

---

return *expr*   §7.4
Returns from the current procedure, producing the outcome of *expr*.

---

suspend *expr*   §11.7
Suspends from the current procedure, producing each result produced by resuming *expr*.

---

until *expr$_1$* **do** *expr$_2$*   §2.1
Evaluates *expr$_2$* each time *expr$_1$* fails; fails when *expr$_1$* succeeds.

---

while *expr$_1$* **do** *expr$_2$*   §1.3, 2.1, 8.1
Evaluates *expr$_2$* each time *expr$_1$* succeeds; fails when *expr$_1$* fails.

---

expr$_1$ | *expr$_2$*   §11.5.1
Generates the outcome for *expr$_1$*, followed by the outcome for *expr$_2$*.

|*expr*   §11.5.4
Generates the outcome for *expr* repeatedly, terminating if *expr* fails.

---

expr \ **i**   §11.5.3
Generates at most **i** results from the outcome for *expr*.

Error:
205   **i** < 0 or **i** > *maxshort*

---

s ? x   §12.1, 12.2
Establishes **s** as the subject of scanning and evaluates **x**; produces the outcome of **x**.

Error:
103   **s** not **string**

---

s ?:= x   §12.2
Establishes **s** as the subject of scanning and evaluates **x**; assigns the result of **x** to **s** and produces the variable **s**.

Errors:

103   s not **string** or s is subscripted **string** or &subject, but x not **string**
111   s not a variable

Keywords.

&ascii   §4.1.2

Produces a cset consisting of the 128 ASCII characters.

&clock   §10.7

Produces a string consisting of the current time of day.

&cset   §4.1.2

Produces a cset consisting of all 256 characters.

&date   §10.7

Produces a string consisting of the current date.

&dateline   §10.7

Produces a string consisting of the current date and time of day.

&errout   §9.1

Produces the standard error output file.

&fail   §8.1

Fails.

&host   §10.7

Produces a string that identifies the host computer.

&input   §9.1

Produces the standard input file.

&lcase   §4.1.2

Produces a cset consisting of the 26 lowercase letters.

&level   §10.6

Produces the integer level of the current procedure call.

&main   §13.4.1

Produces a co-expression for the initial call of main.

&null   §6.3

Produces the null value.

&output   §9.1

Produces the standard output file.

&pos   §12.4

Produces a variable whose value is the integer position of scanning in &subject.

&random   §3.5

Produces a variable whose value is the seed for the pseudo-random sequence.

&source   §13.4.1

Produces a co-expression for the activator of the current co-expression.

&subject   §12.4

Produces the variable whose value is the string being scanned.

&time   §10.7

Produces the integer number of milliseconds since beginning of program execution.

&trace   §10.5

Produces a variable whose value controls procedure tracing.

&ucase   §4.1.2

Produces a cset consisting of the 26 uppercase characters.

&version §10.7
Produces a string that identifies the version of Icon.

Other operations. Arguments in the following operations are evaluated from left to right before the operation is performed. The arguments are not dereferenced until all of them are evaluated. An operation fails if any one of its arguments fails. Any of these operations may generate a sequence of results if any of its arguments generates a sequence of results.

---

i to j by k §11.5.2
Produces the sequence of integers from i to j in increments of k.

Default:
k   1 if **by** clause is omitted

Errors:
101   i, j, or k not **integer**
211   k = 0

---

i(x1, x2, ..., xn) §8.4
Produces the outcome of xi, but fails if i is out of range; produces a variable if xi is a variable; i may be nonpositive.

Default:
i   −1

Error:
106   i not **integer** (see p(x1, x2, ..., xn) following)

---

p(x1, x2, ..., xn) §7.3, 8.2, 8.4, 11.7
Produces the outcome of applying p to x1, x2, ..., xn.

Errors:
106   p not **procedure** (see i(x1, x2, ..., xn) preceding)
117   p is **main**, but there is no main procedure

---

s[i] §4.2.4
Produces a one-character string consisting of the ith character of s, but fails if i is out of range; i may be nonpositive; produces a variable if s is a variable.

Errors:
101   i not **integer**
114   s not **string** (see t[x] and x[i] following)

---

s[i:j]   §4.2.4
Produces the substring of s between positions i and j, inclusive, but fails if a position is out of range; i and j may be nonpositive; produces a variable if s is a variable.

Errors:
101   i or j not **integer**
110   s not **string** (see a[i:j] following)

---

s[i+:j]   §4.2.4
Produces the substring of s between positions i and **poseq**(i, s) + j, but fails if a position is out of range; i may be nonpositive; produces a variable if s is a variable.

Errors:
101   i or j not **integer**
110   s not **string** (see a[i+:j] following)

---

s[i−:j]   §4.2.4
Produces the substring of s between positions i and **poseq**(i, s) − j; fails if a position is out of range; i may be nonpositive; produces a variable if s is variable.

Errors:
101   i or j not **integer**
110   s not **string** (see a[i−:j] following)

---

a[i:j]   §5.1.4
Produces the list consisting of the values of a between positions i and j, inclusive, but fails if a position is out of range; i and j may be nonpositive.

Errors:
101   i or j not **integer**
114   a not **list** (see s[i:j] preceding)

---

a[i+:j]   §5.1.4
Produces the list consisting of the values of a between i and **poseq**(i, a) + j; may be nonpositive; fails if a position is out of range.

Errors:
101   i or j not **integer**
114   a not **list** (see s[i+:j] preceding)

---

a[i—:j]   §5.1.4
Produces the list consisting of values of a between i and poseq(i, a) — j,
but fails if a position is out of range; i may be nonpositive.

Errors:
101   i or j not **integer**
114   a not **list** (see s[i—:j] preceding)

---

t[x]   §5.2.1
Produces the xth entry in t; produces a variable if t is variable.

Error:
114   t not **table** (see s[i] preceding and x[i] following)

---

x[i]   §5.1.2, 5.3
Produces the ith element of x if x is a list or record, but fails if i is out of
range; i may be nonpositive; produces a variable if x is a variable.

Errors:
101   i not **integer**
114   x not **list** or a record type (see s[i] and t[x] preceding)

[x1, x2, …, xn]   §5.1.1
Produces a list of the values x1, x2, …, xn.

F

SOLUTIONS TO
SELECTED EXERCISES

The following solutions use only those features of Icon that are described up to
the point of the corresponding exercise. Better solutions can be formulated in
some cases by using additional features.

Exercise 1.1:

```
procedure locate(s)
    count := 0
    lineno := 0
    while line := read() do {
        lineno := lineno + 1
        if find(s, line) then {
            write(lineno, ": ", line)
            count := count + 1
            }
        }
    if count > 0 then return count else fail
end
```

Exercise 2.1:

```
procedure main()
    while line := read()
    write(line)
end
```

Exercise 2.2:

```
procedure main()
    while write(read(line)) do
        if not read() then break
end
```

Exercise 2.3:

```
procedure first(i)
    count := 0
    while line := read() do {
        count := count + 1
        if count = i then break
        write(line)
        }
    if count < i then fail
    else return line
end
```

Exercise 2.7:

```
procedure exor(s1, s2)
    count := 0
    while line := read() do
        if find(s1, line) then {
            if not find(s2, line) then count := count + 1
            }
        else if find(s2, line) then count := count + 1
    return count
end
```

The braces around the inner **if-then** expression are needed to prevent the subsequent **else** clause from grouping incorrectly.

Exercise 3.1b:

```
procedure main()
   sum := 0.0
   count := 0
   while sum +:= read() do
      count +:= 1
   write(sum / count)
end
```

Exercise 3.3:

```
procedure fact(i)
   j := 1
   while i > 0 do {
      j *:= i
      i -:= 1
      }
   return j
end
```

Note the use of augmented assignment in the numerical computation operations.

Exercise 4.1:

```
procedure main()
   chars := ''
   while chars ++:= read()
   write(*chars)
end
```

Exercise 4.3:

In the following procedure, a negative value of i is interpreted to mean rotation
to the right.

```
procedure rotate(s, i)
   if i <= 0 then i +:= *s
   return s[i + 1:0] || s[1:i + 1]
end
```

Exercise 4.7:

```
procedure delete(s, c)
    while s[upto(c, s)] := ""
    return s
end
```

A more efficient solution can be formulated using many and range restriction:

```
procedure delete(s, c)
    while i := upto(c, s) do
        s[i:many(c, s, i)] := ""
    return s
end
```

Exercise 4.10:

```
procedure main()
    wchar := &lcase ++ &ucase ++ '\'-'
    while line := read() do {
        i := 1
        dashes := repl(" ", *line)
        while j := upto(wchar, line, i) do {
            i := many(wchar, line, j)
            dashes[i:j] := repl("-", i - j)
        }
        write(line)
        write(dashes)
    }
end
```

Exercise 5.2:

```
procedure main()
    lines := []
    while push(lines, read())
    while write(get(lines))
end
```

This method is impractical for large files, since the entire file must be stored before any line is written.

Exercise 5.5:

```
procedure main()
   a := sort(wordlengths())          # get sorted list
   i := 0
   while pair := a[i +:= 1] do
      write(left(pair[1] || ":", 4), right(pair[2], 6))
end

procedure wordlengths()
   wchar := &lcase ++ &ucase ++ '\'-'
   lengths := table(0)
   while line := read() do {
      i := 1
      while j := upto(wchar, line, i) do {
         i := many(wchar, line, j)
         lengths[*line[i:j]] +:= 1  # increment count
         }
      }
   return lengths
end
```

Exercise 5.6:

```
procedure strcpx(s)
   i := upto('+-', s, 2)
   return complex(s[1:i], s[i:-1])
end
```

Exercise 5.7:

```
procedure cpxstr(x)
   if x.ipart < 0 then return x.rpart || x.ipart || "i"
   else return x.rpart || "+" || x.ipart || "i"
end
```

Exercise 5.8:

```
procedure cpxadd(x1, x2)
   return complex(x1.rpart + x2.rpart, x1.ipart + x2.ipart)
end
```

```
procedure cpxsub(x1, x2)
    return complex(x1.rpart − x2.rpart, x1.ipart − x2.ipart)
end

procedure cpxmul(x1, x2)
    return complex(x1.rpart * x2.rpart − x1.ipart * x2.ipart,
        x1.rpart * x2.ipart + x1.ipart * x2.rpart)
end

procedure cpxdiv(x1, x2)
    denom := x2.rpart ∧ 2 + x2.ipart ∧ 2
    return complex((x1.rpart * x2.rpart + x1.ipart * x2.ipart)
        / denom, (x1.ipart * x2.rpart − x1.rpart * x2.ipart) /
        denom)
end
```

Exercise 6.2:

```
procedure hexcvt(s)
    return integer("16r" || s)
end
```

Exercise 7.3:

```
procedure acker(i, j)
    if i = 0 then return j + 1
    if j = 0 then return acker(i − 1,1)
    return acker(i − 1, acker(i, j − 1))
end
```

Exercise 7.6:

In order to tabulate Ackermann's function, the pair of arguments must be saved. This is accomplished in the following procedure by forming a string for the argument pair.

```
procedure acker(i, j)
    local args, k
    static ackermem
    initial ackermem := table()
    args := i || "," || j
    if k := \ackermem[args] then return k
    if i = 0 then return ackermem[args] := j + 1
    if j = 0 then return ackermem[args] := acker(i − 1,1)
    return ackermem[args] := acker(i − 1, acker(i, j − 1))
end
```

Exercise 8.3:

```
procedure both(s1, s2)
    local line, count
    count := 0
    while line := read() do
        if (find(s1, line), find(s2, line)) then count +:= 1
    return count
end
```

Exercise 9.2:

```
procedure main()
    while writes(reads(, 1000))
end
```

This procedure copies any file, not just binary files. The value of 1,000 was chosen arbitrarily.

Exercise 10.1: The procedure **shuffle(s)** in §10.3 works for lists as well as strings.

Exercise 10.2:

```
procedure main()
   local chars, charlist, i, pair
   chars := table(0)
   while chars[reads()] +:= 1
   charlist := sort(chars)
   i := 0
   while pair := charlist[i +:= 1] do
       write(left(image(pair[1]), 6), right(pair[2], 6))
end
```

Exercise 10.4:

In order to keep track of the depth of recursion in Ackermann's function, some method is needed to differentiate recursive calls of Ackermann's function from other calls. It is not safe to use **&level**, since Ackermann's function might be called from any level. The identifier **level** is used here to keep the computation of the level local to the function.

```
procedure ackertrace(i, j)
   static level
   local result
   initial level := 0
   write(repl("x", level +:= 1))
   if i = 0 then result := j + 1
   else if j = 0 then result := ackertrace(i − 1, 1)
   else result := ackertrace(i − 1, ackertrace(i, j − 1))
   level −:= 1
   return result
end
```

Exercise 10.6:

```
procedure pause(i)
   local j
   j := &time
   while (&time − j) < i
   return
end
```

Exercise 11.1:

```
procedure main()
   vowel := 'aeiouAEOIU'
   count := 0
   while line := read() do
       every upto(vowel, line) do count +:= 1
   write(count)
end
```

Exercise 11.4:

```
(i := 2) | |(i +:= 2)
```

Exercise 11.5:

```
procedure genpos(a, x)
   local i
   every i := 1 to *a do
      if a[i] === x then suspend i
end
```

Exercise 11.7:

```
procedure qseq()
   local i, qmem
   qmem := table()
   suspend qmem[1 | 2] := 1
   i := 2
   repeat suspend qmem[i +:= 1] :=
      qmem[i − qmem[i − 1]] + qmem[i − qmem[i − 2]]
end
```

Exercise 11.9:

```
(i := 1, j := 1) | |((i := i + j) :=: j)
```

Exercise 11.10:

```
procedure allbal(c, s)
   local i
   every i := 1 to (*s - 1) do
      suspend "" ~== s[i:bal(c, , , s, i)]
end
```

Exercise 12.1:

```
procedure space(s)
   local s1
   s1 := ""
   s ? while s1 ||:= move(1) || " "
   return s1
end
```

Exercise 12.2:

```
procedure enrepl(s)
   local c, s1
   s1 := ""
   s ? while c := move(1) do {
      i := 1 + (*tab(many(c)) | 0)
      if i > 4 then s1 ||:= c || "(" || i || ")"
      else s1 ||:= repl(c, i)
      }
   return s1
end
```

```
procedure derepl(s)
   local c, s1
   s1 := ""
   s ? {
      while s1 ||:= tab(upto('(') − 1) do {
         c := move(1)
         move(1)
         s1 ||:= repl(c, tab(upto(')')')))
         move(1)
         }
      s1 ||:= tab(0)
      }
   return s1
end
```

Exercise 12.5:

```
procedure allbal(c, s)
   s ? repeat {
      suspend "" ~== tab(bal(c))
      move(1) | break
      }
end
```

Exercise 13.3:

```
procedure Repalt(e)
   local x
   repeat {
     while x := @e do suspend x
     if *e = 0 then fail
     e := ^e
     }
end
```

Exercise 13.5:

```
procedure Seqimage(e)
   local s1
   s1 := ""
   while s1 ||:= ", " || image(@e)
   return "{" || s1[3:0] || "}" | "{}"
end
```

Exercise 13.7:

In order to handle a finite input stream, there must be checks for failure when any source runs out. In A this occurs when an end of file is encountered by reads. A corresponding failure occurs in B when A fails. The necessary changes occur where in is activated in compact and by replacing the **repeat** loop in main by a **while** loop.

```
global A, B

procedure main()
   A := create compact("a", "b", create |reads(), B)
   B := create compact("b", "c", A, &main)
   while writes(@B)
end

procedure compact(s1, s2, in, out)
   local s
   repeat {
      s := @in | fail
      if s == s1 then {
         s := @in | {
            out @ s
            fail
            }
         if s == s1 then s := s2
         else s1 @ out
         }
      s @ out
      }
end
```

Exercise 13.8:

If a list is used for the filters, it need not be global. Furthermore, the filters can be placed in the list with "forward references", since the list references are not evaluated until the co-expressions are activated.

```
procedure main()
   local a
   a := list(4)
   a[1] := create compact("a", "b", create |reads(), a[2])
   a[2] := create compact("b", "c", a[1], a[3])
   a[3] := create compact("c", "d", a[2], a[4])
   a[4] := create compact("d", "e", a[3], &main)
   while writes(@a[4])
end
```

The procedure compact can be used without modification.

Exercise 14.1:

```
procedure gensubstr(s)
   local i
   suspend s[(i := 1 to *s):((i + 1) to (*s + 1))]
end
```

Exercise 14.5:

Since it is easier to print the board by rows instead of by columns, the following solution assigns a queen to each row instead of to each column.

```
procedure main()
   every print([q(1), q(2), q(3), q(4), q(5), q(6), q(7), q(8)])
end

procedure q(r)
   suspend place(1 to 8, r)
end
```

```
procedure place(c, r)
   static up, down, col
   initial {
      up := list(15, 0)
      down := list(15, 0)
      col := list(8, 0)
      }
   if col[c] = up[8 + r − c] = down[r + c − 1] = 0
   then suspend col[c] <− up[8 + r − c] <−
      down[r + c − 1] <− c
end

procedure print(a)
   static line, bar
   initial {
      line := repl("+−", 8) || "+"
      bar := repl("| ", 8) || "|"
      }
   every bar[!a*2] <− "Q" do {
      write(line)
      write(bar)
      }
      write(line, "\n\n")
   return
end
```

Note that reversible assignment is used in print to place the queen temporarily in the correct square.

Exercise 15.2:

```
procedure allbal(c, s)
   s ? suspend arb() & ("" ~== tab(bal(c)))
end
```

Exercise 15.3:

```
procedure limit(p, i)
   local j
   j := &pos
   suspend p() \ i
   &pos := j
end
```

Exercise 15.6:

```
procedure main()
   while writes(line := read()) do
      if line ? (ABCD("", "", "", "") & pos(0))
      then write(" accepted")
      else write(" rejected")
end

procedure ABCD(A, B, C, D)
   suspend (=A || =B || =C || =D) |
      (="a" || ABCD(A, "b" || B, C || "c", D) || ="d")
end
```

Exercise 16.1:

```
procedure depth(ltree)
   local count
   count := 0
   every count <:= 1 + depth(ltree[2 to *ltree])
   return count
end
```

Exercise 16.3:

```
procedure tcopy(ltree)
   local a
   a := [ltree[1]]
   every put(a, tcopy(ltree[2 to *ltree]))
   return a
end
```

Exercise 16.4:

```
record bnode(value, left, right)

procedure btree(stree)
   local x
   stree ? if x := bnode(tab(upto('('))) then {
      move(1)
      x.left := btree(tab(bal(', ')))
      move(1)
      x.right := btree(tab(bal(')')))
      }
      else x := bnode(tab(0))
   return x
end

procedure stree(btree)
   local s
   if /btree.left then return btree.value
   s := btree.value || "(" ||
      stree(btree.left) || "," || stree(btree.right) || ")"
   return s
end
```

Exercise 17.4:

```
procedure uscore(s)
   static labels, trans, max
   initial {
      labels := "1"
      trans := "_\b1"
      max := *labels
      trans := uscore(string(&cset -- '\b_'))
      labels := string(&cset -- '\b_')
      max := *labels
      }
   if *s <= max then
      return map(left(trans, 3 * *s), left(labels, *s), s)
   else return uscore(left(s, *s - max)) ||
      map(trans, labels, right(s, max))
end
```

Exercise 17.5:

```
procedure boldface(s)
   local c
   static labels, trans, max
   initial {
      labels := "1"
      trans := "1\b1\b1\b1\b1"
      max := *labels
      trans := boldface(string(&cset -- '\b'))
      labels := string(&cset -- '\b')
      max := *labels
      }
   if *s <= max then
      return map(left(trans, 9 * *s), left(labels, *s), s)
   else return boldface(left(s, *s - max)) ||
      map(trans, labels, right(s, max))
end
```

Exercise 18.2:

The following procedure does not allow for a leading sign, but it does reject the empty string. Note that the procedure **large** in §18.2.2 can be adapted to verify the correctness of the input by failing if conversion to **integer** fails.

```
procedure large(s)
   if many('0123456789', s) = *s + 1 then return s
   else fail
end
```

Exercise 18.3:

```
procedure cdigit(s)
   local s1
   s1 := ""
   s ? {
      &pos := 0
      while s1 := "," || move(-3) || s1
      if pos(1) then s1 := s1[2:0]
      else s1 := tab(1) || s1
      }
   return s1
end
```

An interesting alternative solution can be formulated using mapping techniques.

Exercise 18.9:

```
procedure palseq(i)
   local j
   j := reverse(i)
   repeat {
      i := add(i, j)
      j := reverse(i)
      if i == j then return i
      else suspend i
      }
end
```

The procedure **add** is from §18.2.1.

Exercise 19.1:

```
procedure main()
   while write(infix(read()))
end

procedure infix(exp)
   return (exp ? form(tab(upto('(')), move(1) & tab(bal(',')),
      move(1) & tab(−1))) | exp
end

procedure form(op, arg1, arg2)
   return "(" || infix(arg1) || op || infix(arg2) || ")"
end
```

Exercise 19.2:

The following simplification procedures for multiplication and subtraction are typical.

```
procedure mpy(arg1, arg2)
   return {
      (integer(arg1) * integer(arg2)) |
      (if (arg1 | arg2) == "0" then "0") |
      (if arg1 == arg2 then symop(arg2, "∧", "2")) |
      (if arg1 == "1" then arg2) |
      (if arg2 == "1" then arg1) |
      symop(arg1, "*", arg2)
      }
end
```

```
procedure sub(arg1, arg2)
    local i
    if i := integer(arg1) − integer(arg2) then
        if i >= 0 then return i else return symop("0", "−", −i)
    return {
        (if arg2 == "0" then arg1) |
        (if arg1 == arg2 then "0") |
        symop(arg1, "−", arg2)
        }
end
```

Note that negative integers are kept in symbolic form. If this were not done, the minus sign for a negative integer would appear as a prefix operation. An alternative approach is to add support for functional notation as suggested in Exercise 19.4 and to represent negative integers in this notation.

Exercise 19.4:

```
procedure fix(exp)
    while exp ?:= 2(="("", tab(bal(')'))), pos(−1))
    return lassoc(exp, '+−' | '*/') | rassoc(exp, '∧') |
        func(exp) | exp
end

procedure func(exp)
    return exp ? tab(upto('(') + 1) || fix(tab(−1)) || tab(0)
end
```

Exercise 19.6:

```
procedure form(arg1, op, arg2)
    arg1 := fix(arg1)
    arg2 := fix(arg2)
    return case op of {
        "+"     :   add(arg1, arg2)
        "−"     :   sub(arg1, arg2)
        "*"     :   mpy(arg1, arg2)
        "/"     :   div(arg1, arg2)
        "~"     :   drv(arg1, arg2)
        default :   symop(arg1, op, arg2)
        }
end
```

Exercise 20.2:

If the value assigned to count is zero, no string is generated. On the other hand, if the value assigned to count is negative or not convertible to an integer, a run-time error occurs in the limitation control structure. Furthermore, the string scanning expression may fail if the generation specification is syntactically incorrect, leaving the value of goal or count unchanged. An improved version of the procedure is

```
procedure generate(line)
    local goal, count
    if line ? {
        ="<" &
        goal := tab(upto('>')) &
        move(1) &
        count := (0 <= integer(tab(0)))
        }
    then {
        every write(gener(goal)) \ count
        return
        }
    else fail
end
```

Exercise 20.3:

With the modified version of generate given in the solution to Exercise 20.2, an input line that is neither a valid definition nor a valid generation specification is ignored. A diagnostic message can be produced by modifying the main procedure as follows:

```
procedure main()
    local line
    defs := table()
    while line := read() do
        (define | generate | diagnose)(line)
end

procedure diagnose(s)
    write("**** erroneous input: ", s)
    return
end
```

Exercise 20.5:

The easiest way to allow the characters <, >, and | to be specified is to provide predefined nonterminal symbols for them. The necessary lists can then be constructed in the main procedure:

```
procedure main()
    local line
    defs := table()
    defs["vbar"] := [["|"]]
    defs["left"] := [["<"]]
    defs["right"] := [[">"]]
       .
       .
       .
end
```

Now <vbar> produces |, and so forth.

REFERENCES

1. GRISWOLD, R. E., J. F. POAGE, and I. P. POLONSKY, *The SNOBOL4 Programming Language*, 2nd ed. Englewood Cliffs, N. J.: Prentice-Hall, Inc., 1971.

2. VAN WIJNGAARDEN, A., et al, "Revised Report on the Algorithmic Language Algol 68", *Acta Informatica*, 5, no. 1 (1975), 1-236.

3. WIRTH, N., "The Programming Language Pascal", *Acta Informatica*, 1, no. 1 (1971), 35-63.

4. INTERNATIONAL BUSINESS MACHINES CORPORATION, *IBM System/360 PL/I Language Reference Manual*. Form C28-8201-2, 1969.

5. LISKOV, B., et al., *CLU Reference Manual*. New York: Springer-Verlag, 1981.

6. KERNIGHAN, BRIAN W. and DENNIS M. RITCHIE, *The C Programming Language*. Englewood Cliffs, N. J.: Prentice-Hall, Inc., 1978.

7. BELL TELEPHONE LABORATORIES, INCORPORATED, *UNIX Programmer's Manual, Seventh Edition*, Murray Hill, N. J., 1979.

8. GRISWOLD, R. E., *Differences between Versions 2 and 5 of Icon*. Technical report, Department of Computer Science, The University of Arizona, Tucson, 1983.

9. BIRD, R. S., "Tabulation Techniques for Recursive Programs", *Computer Surveys*, 12, no. 4 (1980), 403-417.

10. HOFSTADTER, D. R., *Gödel, Escher, Bach: An Eternal Golden Braid.* New York: Basic Books, 1979.

11. DURSTENFELD, R., "Algorithm 235; Random Permutation", *Communications of the ACM*, 7, no. 7 (1964), 420.

12. GRUNE, D., "A View of Coroutines", *SIGPLAN Notices*, 12, no. 7 (1977), 75-81.

13. DAHL, O.-J., E. W. DIJKSTRA, and C. A. R. HOARE, *Structured Programming.* New York: Academic Press, 1972.

14. GIMPEL, J. F., *Algorithms in SNOBOL4.* New York: John Wiley & Sons, 1976.

15. WETHERELL, C. S., "Probabilistic Languages: A Review and Some Open Questions", *Computer Surveys*, 12, no. 4 (1980), pp. 361-379.

16. COUTANT, C. A. and S. B. WAMPLER, *A Tour through the C Implementation of Icon; Version 5.* Technical Report TR 81-11a, Department of Computer Science, The University of Arizona, Tucson, 1981.

INDEX

abs(n), 21, 252
Absolute value, 21, 252
Activating co-expressions, 133-134, 262
Addition, 20
Additive operations, 20, 223, 226
Algebra, symbolic, 201-209
Alphabetical comparison, 33-34, 54, 55, 63, 65, 67, 98, 266, 271-273
Alphabetical order, 33-34, 54, 55, 63, 65, 67, 98, 266, 271-273
Alternation expressions, 109-110, 137, 143, 144, 162, 163, 205, 223, 227, 233, 234, 275
distributivity of, 143-144
Alternation, repeated, 112, 233, 234, 275
Ambiguous failure, 30
any(c, s, i, j), 40, 41, 128, 252
Argument evaluation, 82-83, 107-108, 142, 151, 161
Argument transmission, 73
Arguments, 5, 8, 10, 11, 21, 33, 65, 72, 73, 74, 82-83, 84, 86, 107-108, 119, 128, 142, 151, 161, 241, 245, 251, 252, 261, 263, 274, 278
extra, 83
null-valued, 65, 83, 251
omitted, 34, 37, 65, 83, 128, 251-260
trailing, 83, 128
Arithmetic, 20-21, 263-265
integer, 20-21
mixed-mode, 19, 21
real, 20-21

Arrays, 51-52
ASCII, 24, 25, 33, 142, 188, 232, 234-237, 276
Assignment operations, 3, 80, 96-97, 223, 227-228, 267-274
Assignment, reversible, 120
Associativity, 9, 20, 21, 26, 28, 33, 59, 96, 109, 111, 120, 124, 138, 201, 202, 203, 204, 206, 208, 222
Augmented assignment operations, 22, 27, 29, 34, 52, 56, 124, 190, 263, 268-274, 275
Auxiliary identifiers, 27, 105, 107, 111, 123, 130, 141, 157, 158

Backslashes, 25, 28, 232
Backtracking, 119-120, 126, 148-153, 159, 164
control, 119-120
data, 120
bal(c1, c2, c3, s, i, j), 42-44, 115, 128, 252
Balanced strings, 42, 43, 44, 115, 128, 172, 202, 252
Braces, use of, 7, 16, 224, 248
Break expressions, 13, 14, 81-82, 106, 130, 223, 228, 274
Built-in csets, 25

C programming language, 242-243
Case clauses, 16, 17, 64, 95, 229, 274
Case control expressions, 16, 119

Case expressions, 16-17, 77, 81, 95, 223, 229, 274
center(s1, i, s2), 36, 253
Chaotic sequence, 79, 121
Character codes, 24, 33, 232, 234-237
Character graphics, 24, 25, 234
Character sets, 24-27
Characters, 24-27, 33, 231-232, 234-237
close(f), 90, 253
Closing files, 90, 253
Co-expression data type, 61, 62, 67
Co-expressions, 132-139
  activating, 133-134, 262
  creating, 132-133, 223, 228, 274
  refreshing, 134-135, 262
  size of, 134, 262
  using as coroutines, 138-139
Collating sequence, 24, 33
Command lines, 241, 245
Commands, UNIX, 240, 242, 245
Comments, 3, 4, 233
Comparing values, 94-95
Comparison operations, 226
  alphabetical, 33-34, 54, 55, 63, 65, 67, 98, 266-267, 271-273
  lexical, 33-34, 54, 55, 63, 65, 67, 98, 266-267, 271-273
  numerical, 21-22, 264-265
  value, 94-95, 268
Compiler, Icon, 240, 242-243, 244-245, 248
Compound expressions, 7, 119, 223, 224
Concatenation, lists, 52, 267
Concatenation, strings, 28-29, 36, 266
Concatenation operations, 223, 226, 266, 267
Conditional operations, 4-5, 6, 12, 21-22, 33, 94-95
Conjunction operations, 85-86, 124, 127, 156, 159, 223, 228
Continuation, of quoted literals, 234
Control backtracking, 119-120
Control characters, 232
Control expressions, 12-13, 119
Control structures, 6, 12-17, 274-276
  alternation expressions, 109-110, 137, 143, 144, 162, 163, 205, 223, 227, 233, 234, 275
  break expressions, 13, 14, 81-82, 106, 130, 223, 228, 274
  case expressions, 16-17, 77, 81, 95, 223, 229, 274
  create expressions, 132-133, 223, 228, 274
  every-do expressions, 104-106, 117, 229, 274
  fail expressions, 8, 73, 116, 130, 143, 228, 274

Control structures *(cont.)*:
  if-then-else expressions, 6, 15, 16, 81, 109, 119, 223, 229, 274
  limitation expressions, 111, 138, 144, 223, 225, 275
  next expressions, 13, 106, 130, 223, 228, 274
  not expressions, 15, 225, 274
  repeat expressions, 14, 229, 275
  repeated alternation expressions, 112, 233, 234, 275
  return expressions, 7, 73-74, 82, 84, 116, 130, 143, 223, 228, 275
  scanning expressions, 123-130, 223, 228, 275
  suspend expressions, 116-118, 129, 130, 145, 228, 275
  until-do expressions, 12, 13, 229, 275
  while-do expressions, 6, 12, 13, 125, 137, 229, 275
Conversion, data type, 62-65, 251
  automatic,, 7, 63-64
  cset, 63, 64, 65
  explicit, 63, 64-65
  implicit, 7, 63-64
  integer, 63, 65
  numeric, 63, 64, 65
  real, 64
  string, 26-27, 63, 64, 65
copy(x), 96, 253
Copying structures, 55, 96
Copying values, 96
Coroutine programming, 138-139
Create expressions, 132-133, 223, 228, 274
Cset data type, 61, 62, 67
Cset literals, 25, 231
cset(x), 64, 65, 253
Csets, 25-27
Csets, built-in, 25
Csets, operations on, 26, 261, 265-266

Dags, 174-176
Data backtracking, 120
Data type determination, 61-62
Data types, 61-67
  co-expression, 61, 62, 67
  cset, 61, 62, 67
  file, 61, 62, 67
  integer, 61, 62, 67
  list, 61, 62, 67
  null, 61, 62, 65, 67
  procedure, 61-62, 67
  real, 61, 62, 67

Data types *(cont.)*:
  record, 66
  string, 61, 62, 67
  table, 61, 62, 67
Data types, conversion of, 62-65, 251
  automatic, 7, 63-64
  cset, 63, 64, 65
  explicit, 63, 64-65
  implicit, 7, 63-64
  integer, 63, 65
  numeric, 63, 64, 65
  string, 26-27, 63, 64, 65
Data types, notation, 10-11
Date, 101
Debugging, 61, 97, 99
Decimal literals, 231
Decimal notation, 19, 231
Declarations, 1, 58, 59, 61, 68-71, 221-222
  dynamic, 69, 222
  external, 222, 242-243
  global, 69-70, 221, 222
  local, 68-71, 222
  procedure, 68-69, 221, 222
  record, 58-59, 61, 62, 221, 222
  static, 70, 71, 72, 75, 116, 222
Default clauses, 17, 229
Defaults, 251-261, 278
  null-valued arguments, 65, 83, 251
  omitted arguments, 34, 37, 65, 83, 128, 251-260
Deques, 54
Dereferencing, 84-85, 263
Differentiation, symbolic, 207-209
Digit literals, 19, 231
Digraphs, 174-179
display(i, f), 100-101, 253
Division, 20, 21
Dynamic declarations, 69, 222

Efficiency, 36, 64, 75, 91, 164, 183, 185, 186, 209
Element generation, 112-114, 262
Elements, 112-114
Empty lists, 49
Empty string, 28
Empty tables, 57
Encapsulation, procedural, 145, 160, 164
Ends of file, 4, 90, 91
Environment variables, 244
Environmental information, 101-102
Equivalent characters, 231, 232

Error messages, 10, 21, 64, 65, 88, 92, 164, 243, 245, 246-250
Error output, standard, 88, 93, 99, 100
Error termination, 10, 21, 64, 65, 92, 143, 164, 249-250
Errors, 10, 21, 30, 64, 65, 70, 72, 92, 123, 125, 130, 164, 246-250, 251-276, 278-280
  capacity exceeded, 250
  during linking, 248
  during loading, 248
  during program execution, 249-250, 251-276, 278-280
  during translation, 246-248
  syntactic, 246-248
Escape sequences, 25, 28, 232
Evaluation, goal-directed, 104, 106-107, 116, 119, 132, 135, 141, 204
  order of, 107-108
Evaluation, mutual, 85-87, 127, 278
Evaluation of arguments, 82-83, 107-108, 142, 151, 161
Evaluation of expressions, 80-87, 104
  outcome of, 80-82, 104
Evaluation, symbolic, 206-209
Every-do expressions, 104-106, 117, 229, 274
Exchange, reversible, 120
Exchanging values, 96-97, 120
Exit status, 245, 253, 259
exit(i), 245, 253
Exponent literals, 19, 231
Exponent notation, 19, 231
Exponentiation operations, 20, 223, 225
Expressions, 8-10, 11, 222-232
  alternation, 109-110, 137, 143, 144, 162, 163, 205, 223, 227, 233, 234, 275
  compound, 7, 119, 223, 224
  condensing of, 142-144
  evaluation of, 80-87, 104
  parenthesized, 9, 223
  resumption of, 108, 116, 117, 118, 119, 120, 125, 126, 129, 130, 132, 133, 134, 136, 137, 142, 145, 146, 151, 153, 159, 160, 256, 259, 262, 267, 268, 274, 275
  syntax of, 8-10, 222-234
External declarations, 222, 242-243
External procedures, 222, 242-243

Fail expressions, 8, 73, 116, 130, 143, 228, 274
Failure, 4-5
  ambiguous, 30
Fibonacci sequence, 74, 75, 79, 99, 111, 117,

Fibonacci sequence *(cont.):*
  118, 121, 146, 199
Field names, 58-60, 70, 224, 229
Field references, 59-60, 223, 224
File data type, 61, 62, 67
File names, 88-89, 239, 240-243
File option specifications, 89, 239
Files, 88-90, 239, 240
  closing, 90, 253
  opening, 89-90, 256
find(s1, s2, i, j), 5, 39, 41, 45, 103, 106, 115,
  128, 254
Floating-point representation, 19, 238
Function calls, 2, 82-83
Functions, 2, 68, 252-261
  abs(n), 21, 252
  any(c, s, i, j), 40, 41, 128, 252
  bal(c1, c2, c3, s, i, j), 42-44, 115, 128, 252
  center(s1, i, s2), 36, 253
  close(f), 90, 253
  copy(x), 96, 253
  cset(x), 64, 65, 253
  display(i, f), 100-101, 253
  exit(i), 245, 253
  find(s1, s2, i, j), 5, 39, 41, 45, 103, 106, 115,
    128, 254
  get(a), 53, 54, 254
  image(x), 97-99, 101, 180, 254
  integer(x), 64-65, 254
  left(s1, i, s2), 35-36, 194, 254
  list(i, x), 49, 255
  many(c, s, i, j), 41-42, 128, 179, 255
  map(s1, s2, s3), 37-38, 181-188, 255
  match(s1, s2, i, j), 5, 39-40, 41, 128, 255
  move(i), 126, 156, 158, 160, 169, 256
  numeric(x), 64, 65, 256
  open(s1, s2), 89-90, 256
  pop(a), 54, 256
  pos(i), 127, 202, 256
  pull(a), 54, 257
  push(a, x), 54, 257
  put(a, x), 53, 54, 257
  read(f), 4, 5, 90, 239, 257
  reads(f, i), 91, 239, 257
  real(x), 64, 258
  repl(s, i), 36, 258
  reverse(s), 36, 258
  right(s1, i, s2), 34-35, 194, 195, 258
  sort(a), 54-55, 258
  sort(t, i), 57-58, 258
  stop(x1, x2,..., xn), 14, 93, 245, 259
  string(x), 64, 65, 113, 259
  system(s), 240, 242, 245

Functions *(cont.):*
  tab(i), 123, 126, 128, 156, 158, 159, 160, 259
  table(x), 56, 259
  trim(s, c), 37, 260
  type(x), 61-62, 97, 260
  upto(c, s, i, j), 40-41, 42, 44, 103, 115, 123,
    128, 179, 260
  write(x1, x2,..., xn), 1, 74, 91-92, 158, 260
  writes(x1, x2,..., xn), 92-93, 260-261
Functions, matching, 126-128, 158
Functions, record constructor, 59
Functions, string-analysis, 38-45, 128
Functions, string-valued, 34-45

Generation, 103-118, 141-153
  limiting, 111, 112, 144
Generative control structures, modeling, 137-
  138
Generator expressions, 109-114
Generators, 103-118, 141-153
  applicability of, 141-142
  in string analysis, 115-116
  limitations on use of, 146
  recursive, 145-146
get(a), 53, 54, 254
Global declarations, 69-70, 221, 222
Global identifiers, 69-70
Goal-directed evaluation, 104, 106-107, 116,
  119, 132, 135, 141, 204
Grammar input, 211-212
Grammars, 161-168, 211-214
  generating random strings from, 211-218
  generation specifications, 216-217
  internal representation of, 212-213
  processing, 213-216
  representing, 211-213
Grammars and languages, 161-168
Graphs, 174-179
Graphs, manipulating, 189-190

Hexadecimal codes, 232, 234-237

Identifier list, 69, 70, 222
Identifiers, 68-72, 223, 229-230, 234
  auxiliary, 27, 105, 107, 111, 123, 130, 141,
    157, 158
  scope of, 68, 69-72
  undeclared, 70, 243, 248
If-then-else expressions, 6, 15, 16, 81, 109, 119,
  223, 229, 274

image(x), 97-99, 101, 180, 254
Infinite result sequences, 144-146
Infix operations, 8-9, 225-228, 263-274
Infix-to-prefix conversion, 201-206
Initial clauses, 68, 71-72
Initial substrings, 5, 33, 37, 39, 40, 41, 43, 115
Initial values, 23, 56, 57, 65, 66, 73, 76, 99, 100, 127, 244, 259
Initiating execution, 1, 245
Input, 88-91
Input files, 88-90
Input line length, 239
Input options, 89, 239
Input, standard, 88, 257, 276
Integer arithmetic, 20-21
Integer comparison, 21-22
Integer data type, 61, 62, 67
Integer division, 20, 21
Integer literals, 19, 230-231
Integer sequences, 110-111, 142, 223, 227, 278
integer(x), 64-65, 254
Integers, 19-23
  long, 238
  short, 238, 239
Integers, large, 192-199
  addition of, 193-198
  linked-list representation, 197-198
  list representation, 195-197
  multiplying, 198-199
Interpreter, Icon, 240-242, 244-245
Invocation expressions, 72-73, 86, 223, 225, 278
Iteration, 104-106, 147-148
Iteration, nested, 147-148

Keywords, 10, 23, 25, 65, 80, 88, 99-102, 127, 128, 130, 138, 223, 229, 230, 276-278
  &ascii, 25, 276
  &clock, 102, 276
  &cset, 25, 26, 43, 276
  &date, 101, 276
  &dateline, 101, 276
  &errout, 88, 100, 253, 276
  &fail, 80, 276
  &host, 102, 276
  &input, 88, 257, 276
  &lcase, 25, 255, 276
  &level, 100, 253, 277
  &main, 138, 277
  &null, 65, 277
  &output, 88, 277
  &pos, 127, 128, 129, 130, 159, 252, 254, 255, 256, 260, 277

Keywords *(cont.):*
  &random, 23, 277
  &source, 138, 277
  &subject, 127, 128, 129, 130, 158, 159, 252, 254, 255, 256, 260, 277
  &time, 10, 102, 277
  &trace, 99, 238, 243, 244, 277
  &ucase, 25, 255, 277
  &version, 102, 278
Keywords, scanning, 127-128
Keywords, environmental, 101-102

Labelings, 186-190
Languages and grammars, 161-168
Large integers, 192-199
left(s1, i, s2), 35-36, 194, 254
Letters, 3, 25, 229
Lexical analysis, 40-45
Lexical comparison, 33-34, 54, 55, 63, 65, 67, 98, 266, 271-273
Lexical order, 33-34, 54, 55, 63, 65, 67, 98, 266, 271-273
Limitation expressions, 111, 138, 144, 223, 225, 275
Limiting sequences, 111
Line breaks, 233-234
Line terminators, 90, 91, 92
Linefeed, 25, 90, 91, 92, 232, 260
Linking, 241-243, 248
List concatenation, 52
List data type, 61, 62, 67
List expressions, 48-49, 223, 224, 281
List processing, 170-179
List sections, 53
list(i, x), 49, 255
Lists, 48-56
  empty, 49
  properties of, 55-56
  queue access, 53-54
  referencing, 50-52, 53
  sections, 53
  size, 49
  sorting, 54-55
  stack access, 53-54
  subscripting, 50-52, 53
Literals, 19, 25, 27-28, 223, 229, 230-232, 233, 234
Literals, numeric, 19, 230, 231
  decimal, 231
  digit, 19, 231
  exponent, 231
  integer, 19, 230-231

Literals, numeric *(cont.):*
  radix, 19, 231
  real, 19, 230, 231
Literals, quoted, 25, 27-28, 230, 231-232, 233, 234
  continuation of, 234
  cset, 25, 231
  string, 27-28, 231-232, 234
Loading, 242-243, 248
Local declarations, 68-71, 222
Local identifiers, 3, 70-72
Long integers, 238
Loop expressions, 12-15, 81, 223, 229

Machine dependencies, 238-239
Main procedure, 1, 2, 245
many(c, s, i, j), 41-42, 128, 179, 255
map(s1, s2, s3), 37-38, 181-188, 255
Mapping characters, 37-38, 181-188, 255
Mapping techniques, 181-186
match(s1, s2, i, j), 5, 39-40, 41, 128, 255
Matched substrings, order of, 156-158
Matching expressions, 158-161
Matching functions, 126-128, 158
Matching procedures, 160-161, 163-168
Mixed-mode arithmetic, 19, 21
move(i), 126, 156, 158, 160, 169, 256
Multiplication, 20
Multiplicative operations, 223, 225
Mutual evaluation expressions, 85-87, 127, 278

Nested iteration, 147-148
Nested scanning, 129
Newline, 25, 90, 91, 92, 232, 260
Next expressions, 13, 106, 130, 223, 228, 274
Nonterminal symbols, 76, 162, 163, 164, 167, 211, 212, 213, 214, 215, 216, 218
Not expressions, 15, 225, 274
Null-valued arguments, 65, 83, 251
Null data type, 61, 62, 65, 67
Null value, 65-66
Numbers, 19-23
  real, 19, 230, 231
Numeral strings, 63
Numeric literals, 19, 230, 231
numeric(x), 64, 65, 256
Numerical comparison, 21-22
Numerical computation, 20-21, 238, 263-264
Numerical operations, 20-23

Octal codes, 33, 232, 234-237
Omitted arguments, 34, 37, 65, 83, 128, 251-260
Open options, 89, 239
open(s1, s2), 89-90, 256
Opening files, 89-90
Operations, 8-9
  conditional, 4-5, 6, 12, 21-22, 33, 94-95
  infix, 8-9, 225-228, 263-274
  prefix, 8, 223, 225, 261-263
Options, file specification, 89, 239
Options, running, 243
Order of evaluation, 82-83, 107-108, 142, 151, 161
Out-of-range references, 29-30, 50
Outcome of evaluation, 80-82, 104
Output, 88-93
Output files, 88, 277
Output options, 89, 239
Output, standard, 88, 277
Overflow conditions, 238, 248, 261, 263, 264, 269

Parameters, 2, 68, 72-73
Parentheses, 9, 223
Parenthesized expressions, 9, 223
Parse trees, 166-168
Parsers, 166-168
Pattern matching, 158-161
Pipes, 239
Pointers, 55, 73
pop(a), 54, 256
pos(i), 127, 202, 256
Positional transformations, 185-186
Positioning of strings, 34-36
Positions in strings, 29-32, 44-45
  nonpositive specification, 31, 44-45
  positive specification, 29, 31, 44
Precedence, 8-9, 222-228
Precision of real numbers, 238
Prefix operations, 8, 223, 225, 261-263
Procedural encapsulation, 145, 160, 164
Procedure bodies, 68, 69
Procedure calls, 2, 82-83
Procedure data type, 61-62, 67
Procedure declarations, 68-69, 221, 222
Procedure invocation, 72-73
Procedure level, 100, 253, 277
Procedure names, 68, 70, 74
Procedures, 1, 2, 6-8, 68-78
  as generators, 116-118

Procedures *(cont.):*
  as values, 62, 74
  computed, 74
  external, 222, 242-243
  main, 1, 2, 245
  matching, 160-161, 163-168
  recursive calls of, 74-78, 145-146
  returning from, 73-74
  suspending from, 116-118, 145
Program character set, 234-237
Program errors, 249-250, 251-276, 278-280
Program execution, 240, 242, 245
Program organization, 1-4, 221
Program termination, 2, 245
Pseudo-random sequence, 23, 32, 52, 57, 60
pull(a), 54, 257
push(a, x), 54, 257
put(a, x), 53, 54, 257

Queues, 53-54
Queues, access methods, 53-54
Quoted literals, 25, 27-28, 230, 231-232, 233, 234
  continuation of, 234
  cset, 25, 231
  string, 27-28, 231-232, 234
Quotation marks, 2, 25, 27-28, 232

Radix literals, 19, 231
Random elements, 52, 57, 60
Random number seed, 23, 277
Random numbers, 23
Random strings, 211-218
Random subscripts, 32, 263
Range restriction, 44-45
Range specifications, 29-32, 224
read(f), 4, 5, 90, 239, 257
Reading data, 4, 90-91, 239
reads(f, i), 91, 239, 257
Real arithmetic, 20-21
Real comparison, 21-22
Real data type, 61, 62, 67
Real literals, 19, 230, 231
Real numbers, 19, 230, 231
  floating-point representation, 19, 238
  precision of, 238
real(x), 64, 258
Recognizers, 163-166
Record constructor, 59
Record declarations, 58-59, 61, 62, 221, 222
Record types, 66

Records, 58-60
  creation, 59
  field names, 58-60, 70, 224, 229
  names, 58, 70
  referencing, 59-60, 223, 224
  size, 60
  subscripting, 59-60, 223, 224
Recursion, 74-78, 145-146
Recursion, left, 164
Recursive generators, 145-146
Referencing expressions, 29-32, 50-52, 56-57, 59-60, 223, 224, 278-280
Referencing, lists, 50-52, 53
Referencing, field, 59-60, 223, 224
Referencing, records, 59-60, 223, 224
Referencing, tables, 56-57
Refreshing co-expressions, 134-135, 262
Remaindering, 20, 264, 269
Repeat expressions, 14, 229, 275
Repeated alternation expressions, 112, 233, 234, 275
repl(s, i), 36, 258
Replication of strings, 36, 258
Reserved words, 1, 6, 7, 8, 229-230
Result sequences, 104
Results, 80-82, 104
Resumption, 108, 116, 117, 118, 119, 120, 125, 126, 129, 130, 132, 133, 134, 136, 137, 142, 145, 146, 151, 153, 159, 160, 256, 259, 262, 267, 268, 274, 275
Return expressions, 7, 73-74, 82, 84, 116, 130, 143, 223, 228, 275
Return from procedures, 73-74
reverse(s), 36, 258
Reversible assignment, 120
Reversible effects, 119-120, 126-127
Reversible exchange, 120
Reversing strings, 36, 258
right(s1, i, s2), 34-35, 194, 195, 258
Running a program, 240-245
  compilation, 240, 242-243, 244-245, 248
  execution, 240, 242, 245
  interpretation, 240-242, 244-245
  linking, 241-243, 248
  loading, 242-243, 248
  translation, 240-242

Scanning expressions, 123-130, 223, 228, 275
Scanning, string, 122-130, 155-168
  functions, 128
  keywords, 127-128
  matching functions, 126-128, 158

Scanning, string *(cont.)*:
  nested, 129
  returning from, 129-130
  string-analysis functions, 38-45, 128
Scope declarations, 69-72
  dynamic, 68-71, 222
  external, 222, 242-243
  global, 69-70, 221, 222
  local, 68-71, 222
  static, 70, 71, 72, 75, 116, 222
Scope of identifiers, 68, 69-72
Selecting expressions, 15-17
Semicolons, use of, 9, 233-234
Short integers, 238, 239
Shuffling values, 97, 187
Size limitations, 238, 239
Size, co-expressions, 134, 262
Size, lists, 49
Size, records, 60
Size, strings, 28
Size, tables, 57
SNOBOL4 programming language, 155, 156, 160
sort(a), 54-55, 258
sort(t, i), 57-58, 258
Sorting, 54-55, 57-58, 66-67
  lists, 54-55
  tables, 57-58
Spaces, 25, 34, 37, 63, 188, 212, 232, 233, 234
Stack access methods, 53-54
Stacks, 53-54
Standard error output, 88, 93, 99, 100
Standard input, 88, 257, 276
Standard output, 88, 277
Static declarations, 70, 71, 72, 75, 116, 222
Static identifiers, 70-72
stop(x1, x2,..., xn), 14, 93, 245, 259
Storage allocation, 250
Storage limits, 244, 250
String analysis, 38-45
String analysis functions, 38-45, 128
String comparison, 33-34, 54, 55, 63, 65, 67, 98, 266, 271-273
String concatenation, 28-29, 36
String conversion, 26-27, 63, 64, 65
String data type, 61, 62, 67
String, empty, 28
String images, 97-99
String literals, 27-28, 231-232, 234
String replication, 36, 258
String scanning, 122-130, 155-168
  keywords, 127-128

String scanning *(cont.)*:
  matching functions, 126-128, 158
  nested, 129
  returning from, 129-130
  string-analysis functions, 38-45, 128
String size, 28
String-valued functions, 34-45
string(x), 64, 65, 113, 259
Strings, 27-45
Strings, random, 211-218
Structures, 48-60
  copying, 55, 96
Subscripting lists, 50-52, 53, 279-280
Subscripting records, 59-60, 223, 224, 280
Subscripting tables, 56-57, 280
Subscripting expressions, 29-32, 50-52, 56, 59-60, 223, 224
Substrings, 29-32, 112-113, 278-279
  initial, 5, 33, 37, 39, 40, 41, 43, 115
Substrings, locating, 38-40, 44-45
Subtraction, 20
Success, 4-5, 80
Suspend expressions, 116-118, 129, 130, 145, 228, 275
Suspended procedures, 116-118, 145
Symbolic algebra, 201-209
Symbolic differentiation, 207-209
Symbolic evaluation, 206-209
Syntactic errors, 246-248
Syntactic classes, 221
Syntax, of expressions, 8-10, 222-234
system(s), 240, 242, 245

Tabs, 232, 233, 234
tab(i), 123, 126, 128, 156, 158, 159, 160, 259
table(x), 56, 259
Table data type, 61, 62, 67
Tables, 56-58
  assigned values, 56-57
  creation, 56-57
  empty, 57
  entry values, 56-58
  referencing, 56-57
  size, 57
  sorting, 57-58
  subscripting, 56-57
Tabulation, 75-76, 175-176
Terminal symbols, 76, 163, 211, 212, 214, 215, 216
Terminals, computer, 88, 92, 234, 239, 244
Time, 10, 102, 277

To-by operations, 110-111, 142, 223, 227, 278
Trace messages, 99-100, 118, 165-166, 172
Tracing, 99-100, 118, 165-166, 172
Trailing arguments, 83, 128
Transitive closure, in graphs, 189-190
Translation, 240-242
Translation errors, 246-248
Translator, Icon, 240-242
Transmission operations, 138, 223, 225
Transpositions, 181-185
Trees, 166-168, 170-176
trim(s, c), 37, 260
Trimming strings, 37, 260
Truncation, string, 34, 35, 36, 183, 194
Truncation, integer, 20
Type checking, 61-62, 97, 260
Type conversion, 62-65, 251
   cset, 63, 64, 65
   explicit, 63, 64-65
   implicit, 7, 63-64
   integer, 63, 65
   numeric, 63, 64, 65
   real, 64
   string, 26-27, 63, 64, 65
Type determination, 61-62
type(x), 61-62, 97, 260

Undeclared identifiers, 70, 243, 248
Underscores, 3, 229, 234
UNIX, 88, 89, 90, 232, 239, 240, 242, 244, 245,
   259
UNIX commands, 240, 242, 245
UNIX shells, 239, 244, 245
Until-do expressions, 12, 13, 229, 275
upto(c, s, i, j), 40-41, 42, 44, 103, 115, 123, 128,
   179, 260

Value comparison, 94-95
Values, 3, 74, 80
Values, copying, 96
Variables, 3, 31-32, 50, 56, 59, 80
   computed, 84
   identifiers, 68-72, 223, 229-230, 234

While-do expressions, 6, 12, 13, 125, 137, 229,
   275
White space, 232-233
write(x1, x2,..., xn), 1, 74, 91-92, 158, 260
writes(x1, x2,..., xn), 92-93, 260-261
Writing data, 1-2, 91-93